THE ARDEN EDITION OF THE
WORKS OF WILLIAM SHAKESPEARE

JULIUS CÆSAR

Edited by
T. S. DORSCH

ROUTLEDGE
LONDON and NEW YORK

The general editors of the Arden Shakespeare have been
W. J. Craig (1899–1906), R. H. Case (1909–44),
Una Ellis-Fermor (1946–58), Harold F. Brooks (1952–82),
Harold Jenkins (1958–82) and Brian Morris (1975–82)

Present general editor: Richard Proudfoot

This edition of *Julius Caesar*, by T. S. Dorsch,
first published in 1955 by
Methuen & Co. Ltd
Reprinted five times

Reprinted 1988, 1989
by Routledge
11 New Fetter Lane, London EC4P 4EE
29 West 35th Street, New York, NY 10001

First published as a University Paperback 1965
Reprinted ten times
Reprinted 1988

ISBN (hardbound) 0 415 02719 5
ISBN (paperback) 0 415 02684 9

Printed and bound in Great Britain by
Richard Clay Ltd, Bungay, Suffolk

CONTENTS

INTRODUCTION

I. DATE OF COMPOSITION

Shakespeare's *Julius Cæsar* was first published in the First Folio of 1623. It was probably first staged a quarter of a century earlier, in 1599.

Thomas Platter, a Swiss traveller who was in England from 18 September to 20 October 1599, saw two plays in London. Of one he wrote as follows:[1]

> After lunch on September 21st, at about two o'clock, I and my party crossed the river, and there in the house with the thatched roof we saw an excellent performance of the tragedy of the first Emperor Julius Cæsar with about fifteen characters; after the play, according to their custom they did a most elegant and curious dance, two dressed in men's clothes, and two in women's.

Sir Edmund Chambers has shown[2] that the play Platter saw on this occasion must have been Shakespeare's *Julius Cæsar,* and that the theatre in which he saw it was in all probability the Globe, the building of which, begun in January or February 1599, would have been completed by the late summer.

All recent scholars have seen confirmation that the play was produced at about this time in the following lines from John Weever's *The Mirror of Martyrs, or The Life and Death of . . . Sir John Oldcastle,*[3] which seem to be a clear reference to the Forum scene:

> The many-headed multitude were drawne
> By *Brutus* speach, that Cæsar was ambitious,
> When eloquent *Mark Antonie* had showne
> His vertues, who but *Brutus* then was vicious?

1. Platter's account of entertainments he saw in England was published by Gustav Binz in *Anglia,* XXII (1899), pp. 458–62. The passage quoted here is given in the original German in Appendix B, p. 166. The dance that Platter saw was of course the jig.

2. E. K. Chambers, *William Shakespeare,* I, p. 397.

3. Stanza 4. *The Mirror of Martyrs* is reprinted in *The Hystorie of the Moste Noble Knight Plasidas, and Other Rare Pieces . . . Printed for the Roxburghe Club,* 1873. The quotation is on p. 180.

The Mirror of Martyrs was printed in 1601, but a passage in the
Dedication to William Couell says that it "some two yeares agoe
was made fit for the Print", whence it has been inferred that it was
written as early as 1599. But Weever's statement was not true. "*The
Mirror of Martyrs* is literally packed from beginning to end with
oddments stolen from Fairfax's Godfrey of Bulloigne, which was
unknown before 1600."[1] The poem cannot therefore have been lying in a corner of Weever's study for two years, as he claims, in anything like complete form. His allusion to the speeches of Brutus and
Antony is interesting as a comparatively early reference to the play,
but does not help us to date it with any accuracy.

Julius Cæsar does not appear in Francis Meres's famous list of
Shakespeare's plays in *Palladis Tamia: Wits Treasury*, which was
entered in the Stationers' Register in September 1598, and Meres's
failure to mention it is strong presumptive evidence that it had not
appeared when he wrote his list. Meres was not, of course, a chroni-
cler of the stage, and did not profess to list all the works of the dramatists and poets he commended; by his method of presenting his
material, the mention of six comedies by Shakespeare required six
tragedies to balance them. But it is hard to believe that he would
have omitted so striking and popular a play as *Julius Cæsar* if he had
known it.

We may take it, then, on the evidence supplied by Platter, that
Julius Cæsar was among the earliest plays performed in the new
Globe theatre, in the autumn of 1599. In all probability it was writ-
ten earlier in the same year.

2. OTHER CONTEMPORARY ALLUSIONS

Parallels to several passages in *Julius Cæsar* are found in contemporary works. Antony's words,

> O judgment, thou art fled to brutish beasts,
> And men have lost their reason, (III. ii. 106–7)

are mockingly echoed in Jonson's *Every Man out of his Humour*,[2]
when Clove is trying to impress his hearers with his scholarship by
talking "fustian", and says, "Reason long since is fled to animals,
you know." There is a similar echo in *The Wisdome of Doctor Dodypoll*:[3] "Then reason's fled to animals I see." I have not found the

1. *Englands Parnassus*, ed. Charles Crawford (Clar. Press, 1913), notes, p. 388.
2. Ed. Herford and Simpson, III. iv. 33. *E.M.O.* was registered with the
Stationers on 8 April 1600.
3. *The Wisdome of Doctor Dodypoll* (Old Eng. Drama: Students' Facs. Edn.),
Sig. E1^r, l. 26. *Dodypoll* was registered on 7 October 1600.

thought used quasi-proverbially elsewhere, and suppose it to be derived from *Julius Cæsar* in the two later instances.

Cæsar's "Et tu, Brute?" is also used in a humorous context in *Every Man out of his Humour*,[1] when Carlo Buffone is made to lie down by Puntarvolo, and Macilente comes to Puntarvolo's help. It occurs again in Samuel Nicholson's poem *Acolastus his Afterwitte*:[2]

> *Et tu Brute*, wilt thou stab *Cæsar* too?
> Thou art my friend and wilt not see me wrong'd.

The phrase is almost certainly not of Shakespeare's coinage,[3] but his use of it in 1599 would add point to the passages in Jonson and Nicholson.

It is probable that Antony's valedictory words over the body of Brutus (v. v. 73–5) were in Jonson's mind when, in *Cynthia's Revels*,[4] he caused Mercury to describe Crites in the following terms:

> A creature of a most perfect and diuine temper. One, in whom the humours and elements are peaceably met . . . in all, so composde & order'd, as it is cleare, *Nature* went about some ful worke, she did more then make a man, when she made him.

This speech of Antony also influenced Drayton's description of Mortimer in *The Barons Warres* (1603).[5]

Evidence of an alteration made in the text of *Julius Cæsar* between its first production and its publication in the Folio seems to be provided by a comment that Jonson made in his *Timber*. In the Folio Cæsar's words at III. i. 47–8 read as follows:

> Know, *Cæsar* doth not wrong, nor without cause
> Will he be satisfied.

In *Timber*[6] Jonson says of Shakespeare:

> . . . Many times hee fell into those things, could not escape laughter: As when hee said in the person of *Cæsar*, one speaking to him; *Cæsar, thou dost me wrong*. Hee replyed: *Cæsar did never wrong, but with just cause* and such like: which were ridiculous.

Timber seems to be a selection from Jonson's notebooks covering several years, and this comment cannot be dated. I have discussed its implications in my note on III. i. 47–8. In the Induction to *The*

---

1. Ed. Herford and Simpson, v. vi. 79.
2. *Acolastus his Afterwitte* (1600), Sig. E3ʳ, l. 7.   3. See note on III. i. 77.
4. Ed. Herford and Simpson, II. iii. 123–30. Registered 23 May 1601.
5. Canto III, st. 40. *The Works of Michael Drayton*, ed. J. W. Hebel, II, p. 56.
6. *Timber: or, Discoveries; Made upon Men and Matter*, ed. Herford and Simpson, VIII, p. 584.

Staple of News[1] Jonson again makes fun of this passage when the Prologue, in answer to Madame Expectation's admission that she can expect too much, if she has cause, retorts: "*Cry you mercy*, you neuer did wrong, but with iust cause." The use of roman type amid the italics in which the rest of the Induction is printed shows that a quotation is intended.

Finally, there is a reminiscence of the last two lines of the second scene of the play (I. ii. 318-19) in *The Tragedy of Sir John Van Olden Barnavelt*[2] by Massinger and Fletcher:

> and let this *Prince* of *Orange* seat him sure,
> or he shall fall, when he is most secure.

So much for apparent echoes from *Julius Cæsar*.

Echoes in the opposite direction are less clear. It is possible that, in Cassius's prophecy that the assassination of Cæsar will be acted over "in states unborn, and accents yet unknown" (III. i. 111-13), Shakespeare was recalling some lines in Daniel's *Musophilus*:[3]

> And who in time knowes whither we may vent
> The treasure of our tongue, to what strange shores
> This gaine of our best glorie shal be sent,
> T' inrich unknowing Nations with our stores?
> What worlds in th' yet unformed Occident
> May come refin'd with th' accents that are ours?

Musophilus was entered in the Stationers' Register as part of the *Poeticall Essayes* of Daniel on 9 January 1599 and published in the same year.

Malone first drew attention to the resemblance between I. ii. 51-64 in *Julius Cæsar* and a passage in Davies's *Nosce Teipsum*:[4]

> Mine *Eyes*, which [view] all obiects nigh and farre,
> Looke not into this litle world of mine,
> Nor see my face, wherein they fixed are.

Dr Dover Wilson has pointed out[5] that there are further striking parallels earlier in the same poem, in these lines,[6] for instance:

1. Ed. Herford and Simpson, Induction, 36-7. Registered 14 April 1626.
2. Ed. W. P. Frijlinck (Amsterdam, 1922), ll. 748-9. This play was performed in 1619. The scene in which these lines occur (II. i) is generally accepted as Massinger's work.
3. Ll. 957-62. Samuel Daniel, *Poems and a Defence of Ryme*, ed. A. C. Sprague, p. 96.
4. Stanza 48. *The Poems of Sir John Davies* (Facs. from the first edns.), ed. Clare Howard, p. 121; ed. Grosart (Early Eng. Poets), I, p. 25. *Nosce Teipsum* was registered 14 April 1599.
5. *Julius Cæsar*, ed. J. Dover Wilson (N.C.S. edn.), note on I. ii. 52-8, p. 109.
6. *Nosce Teipsum*, st. 23. Howard, p. 116; Grosart, p. 20.

All things without, which round about we see,
We seeke to know, and how therewith to do;
But that whereby we *reason, liue, and be,*
Within our selues, we strangers are thereto;

and in these:[1]

Is it because the minde is like the eye,
(Through which it gathers knowledge by degrees,)
Whose rayes reflect not, but spread outwardly,
Not seeing it selfe, when other things it sees?

Admittedly the thought was something of a commonplace at this period. Nashe uses it in the Dedication of *The Unfortunate Traveller* (1594):[2] "The eye that sees round about it selfe, sees not into it selfe"; it is found in Beaumont and Fletcher's *Cupid's Revenge* (I. iii); and Shakespeare himself repeats it more elaborately in *Troilus and Cressida* (III. iii. 105–11).[3] However, the parallel with Davies is close enough to suggest that Shakespeare may have been reading *Nosce Teipsum* while he was writing his play, even as the earlier parallel suggests an acquaintance with Daniel's *Musophilus*. Both poems must have been rousing interest at about this time.

If Mr Nathan is right,[4] there may be in the Cobbler's remark that he meddles with "no tradesman's matters, nor women's matters" (I. i. 21–3) an allusion to Dekker's *Shoemaker's Holiday*, to which Henslowe referred in his Diary on 15 July 1599.

Though they do not individually provide any conclusive evidence towards the dating of *Julius Cæsar*, these various echoes and parallels do something cumulatively to confirm that it appeared in 1599, if such corroboration were needed.

Cæsar's story was fresh in Shakespeare's mind when he wrote *Hamlet*. I have in the annotations drawn attention to references to it in *Hamlet*, and to some points of correspondence between the two plays. There too I have noted some other Shakespearian references to Cæsar, most of which are listed by MacCallum, in his book on Shakespeare's Roman plays.[5]

That *Julius Cæsar* was popular is attested, not only by the familiarity with it which some of the parallels imply, and presuppose in audiences, but also by some lines in the commendatory verses of

1. *Ibid.*, st. 27. Howard, p. 117; Grosart, p. 20.
2. *The Works of Thomas Nashe*, ed. R. B. McKerrow, II, p. 201.
3. Cf. also Joshua Sylvester, *Bartas his Devine Weekes and Workes* (1605), I. vi. 784, "As the Eye perceives All but it self"; and Marston, *Parasitaster* (1606), IV. i. 584.
4. See note on I. i. 21–3.
5. M. W. MacCallum, *Shakespeare's Roman Plays*, pp. 177–80.

Leonard Digges[1] which John Benson prefixed to his 1640 edition of Shakespeare's *Poems*. Digges compares it with Ben Jonson's Roman plays, to their disadvantage:

> So have I seene, when Cesar would appeare,
> And on the Stage at halfe-sword parley were,
> *Brutus* and *Cassius*: oh how the Audience,
> Were ravish'd, with what wonder they went thence,
> When some new day they would not brooke a line,
> Of tedious (though well laboured) *Catilines*: (*sic*)
> *Sejanus* too was irkesome, they priz'de more
> Honest *Iago*, or the jealous Moore.

Almost everything in this poem of Digges, who died five years before it appeared, is more relevant to Shakespeare's plays than to his poems, and it is very likely that it was intended for the First Folio, and that its disparagement of Jonson led to its being put aside and replaced in the Folio by another set of verses. In these[2] Digges expresses without invidious comparisons his admiration for the Quarrel scene:

> Nor shall I e're beleeue, or thinke thee dead
> (Though mist) untill our bankrout Stage be sped
> (Impossible) with some new straine t' out-do
> Passions of *Iuliet*, and her *Romeo*;
> Or till I heare a Scene more nobly take,
> Than when thy half-Sword parlying *Romans* spake.

Whether his memory had been refreshed by recent performances or not, Digges could still in 1623 speak of vivid impressions that *Julius Cæsar* had made on himself and on its audiences generally.

3. THE SOURCE

Though Shakespeare drew also on other reading, as will be seen from the annotations, the plot of *Julius Cæsar* is wholly derived from Sir Thomas North's translation of Plutarch's *Lives*.[3] North himself translated, not from the original Greek, but from the French version of Jacques Amyot (1559), and the immense popularity of his work is seen in the fact that it ran to seven editions before the end of the seventeenth century. For *Julius Cæsar* Shakespeare must have

1. "Vpon Master William Shakespeare, the Deceased Authour, and his Poems," ll. 41–8.

2. "To the Memorie of the deceased Authour Maister W. Shakespeare," ll. 13–18.

3. Sir Thomas North, *The Lives of the noble Grecians and Romanes*, 1579, 1595, 1603, etc.

THE ARDEN SHAKESPEARE

This book is due for return on or before the last date shown
above; it may, subject to the book not being reserved by
another reader, be renewed by personal application, post, or
telephone, quoting this date and details of the book. 100%
recycled paper.

HAMPSHIRE COUNTY COUNCIL
County Library

THE ARDEN SHAKESPEARE

All's Well That Ends Well: edited by G. K. Hunter
Antony and Cleopatra: edited by M. R. Ridley
As You Like It: edited by Agnes Latham
The Comedy of Errors: edited by R. A. Foakes
Coriolanus: edited by Philip Brockbank
Cymbeline: edited by J. M. Nosworthy
Hamlet: edited by Harold Jenkins
Julius Caesar: edited by T. S. Dorsch
King Henry IV, Parts 1 & 2: edited by A. R. Humphreys
King Henry V: edited by John H. Walter
King Henry VI, Parts 1, 2 & 3: edited by A. S. Cairncross
King Henry VIII: edited by R. A. Foakes
King John: edited by E. A. J. Honigmann
King Lear: edited by Kenneth Muir
King Richard II: edited by Peter Ure
King Richard III: edited by Antony Hammond
Love's Labour's Lost: edited by Richard David
Macbeth: edited by Kenneth Muir
Measure for Measure: edited by J. W. Lever
The Merchant of Venice: edited by John Russell Brown
The Merry Wives of Windsor: edited by H. J. Oliver
A Midsummer Night's Dream: edited by Harold F. Brooks
Much Ado About Nothing: edited by A. R. Humphreys
Othello: edited by M. R. Ridley
Pericles: edited by F. D. Hoeniger
The Poems: edited by F. T. Prince
Romeo and Juliet: edited by Brian Gibbons
The Taming of the Shrew: edited by Brian Morris
The Tempest: edited by Frank Kermode
Timon of Athens: edited by H. J. Oliver
Titus Andronicus: edited by J. C. Maxwell
Twelfth Night: edited by J. M. Lothian and T. W. Craik
Troilus and Cressida: edited by Kenneth Palmer
The Two Gentlemen of Verona: edited by Clifford Leech
The Winter's Tale: edited by J. H. P. Pafford

used either the first edition of 1579, or the second of 1595. The principal passages on which he drew are printed as Appendix A in the present edition of the play, and others are quoted in the annotations.

Shakespeare's wording in a few lines seems to show that he knew the *Caius Iulius Cæsar* that was added to the tragic narratives of *A Mirror for Magistrates* in 1587;[1] and there are occasional echoes from other narratives in the *Mirror*. There has recently been an attempt[2] to establish for the anonymous *Cæsar's Revenge*[3] an "importance as a source . . . only second to Plutarch". But there are no close verbal parallels,[4] and the few general correspondences that are found in the two plays are either commonplaces of Elizabethan revenge tragedy, or typical expressions of Shakespeare's outlook on civil discord and on society as a whole. No doubt Shakespeare was aware that Cæsar's assassination had been the subject of earlier plays; but without being acquainted with any of them he would still have seen the dramatic potentialities of the event and its consequences as he read about them in Plutarch. His own development of the revenge theme may well have been influenced to some extent by the following passage in Plutarch:[5]

But his great prosperity and good fortune that favoured him all his lifetime, did continue afterwards in the revenge of his death, pursuing the murtherers both by sea and land, till they had not left a man more to be executed, of all them that were actors or counsellers in the conspiracy of his death.

4. SHAKESPEARE'S TREATMENT OF THE SOURCE

Shakespeare took his material from three of Plutarch's *Lives*, those of Marcus Brutus, Julius Cæsar, and Marcus Antonius. From three separate accounts of the events leading to and resulting from the assassination of Cæsar, presented with different emphasis and some differences in detail, he put together a plot which is supremely well proportioned in its distribution of interest and wholly consistent in its development of character, and which seems inevitable in its chain of cause and effect. From these *Lives* he took, too, many details of the appearance and personality of his characters, adding,

1. See notes on, e.g., II. iii. 1–5; III. i. 1–2, 6–10, 77.
2. See Ernest Schanzer, 'A Neglected Source of "Julius Cæsar"' (*Notes and Queries*, May 1954, pp. 196–7).
3. See p. xx.
4. For "What, Brutus too?" see note on "Et tu, Brute?" III. i. 77.
5. *Shakespeare's Plutarch*, ed. W. W. Skeat, p. 103.

however, much of his own, and developing in his own way the relationship between them, as will be apparent to anyone who reads more widely in the *Lives* than the extracts in the Appendix.

In North Shakespeare also found many passages which he could transmute into blank verse with only trifling alterations. It might be a matter of the odd line: North's "What art thou then determined to do?" reappearing as "What are you then determined to do?" (v. i. 100), or "Brutus did condemn and note Lucius Pella" as "You have condemn'd and noted Lucius Pella" (iv. iii. 2). It might be the retention of North's phrasing through several consecutive lines. For example, in the *Life of Marcus Brutus* we read:[1]

I dare assure thee, that no enemy hath taken nor shall take Marcus Brutus alive, and I beseech God keep him from that fortune: for wheresoever he be found, alive or dead, he will be found like himself.

In Shakespeare's play this becomes:

> I dare assure thee that no enemy
> Shall ever take alive the noble Brutus.
> The gods defend him from so great a shame!
> When you do find him, or alive or dead,
> He will be found like Brutus, like himself. (v. iv. 21–5)

Or the verbal echoes might be spread more thinly over a longer passage, as in Portia's interview with Brutus (ii. i. 279–303),[2] or Cassius's speech to Messala before the battle of Philippi (v. i. 71–89).[3]

However, it is in his selection of the source material, in what he added, omitted, or changed, and above all in his imaginative treatment, that Shakespeare shows his dramatic genius. He had no model for the Forum speeches of Brutus and Antony. From Plutarch's illustration of Brutus's epistolary style, and his observation that in his Greek letters he affected the "brief compendious manner of speech of the Lacedaemonians",[4] came the unadorned, antithetical manner of Brutus's appeal to the reason of the Roman mob. A passing remark that Antony was an exponent of the Asiatic style of oratory was the starting-point for Antony's more telling appeal to the emotions of the same mob. Nor did Shakespeare find this extremely realistic mob ready-made; Plutarch provided some of its actions, but its fickleness and its passions, its humour and shrewdness and blindness, are almost entirely of his devising.

Likewise there is no warrant for his comparatively full delineation of Casca, and very little for that of Octavius, who, though he

1. Skeat, p. 149; Appendix, p. 164. 2. Cf. Appendix, p. 145.
3. Cf. Appendix, pp. 159, 160. 4. See note on iii. ii. 13–35.

appears late in the play and speaks only about forty lines, is clearly and firmly sketched as the politic, efficient and rather cold figure who was to be developed more fully in *Antony and Cleopatra*.

For the characters of Cæsar, Brutus, and Antony, and to a smaller degree of Cassius, Plutarch furnished large-scale portraits already charged with life; but Shakespeare elaborated on Plutarch's details in his own way, and recreated the characters in his own terms. For example, he was able to emphasize some less noble and impressive attributes in Cæsar without obscuring his essential greatness. He brought out all the envy and the instability of Cassius, and yet found opportunities for making him a sympathetic character. He developed to the full the irony and the opportunism of Antony, and, too, his unselfish love and admiration for Cæsar. And he worked up beautifully the gentle and the idealistic sides of Brutus's nature that he found in Plutarch, and added some less lovable and worthy traits on his own account.

Plutarch also provided the basis for the portraits of Portia, Calphurnia, and Cicero. But he gave little more than the names, and in a few instances an odd action, of the less important characters generally, most of whom nevertheless leave more than a passing impression on our minds when we see or read the play. Shakespeare made the most of the few words he found in Plutarch about, for instance, the sick Ligarius's faith in Brutus, Metellus Cimber's petition to Cæsar, and the poet Cinna's treatment in the hands of the mob; but it is his own touches that give a lively reality to these men for the few moments that they are before us. Similarly, in the short, bustling episodes from the battle of Philippi the various officers are clearly differentiated by the way in which they speak and act. Dowden has pointed out how profoundly true to Roman life and character Shakespeare manages to seem; he also observes[1] that he "was aware that his personages must be men before they were Romans"; and certainly the personages of *Julius Cæsar*, minor as well as major, come to life as real human beings.

As was his practice in dramatizing historical material, whether from the English chroniclers or Plutarch, Shakespeare took liberties in *Julius Cæsar* with the events of history. Historically, for example, Cæsar celebrated his triumph for the defeat of Pompey's sons in October, 45 B.C., and the Lupercalian festival that figures in the play took place in the following February; moreover, it was not until later that the Tribunes were put to silence for disrobing Cæsar's images, and then, as followers of Brutus, they were disrobing them of the diadems with which they were adorned for the pro-

1. Edward Dowden, *Shakspere: His Mind and Art*, 8th edn. (1886), pp. 276–7.

posed coronation of Cæsar, not of trophies hung on them for his
triumph over Pompey's sons. For the sake of dramatic economy,
and to heighten the dramatic effect of his opening scenes, Shakespeare has condensed all these events into one day of varied and
surging emotions, in the course of which the scene and atmosphere
of the play are laid and the personalities and aspirations of its leading figures revealed.

In Act III there has been further compression. According to
Plutarch,[1] "Brutus and his consorts, having their swords bloody in
their hands, went straight to the Capitol," where Brutus made a
speech; then they went down into the market-place and he made a
second speech, which by no means satisfied all those who heard it,
as did his speech in the play. On the following day, and after the
public reading of Cæsar's will, Antony, "making his funeral oration in praise of the dead, according to the ancient custom of
Rome", seized his opportunity of stirring the populace into rage
and mutiny. Furthermore, it was not on this day that Octavius
came to Rome, but about six weeks later; nor did his arrival then
accord with Antony's desires,[2] for the two quarrelled over the man-
agement of affairs, and it was only after a year and a half of bitter-
ness, and even fighting, that they composed their differences and
formed the Triumvirate with Lepidus. One more example of this
telescoping process may be mentioned: the "second fight" in the
battle of Philippi to which Brutus refers (v. iii. 110) occurred nearly
three weeks after the first; Shakespeare emphasizes the complete-
ness and finality of Cæsar's revenge by putting both engagements,
and hence the deaths of both Cassius and Brutus, on the same day.
I have drawn attention in the notes to other occasions on which he
alters or transposes events that he found in Plutarch.

However, a catalogue of Shakespeare's departures from his
source has little value in itself; it is their effect that matters. The
facts of history were for him the raw material which he had a right,
within broad limits, to shape to his own artistic ends. By selection,
compression, and adaptation, now using this source-life, now that,
he immeasurably enriched and deepened his characters, and
wrought them to his own kind of dramatic consistency. This may
be illustrated by one striking example of adaptation. Casca has
struck the first blow at Cæsar. "Then," Plutarch goes on,[3]

Then the conspirators thronging one upon another, because
every man was desirous to have a cut at him, so many swords and
daggers lighting upon one body, one of them hurt another, and

1. Skeat, pp. 120–2; Appendix, pp. 150–3.
2. "He comes upon a wish" (III. ii. 268).   3. Skeat, p. 119; Appendix, p. 149.

among them Brutus caught a blow on his hand, because he would make one in murthering of him, and all the rest also were every man of them bloodied.

Shakespeare turns this into Brutus's words:

Stoop, Romans, stoop,
And let us bathe our hands in Cæsar's blood
Up to the elbows, and besmear our swords:
Then walk we forth, even to the market-place,
And waving our red weapons o'er our heads,
Let's all cry, "Peace, freedom, and liberty!"
(III. i. 105–10)

It is all of a piece with what we have already seen of Brutus that he should turn the assassination of Cæsar into a solemn ritual, and we recall the words he spoke earlier, "Let's be sacrificers, but not butchers, Caius." (II. i. 166).

Another artistic effect of Shakespeare's selection and condensation of his source-material is the transmutation of Plutarch's three comparatively leisurely narratives into a single closely knit and swiftly moving drama which has been aptly called "a political thriller". The play is supremely well constructed, the balance of dramatic power wonderfully well maintained between the conflicting parties. The objection that it falls into two parts, that it must inevitably do so since its titular hero is killed early in the third act, has been met by many writers. The assassination is a central point, not a dividing point; before it takes place our interest is focused on the conspiracy in which it is planned, and afterwards on the steps by which it is avenged. In the dramatic sense Cæsar dead is just as powerful as the living Cæsar; in fact, his spirit dominates the second half of the play more forcefully than his personality the first half, and subjugates the conspirators more truly than did his aspirations before they slew him. After the assassination the star of "Cæsarism" is ever in the ascendant, while the fortunes of Brutus and Cassius are ever on the decline. We see this especially in their misunderstandings and errors of judgement, and in the omens that dismay their soldiers; and indeed, both Brutus and Cassius seem to find release from some not fully understood oppression of their spirits only when they die upon the swords with which they killed Cæsar, and with his name on their lips.

Examining the structure from another angle, we may see how the action rises on mounting waves of emotion and suspense to the great twin climaxes of the Capitol and Forum scenes, the second overtopping the former in tension as the summit of Everest overtops the South Peak. Then, through the grimly comic scene in which the Roman mob harries the poet Cinna and rushes off to burn the houses of the conspirators, exciting enough, but exciting on a lower level than what has gone before, we are dropped down to the cold formality of the meeting of the Triumvirs. In the last two acts the emotional content is deliberately kept on a lower plane than in the first three, but the interest never flags. After the conflict of sympathies in the quarrel scene, we are carried through the varying hopes and fortunes of the battle episodes to the twin anti-climaxes of the deaths of Cassius and Brutus, and the play ends with Antony's generous tribute to his fallen enemy and Octavius's desire that he should be given military honours "according to his virtue".

I have spoken of the assassination of Cæsar as the central point of the play. Moulton,[1] and after him Granville-Barker,[2] rightly, I think, place the decisive turning-point of the action a little later, when Antony's servant halts the conspirators as they turn from the symbolic bathing of their hands in Cæsar's blood to go to the mar-ket-place. "*Enter a servant*: this simple stage-direction is the . . . turning-round of the whole action; the arch has reached its apex and the Reaction has begun. So instantaneous is the change, that though it is only the servant of Antony who speaks, yet the first words of his message ring with the peculiar tone of subtly poised sentences which are inseparably associated with Antony's elo-quence; it is like the first announcement of that which is to be a final theme in music, and from this point this tone dominates the scene to the very end."[3]

> Thus he bade me say:
> Brutus is noble, wise, valiant, and honest;
> Cæsar was mighty, bold, royal, and loving:
> Say I love Brutus, and I honour him;
> Say I fear'd Cæsar, honour'd him, and lov'd him.
> If Brutus will vouchsafe that Antony
> May safely come to him, and be resolv'd
> How Cæsar hath deserv'd to lie in death,
> Mark Antony shall not love Cæsar dead
> So well as Brutus living. (III. i. 125–34)

Hitherto we have seen very little of Antony, and the few words he has spoken have tended to confirm Brutus's impression that he is "but a limb of Cæsar". With the message that he sends by his servant we begin to have an inkling that, as on other occasions, Cassius may once again have been wiser than his friend in his esti-

1. R. G. Moulton, *Shakespeare as a Dramatic Artist*, 2nd edn. (1888), p. 198.
2. Harley Granville-Barker, *Prefaces to Shakespeare*, 1st Series, p. 71.
3. Moulton, *loc. cit.*

mate of him as "a shrewd contriver". Though the misgivings of Cassius are in no wise allayed by the tenor of the message, Brutus accepts it at its face-value, and warmly welcomes Antony as a friend and potential ally. Antony's handling of the situation is masterly in the extreme. We cannot doubt the sincerity of his grief when he sees the body of Cæsar, but it does not cloud his judgement of the men with whom he has to deal. He knows only too well that his credit stands on slippery ground; he also knows that if he can win the countenance of Brutus he will be safe. Evading Cassius's attempts to bring him to a compact, he concentrates on Brutus all the power of his subtle flattery and his irony; and when he has gained permission to speak his funeral oration he knows he has won his battle. Cæsar's vengeance has begun.

5. OTHER PLAYS ABOUT CÆSAR

The dramatic potentialities of Cæsar's career had been seen by English writers earlier than Shakespeare. According to the Revels Accounts, the "children of Pawles" played "a storie of Pompey" at Court on Twelfth Night, 1581,[1] and this may perhaps have embraced Cæsar's part in Pompey's downfall. In Stephen Gosson's *Playes Confuted in fiue Actions*, which was registered in 1582, mention is made of a "history of Cæsar and Pompey",[2] which may have been staged at the Theatre, though Gosson's words are not clear on this point. Gosson was a renegade actor-dramatist who, having taken orders, devoted much energy to "prouing that [plays] are not to be suffred in a Christian common weale". He cites this play to illustrate one of his many objections to drama, the fact that dramatists all too often swell a slender theme with bombast, or, to use his own words, "followe the practise of the cobler, and set their teeth to the leather to pull it out".

There survives the Epilogue, in Latin prose, of a play called *Cæsar Interfectus*,[3] which was probably acted at Christ Church, Oxford, in 1582. This Epilogue was written by Richard Edes of Christ Church, who was named by Meres among "our best for Tragedie", and it is likely that he was responsible for the play as a whole.

Henslowe's *Diary* records[4] a "seser & pompie" on 8 November 1594, and "the 2 pte of sesore" on 18 June 1595, but of these plays nothing is known. Chambers points out[5] that an entry in Henry Machyn's *Diary*, which may record an English "Julyus Sesar" as

1. E. K. Chambers, *The Elizabethan Stage*, IV, p. 158.   2. *Ibid.*, IV, p. 216.
3. *Ibid.*, III, p. 309.   4. *Henslowe's Diary*, ed. W. W. Greg, I, pp. 20, 24.
5. *William Shakespeare*, I, p. 400, and II, p. 386.

early as 1562, is probably in part a forgery. Kyd's *Cornelia*,[1] registered and printed in 1594, is a translation of Robert Garnier's
Cornélie (1574). None of these works can be shown to have had any
influence on Shakespeare's *Julius Cæsar*; but it is possible that some
of the contemporary literary allusions to Cæsar are drawn from
them.

It may have been the continued success of Shakespeare's play
that in 1602 stirred the rival company to emulation. On 22 May in
this year Henslowe notes[2] the advance of five pounds "to geue vnto
antoney monday & mihell drayton webester & the Rest in earneste
of a Boocke called sesers ffalle"; but no record exists of the production of this work. *The Tragedie of Iulius Cæsar*[3] by Sir William Alex-
ander, Earl of Stirling, was printed in 1607, but probably composed a year or two earlier.

One other Cæsar play of this period has survived, the anonymous
Cæsar's Revenge,[4] registered in June, 1606, and twice printed, in an
undated edition and an edition dated 1607. The 1607 title-page
tells us that this play had been "Priuately acted by the Studentes of
Trinity Colledge in Oxford"; and indeed in tone and in the pro-
fusion of classical references it bears the marks of an academic origin. Dr Boas suggests that it may have been written before the turn
of the century; but there are no signs that it was known to Shakespeare.

Finally there is Chapman's *Cæsar and Pompey*, registered and
printed in 1631, but according to Chapman written "long since"
and "never touched at the stage". Chambers[5] conjecturally dates
its composition in about 1613.

Apart from Garnier's *Cornélie*, Continental plays on Cæsar that
have from time to time been canvassed as possible influences on
Shakespeare are the Latin *Julius Cæsar* of Marc Antoine Muret,
published in 1553, and the *César* of Jacques Grévin, published in
1561.[6] No one has succeeded in establishing any connection between these plays and that of Shakespeare.

---

1. See *The Elizabethan Stage*, III, p. 397. Dr Boas thinks that, as Shakespeare
shows some acquaintance with others of Kyd's works, he had probably also read
his *Cornelia*; but he gives no clear evidence of its influence on *Julius Cæsar*. (See
The Works of Thomas Kyd, ed. F. S. Boas, Introduction, p. lxxxiii). This question
is again discussed by Joan Rees, in *Mod. Lang. Rev.*, L, 2, April 1955.

2. *Henslowe's Diary*, ed. Greg. I, p. 166.

3. Reprinted in the Appendix to Furness's Variorum *Julius Cæsar*.

4. *The Tragedie of Cæsar and Pompey, Or Cæsars Reuenge*, ed. F. S. Boas for the
Malone Society. See p. xiii.

5. *The Elizabethan Stage*, III, p. 259.

6. Summaries of these two plays are given in Furness's Variorum *Julius
Cæsar*, pp. 461–3.

6. THE DISINTEGRATORS

Even without the testimony of Ben Jonson and Leonard Digges, I find it very strange that any one who reads *Julius Cæsar* with an attentive mind and ear could doubt that it was wholly written by Shakespeare. Yet in the last three-quarters of a century several attempts have been made to prove that much of the play as we now have it was written, or revised, by other hands. These attempts do not deserve much space in the present edition, but perhaps their general tenor ought to be stated.

The process of disintegration began with Fleay,[1] who believed "that this play as we have it is an abridgment of Shakespeare's play, made by Ben Jonson". He founded this belief on such tenuous evidence—to say the best of it—as the comparative frequency of short lines in *Julius Cæsar*, which he felt pointed to abridgement, the presence of a few phrases which were also used by Jonson, and the spelling of the name Antony without an *h*, according to the practice of Jonson, but contrary to that of Shakespeare in other plays. He concluded that "there is a strange feeling about the general style of this play; which is not the style of Jonson: but just what one would fancy Shakespeare would become with an infusion of Jonson." It seems to me that the final answer to Fleay is provided by that sanest of Shakespearian editors, William Aldis Wright:[2]

The arguments adduced in support of this theory are certainly not such as the readers of Shakespeare have a right to demand, and to any one who wishes to investigate the subject I cannot recommend a more instructive study than a comparison between the Roman plays of Shakespeare and Ben Jonson.[3]

Next in the field was that prince of disintegrators, J. M. Robertson,[4] who likewise saw compression on the part of Jonson. But Robertson could scarcely be expected to be satisfied with so simple a hypothesis as that of the compression of a single play of Shakespeare by Jonson alone. He set out to find as many collaborating and revising hands as possible, basing his arguments largely on inconsistencies in the characterization and chronology, on what he

1. F. G. Fleay, *Shakespeare Manual* (1878), pp. 262–70.
2. *Julius Cæsar*, ed. W. A. Wright, Clarendon Press Series (1896), Preface, p. xlv.
3. Fleay (*op. cit.*, p. 264) also makes the remarkable statement: "Shakespeare and Jonson probably worked together on *Sejanus* in 1602–3. He having helped Jonson then in a historical play, what more likely than that Jonson should be chosen to remodel Shakespeare's *Cæsar*, if it needed to be reproduced in a shorter form than he gave it originally?"
4. J. M. Robertson, *The Shakespeare Canon* (1922), I, pp. 66–154.

was pleased to call "flaws of construction" and "primitive elements", and on passages paralleled in other writers. Briefly, his
conclusions are as follows. Marlowe, possibly in association with
Kyd, wrote a Cæsar play in three parts. The first part, dealing with
the struggle of Cæsar and Pompey, was revived in 1594 by the
Admiral's Men, and was in fact the play which Henslowe, under the
title "seser & pompie", recorded in that year as *ne* (that is, *new*),
though Robertson states[1] that neither this play nor its sequel in the
following year was marked as *ne* by Henslowe. The second part, revised by Drayton and Chapman, and possibly Heywood, was Henslowe's "2 pte of sesore" of 1595. The third part was revised as the
"Boocke called sesers ffalle" for which Henslowe in 1602 advanced
money to Munday, Drayton, Webster "and the Rest"—though
from this group Robertson seeks only to find Drayton's work in
Julius Cæsar. It was the second and third parts of this strange com-
posite trilogy which Shakespeare revised in about 1603, and which
Jonson, perhaps in about 1607 or perhaps some years later, further
condensed, adding yet another stylistic layer to the earlier ag-
glomeration.

After Robertson comes his friend William Wells.[2] Wells shows
none of the comparative caution of his predecessors. "The very
small piece of Shakespeare's work in *Julius Cæsar*", he says,[3] "is
fairly distinct. It comprises lines 1 to 57 . . . of the first scene of the
first act." Like Robertson, Wells begins with an "old and appar-
ently good Marlowe play" which, *after* the success of *Antony and
Cleopatra* and *Coriolanus*, "Shakespeare no doubt thought it worth
while to overhaul" in about 1609. But "for some reason not defin-
itely known" he abandoned the task at I. i. 57, and from this point
the revision was carried out by Francis Beaumont. Wells also bases
his theory largely on verbal parallels; but as Chambers points out,[4]
there is no special resemblance to Marlowe in the language of
Julius Cæsar, and "the derivation of Beaumont's diction from
Shakespeare's has long been recognized."

Finally, there is E. H. C. Oliphant, who is much more circum-
spect. He is content with a Shakespearian revision of an earlier
play, probably by Marlowe, with a few touches added by Beaumont, largely in Act IV, Scene iii.

The theories of these misguided men rest almost entirely on the
very dangerous evidence of linguistic parallels, with support from
allegedly un-Shakespearian practices in structure and characterization. As Chambers drily remarks,[5] "These conflicting theories

1. Robertson, *op. cit.*, p. 95.
2. William Wells, *The Authorship of Julius Cæsar* (1923).
3. *Op. cit.*, p. 25.   4. *William Shakespeare*, I, p. 399.   5. *Ibid.*

may perhaps be left to cancel each other out." It is perhaps worth recalling that before the time of Fleay no one ever hinted a doubt about the authorship of the play, that Jonson and Digges attributed it clearly enough to Shakespeare, and that Shakespeare's fellow-actors and intimate friends, Heminge and Condell, gave it to him in their authoritative edition of his plays, the First Folio.

7. THE TEXT OF "JULIUS CÆSAR"

The substantive text of *Julius Cæsar* is provided by the 1623 Folio, and no other text has any authority. Those of the three later Folios (1632, 1664, 1685) show the usual spelling-variants and the usual accretion of compositors' errors, with only rare attempts to correct what appear to be errors in the First Folio. They have no value for the determination of the text. There are no early Quarto editions, but towards the end of the seventeenth century six Quartos were printed, four of them undated, one dated 1684, and one 1691.[1]

From the cleanness of the First Folio text it is clear that Jaggard's compositors were printing from exceptionally tidy copy. There are comparatively few misprints, even of the trifling kind that every compositor is bound to make;[2] the punctuation is on the whole sound, and seldom goes so far astray as to cause confusion;[3] there is remarkably little mislineation, and what there is is due largely, not to bad copy, but to the splitting of lines in order to fit them into the rather narrow Folio column; and the misattribution of speeches is rare.[4] Moreover, there are fewer manifest corruptions[5] than in any other play in the Folio.

The claim of the old Cambridge editors[6] that *Julius Cæsar* may have been set up from "the original manuscript of the author" seems inadmissible. Dr Dover Wilson and Sir Walter Greg have pointed out[7] that there are no traces of Shakespearian spelling, and that the stage-directions suggest those of a prompt-copy. Greg de-

---

1. See Henrietta C. Bartlett, 'Quarto Editions of Julius Cæsar' (*The Library*, 3rd Series, IV, pp. 122 ff), 1913.
2. e.g., condltion, II. i. 254; Brntus, II. i. 255; tho bond, II. i. 280; ill remper'd too.s, IV. iii. 115; slumbler, IV. iii. 266.
3. See apparatus criticus on, e.g., I. i. 37, 39; I. ii. 164, 251; II. i. 15; V. v. 33.
4. e.g., I. i. 15, IV. ii. 34–6, V. iv. 7.
5. Such as I. iii. 129; II. i. 40; III. i. 39, 283.
6. *The Works of William Shakespeare*, ed. Clark and Wright, vol. VII, Preface, p. xii.
7. Wilson in Introduction to Folio Facsimile edition of *Julius Cæsar* (1929), and Notes on Copy in N.C.S. *Julius Cæsar*, pp. 92–3; Greg in *The Editorial Problem in Shakespeare* (2nd edn., 1951), pp. 143–4.

clares that "the latter are business-like without being bare: 'Enter
Boy with wine and tapers' is in character for the book-keeper, and
so are some flourishes and the like—'Low alarums. . . Alarm still.'
A few touches more literary," he goes on, "appear to have survived
from the author's manuscript: 'in his orchard', 'in his night gown',
'goes into the pulpit'."

Wilson, while confident that there has been prompt-book influence, thinks that "the actual copy was a transcript from the prompt-
book rather than that document itself." Apart from the unlikeli-
hood that the players would risk the loss of an "allowed book" by
sending it to press, he suspects "corruption here and there" by a
copyist in the Folio text. Judging from the usual results of multiply-
ing manuscripts from one another, I think it probable that there
would have been more corruption in this text than there is, if it had
been set up from a second transcript. Here if anywhere Heminge
and Condell seem to be justified in their boast that they were presenting their friend's plays "perfect of their limbes"; and copy at
only one remove from Shakespeare's "foul papers" is more likely
to be perfect of its limbs than that which is a further stage removed.
I suggest that the copy for *Julius Cæsar* was a careful scribal copy of
Shakespeare's "foul papers" which had been used as the prompt-
book.

In my notes I discuss two passages in which there may have been
some revision between the original writing of *Julius Cæsar* and its
publication in the Folio. It is possible that the former,[1] containing
originally the words, "Cæsar did never wrong, but with just cause,"
was out of deference to criticism from Jonson altered or abridged to
the Folio reading,

> Know, Cæsar doth not wrong, nor without cause
> Will he be satisfied.

In the two contradictory accounts of Portia's death[2] there appears
to be more certainty that revision has taken place. It seems probable that the earlier passage, in which Brutus himself tells Cassius of
Portia's death, represents Shakespeare's second thoughts, and presumably the later announcement by Messala was not removed because some mark of deletion was overlooked or misunderstood—
whether the alteration was made in Shakespeare's "foul papers" or
in the prompt-book. There are no other clear signs of revision,
though Dr Wilson thinks it possible that apparent inconsistencies
in Casca's character in the second and third scenes of Act I may be

1. III. i. 47–8.   2. IV. iii. 146–56 and 180–94.

due to some rewriting.[1] I do not myself see these inconsistencies.

There is one further point in connection with the text of *Julius Cæsar* that calls for mention. It has been a common practice to speak of the First Folio as a single text, as though it were identical in all its copies, although it has long been known that this is not so.[2] Professor Charlton Hinman's researches in the Folger Library are showing that, to a greater extent than has hitherto been realized, it is unsafe to speak thus: that the text in fact varies considerably in different surviving copies of the Folio.[3]

In the present state of our knowledge it would be unwise to generalize about printing-processes in the sixteenth and seventeenth centuries.[4] For the substance of what follows I have drawn on the article by Professor Hinman to which I have just reíerred.

In the printing-houses of the period, the first impression from a "forme", that is, the letterpress for one side of a full, unfolded sheet (two folio type-pages), was as a rule used as a proof-sheet and handed to the proof-reader for correction; but printing went on all the time that the proof was being read. When a proof had been read press-work was stopped to allow corrections to be made in the body of type locked up in the chase (i.e., the frame in which the pages of type were wedged to hold them firmly together on the press). Since both paper and labour were expensive, the uncorrected as well as the corrected sheets, and even at times the proof-sheets bearing the reader's correction-marks,[5] were bound into the complete volumes—not necessarily or even normally combined in the same order in all copies. Indeed almost every conceivable combination of corrected and uncorrected sheets may be found in different copies of the same book. This is so in surviving copies of Shakespeare's First Folio.

By an ingenious photographic process Professor Hinman had, up to April 1953, collated twenty-two copies of the First Folio through-

1. See Notes on the Copy, N.C.S. *Julius Cæsar*, pp. 96–7.

2. Sir Sidney Lee (in somewhat risky terms) declared, in the Introduction (p. xxx) to his Facsimile of the First Folio (1902), that "the variations among different copies of the First Folio are more numerous than those among copies belonging to the same edition of any other known book of the day."

3. See Charlton Hinman, 'Variant Readings in the First Folio of Shakespeare' (*Shakespeare Quarterly*, vol. IV, no. 3, July 1953, pp. 279–88).

4. For further information see, e.g., E. E. Willoughby, *The Printing of the First Folio of Shakespeare* (O.U.P., 1932); Fredson Bowers, 'Elizabethan Proofing' (*Joseph Quincy Adams Memorial Studies*, Folger Shak. Library, 1948); and Hinman's article just cited.

5. Four proof-sheets have already been discovered in different copies of the First Folio.

out the section embracing the Tragedies, and many more copies in the formes in this section which had already proved variant. He had not yet found a single copy made up wholly of corrected sheets, nor any pair of copies showing the same mixture of corrected and uncorrected states. If the gigantic task of collating the 230-odd extant copies of the Folio is ever completed, it may well be that some wholly corrected copies, or some twins, will reveal themselves. Meanwhile, on the evidence so far obtained, Hinman has been able to establish two general principles: that no two copies of the Folio, selected at random, should ever be supposed to be textually identical; and that no single copy can reasonably be regarded as providing "*the* First Folio Text".

The bearing of these investigations on the text of *Julius Cæsar* cannot be known until Hinman has carried them further and published his findings. It is at least possible that they may throw some light on the hitherto unsolved cruces in this text.

After these remarks, I should mention that I have worked from Dr Dover Wilson's facsimile of the First Folio text of *Julius Cæsar*, which is prepared from a copy of the First Folio in the Grenville Library at the British Museum.[1] I have often checked readings also in Sir Sidney Lee's facsimile of the whole Folio:[2] for instance, in all passages where there appears to be textual corruption, and wherever in Wilson's facsimile I have found badly broken letters, or gaps due possibly to faulty inking, possibly to dropped letters, or especially strange misprints.[3] This checking has filled in or completed a few letters, but has thrown no light on the corruptions. I have not collated the two copies, and do not know whether they vary in passages that I have not checked.

8. THE CHARACTERS

There are four fully developed figures of absorbing interest in *Julius Cæsar*: Cæsar himself, Brutus, Cassius, and Antony. For each

1. *Julius Cæsar, by William Shakespeare: A Facsimile of the First Folio Text, with an Introduction by J. Dover Wilson, Litt.D.* (Faber & Gwyer, 1929). Wilson does not state by what process his text is reproduced. I have assumed that it is a perfect facsimile.

2. *Shakespeares Comedies, Histories, & Tragedies: Being a Reproduction in Facsimile of the First Folio Edition, 1623, from the Chatsworth Copy in the Possession of the Duke of Devonshire, K.G. . . .* By Sidney Lee (Oxford, 1902).

3. e.g., at I. ii. 138 Lee gives "fault" clearly, where in Wilson the *a* and the *u* and most of the *l* are missing; at IV. iii. 267 Lee reads "Leaden" where in Wilson only the downstroke of the *L* is visible; at IV. iii. 115 both facsimiles read "ill remper'd too.s."

of them Shakespeare arouses in us some admiration and some degree of sympathy; in each he brings out some conspicuous defects of character. Cæsar is the titular hero, Brutus the dramatic hero.

Julius Cæsar. Cæsar's part in the play is small in comparison with those of Brutus, Cassius, and Antony, and he cannot therefore reveal himself fully in his speeches and actions. A good deal of what we learn about him emerges from the remarks of other men, whose opinions of him differ widely; and in piecing together the impression that Shakespeare wishes us to form of him, we must depend to some degree on passing remarks, hints, and implications. We must also try to differentiate between reliable and prejudiced judgement on the part of those who speak of him.

Nearly a century and a half ago Hazlitt wrote[1] of the play *Julius Cæsar:*

It . . . is remarkable for the profound knowledge of character, in which Shakespear could scarcely fail. If there is any exception to this remark, it is in the hero of the piece himself. We do not much admire the representation here given of Julius Cæsar, nor do we think it answers to the portrait given of him in his Commentaries. He makes several vapouring and rather pedantic speeches, and does nothing.

The view that Shakespeare has drawn his Cæsar merely as "a grand, strutting piece of puff-paste, . . a glorious vapourer and braggart, full of lofty airs and mock-thunder",[2] has, with a few dissentient voices, persisted to the present day. Dr Dover Wilson carries it further, indeed, and represents Shakespeare's Cæsar as a ruthless tyrant in the decline of his physical and moral powers. Drawing parallels from earlier and contemporary treatments of Cæsar, and assuming that Shakespeare accepted the current estimate of him as "an almost supernatural conqueror who out of lust for power ruined the Roman Republic" and was nobly slain by Brutus, Wilson begins his character-sketch thus:[3]

A Roman Tamburlaine of illimitable ambition and ruthless irresistible genius; a monstrous tyrant who destroyed his country and ruined 'the mightiest and most flourishing commonwealth that the world will ever see'—one feature remained to add before the sixteenth century stage-figure of the great dictator was complete,

---

1. William Hazlitt, *Characters of Shakespear's Plays*, 1805. Quoted from *The Complete Works of William Hazlitt*, ed. P. P. Howe, IV, p. 195.
2. H. N. Hudson, *Shakespeare: His Life, Art, and Characters*, 1872, II, p. 224.
3. Introduction to N.C.S. *Julius Cæsar*, p. xxv.

that of a braggart, of the 'thrasonical Cæsar,' to whom Shakespeare refers more than once.[1]

Wilson goes on to give a well-worn list of Cæsar's moral and physical deficiencies, and points out where Shakespeare has distorted Plutarch to give them prominence or increase them.

I do not believe that Shakespeare would ever have been content, as Wilson implies, to accept conventional judgements on a historical personage whom he intended to dramatize. He did not take his Cæsar from Muret's Latin play or Grévin's *César*, neither of which he is likely to have known, nor from Kyd's version of Garnier's *Cornélie*, nor the anonymous *Cæsar's Revenge*—all of them plays which do show, indeed, a more or less hostile attitude to Cæsar. His source was Plutarch. He had read North's *Plutarch* carefully, and had it open beside him while he was writing his play.

But he did not even accept Plutarch's Cæsar entire; he selected and adapted according to the emphasis that he wanted to give to his plot. He gave Cæsar a defect not found in Plutarch in making him deaf in one ear; he allowed him to succumb to the falling-sickness at a very awkward moment; and he caused Cassius to tell stories against him—stories which we are intended to see, however, as being strongly coloured by Cassius's rancour. If he had really wished to denigrate Cæsar, as so many critics feel he did, he could have found plenty of material in Plutarch on which to build: the suspicion that Cæsar was implicated in Catiline's conspiracy; his dishonourable treatment of Cato; his "shamefullest part" in choosing as Tribune Publius Clodius, "that had offered his wife such dishonour"; his sacrilegious robbery of the Temple of Saturn; his dishonourable motives in the Egyptian wars. Moreover, he could have intensified his arrogance by citing, for example, the occasion on which he disdained to rise before the officers of state who came to tell him of honours that the Senate had decreed for him. These things Shakespeare ignored; and his alterations and additions to Plutarch do not, taken as a whole, suggest a desire to blacken Cæsar's character. On the contrary, his presentation is more favourable than that of Plutarch.

Following Plutarch, he could have depicted Cæsar as a man universally hated in Rome, not merely by a few malcontents. "But the chiefest cause that made him mortally hated was the covetous desire he had to be called king: which first gave the people just cause, and next his secret enemies honest colour, to bear him ill-will." Thus Plutarch:[2] "Gave *the people* just cause . . . to bear him ill-will."

---

1. Wilson here gives references to *Cym.*, III. i. 23; *AYL.*, v. ii. 30; and *2 H 4,* IV. iii. 41.   2. Skeat, p. 94. See Appendix, p. 132.

Yet in the first scene of the play the people of Rome are seen rejoicing in Cæsar's triumph. After his assassination these same people
are "beside themselves with fear" (III. i. 180), not transported with
delight at the death of a hated ruler. Brutus persuades them, indeed,
that Cæsar was a tyrant; but it does not take Antony long to make
them feel that he was worthy of the love and reverence they had
formerly had for him. It is sometimes said that the opening scene of
the play significantly introduces a Cæsar so ruthless that he will
celebrate a triumph even over his own countrymen. The triumph
was a fact of history which Shakespeare could not annul, but he
made of it at least something in favour of Cæsar. Plutarch tells us[1]
that it "did as much offend the Romans, and more, than any thing
that ever he had done before: because he had not overcome captains that were strangers, nor barbarous kings, but had destroyed
the sons of the noblest man of Rome, whom fortune had overthrown". Shakespeare shows him as the darling of the commons.
The Tribunes upbraid them, indeed, but these Tribunes are represented as adherents of Pompey, naturally hostile to his conqueror,
and angry at the "ingratitude" shown towards him by the fickle
populace.

Cæsar is so much "the foremost man of all this world"—to bor-
row Brutus's description—that his greatness and nobility do not
need to be emphasized; they are implicit in the attitude towards
him of every one else in the play. "The force and strength of his
character is seen in the impression he makes upon forceful and
strong men," says Moulton,[2] referring to Brutus and Antony, both
of whom love and admire Cæsar. I shall return to this point.

In the second scene Cæsar makes his first appearance, attended
by the leading men of Rome and followed by a great crowd. We
see at once that he is a man of immense authority. When he speaks
Casca bids every noise be still; when he gives orders Antony says,
"When Cæsar says, 'Do this,' it is perform'd." We are told by some
commentators that he is superstitious, because he believes that if
Calphurnia is touched by Antony during the "holy chase" she may
be cured of her barrenness. But this was a belief common to all the
Romans of his day, and his subscription to it has no significance in
a consideration of his character. Shakespeare took it from Plutarch. When the Soothsayer bids Cæsar beware the ides of March,
he brushes him aside as a "dreamer". A really superstitious man
would have taken the warning seriously; but Cæsar will not regard
a threat to his personal safety, even if it comes from a soothsayer.
The interview between Brutus and Cassius that follows is highly

1. Skeat, p. 91. See Appendix, p. 138. 2. *Shakespeare as a Dramatic Artist*, p. 176.

interesting, and critics who are intent on finding fault with Cæsar
have made much of it, accepting Cassius's account of Cæsar's shortcomings as a sign of Shakespeare's intention to belittle him. This is
scarcely fair to his presentation of either man. We have just had a
glimpse of a Cæsar who has such authority that "many of the best
respect in Rome", including Brutus and Antony and Casca, are
anxious to serve him. In a few minutes we are to have a pre-emin-
ent example of his sagacity and judgement. Meanwhile a glance at
some of his weaknesses can do him no real harm. Cassius tells us
about them, and they are not serious weaknesses. Once in a fit of
bravado he challenged Cassius to swim against him in the swollen
Tiber and got the worst of the contest. Another time, in Spain, he
had a high fever, and Cassius marked "how he did shake; 'tis true,
this god did shake," and became like any other human being, and
cried out for water.

These speeches of Cassius do not detract from the greatness of
Cæsar; they tell us much about the littleness of Cassius, the envious
malcontent who is obsessed with a sense of his inferiority to Cæsar.
He is trying to work on the feelings of Brutus, and he cannot control the rush of his own feelings. He is conscious that beside Cæsar,
the Colossus, he is a petty underling; he cannot endure that Cæsar
should "so get the start of the majestic world, and bear the palm
alone". As will happen with such unstable natures, chafing under a
sense of inferiority, he works himself into a fury over these two instances of ungodlike physical weakness in Cæsar, and magnifies
them beyond all proportion. That he is able to impose on Brutus
is rather an indication of Brutus's lack of insight into character than
of any deficiency in Cæsar.

It would not be fair to assume that Cassius is insincere. He could
scarcely consider Cæsar's infirmities to be serious faults in themselves; what he wants to do is to enforce the contrast between the
self-styled demigod Cæsar, and Cæsar the man of ordinary human
frailties. He would regard himself as trying to break the hypnotic
spell which holds the Romans in an exaggerated awe of such a man.
But his judgement is warped by his private motives for wishing to
be rid of Cæsar, and instead of a reasoned exposition of his point of
view, he becomes hysterical about it and gives a thoroughly distorted picture of Cæsar as a weakling.

This contrast in Cæsar is so heavily stressed by Shakespeare that
he must have intended it to be an important part of his dramatic
theme. We are prepared for his treatment of Cæsar by the concern
with kingship that he shows in his English history plays. Like
Richard II, but of course with infinitely greater reason, Cæsar

lapses into the fault habitual with Richard of attributing to himself as a man the inviolability proper to the divinely ordained ruler. Indeed, Cæsar himself, Cassius in the passage under discussion, and Brutus in his soliloquy in his garden, each in his own characteristic way misinterprets the relation between Cæsar's spirit, which informs his magistracy and vocation, and the imperfect, vulnerable man Cæsar. Brutus thinks how admirable it would be if the spirit of Cæsar, which he has wrongly become convinced is evil, could be destroyed without killing the man, and concludes that it is vulnerable only through the man. He is to find that the spirit of Cæsar is invulnerable, even though the man, and only the man, whom he did not wish to kill, is mortal.

Hard upon Cassius's outburst, which has been punctuated, and given some weight in the mind of Brutus, by excited shouting in the market-place, Cæsar returns; and at first he does not appear to advantage. He is in a very bad temper. He has been offered a crown, which of course he would like to accept; but he has felt compelled, or has felt it expedient, to refuse it, though three times offered. He is mortified by the applause that greeted his refusal. Moreover, he has made something of an exhibition of himself by being overcome by the stinking breath of the rabble and having an epileptic seizure. His eye lights on Cassius, whose feelings are still inflamed and who doubtless is glaring malevolently at him, and suddenly a new Cæsar is revealed. He treats us to a brilliant piece of character-reading which is in marked contrast with the frequently displayed naïveté of Brutus. His analysis of Cassius is one of the most impressive passages in the play, and we feel that a man who can judge his fellow men with this penetration should rightly stand at the head of his nation. Antony here makes the kind of mistake that he is not to make in the second half of the play; he does not think Cassius dangerous. Cæsar is not deceived:

> Such men as he be never at heart's ease
> Whiles they behold a greater than themselves,
> And therefore are they very dangerous. (I. ii. 205–7)

Here is the very soul of Cassius laid bare, by the man he has just been blackguarding in the pettiest fashion. Cæsar delivers this judgement with a touch of his characteristic arrogance:

> I rather tell thee what is to be fear'd
> Than what I fear; for always I am Cæsar.

But we have good-humouredly accepted arrogance of this kind in recent English leaders who have served us conspicuously; why not in Shakespeare's Cæsar? Nor does the immediately succeeding reference to his deafness take away from the greatness shown in the speech as a whole, as is so often implied. Cæsar's moral ascendancy over the Romans has already been sufficiently established by Shakespeare, and neither the deafness, nor the epileptic fit that Casca is about to describe, will make us think of him as "a sick girl" or a man of "a feeble temper".

Casca's account of the scene in the market-place, with its scarcely veiled hostility to Cæsar, must not, for what it can tell us of Cæsar's character, be taken any more seriously than Cassius's tirade. We are told beforehand (I. ii. 178) that Casca will describe the affair "after his sour fashion"; and when he has done so, we learn that, though he is really "quick mettle", he puts on a "tardy form", and that his "rudeness is a sauce to his good wit". The envious Casca is in fact, like Cassius, a malcontent, but has his feelings under better control; he tries to hide them beneath the affectation of bluntness and good-humoured surliness. He is not to be trusted. He is obsequious in Cæsar's presence, and jeers at him behind his back. Later he is to stab him from behind.

This important and revealing scene ends with the soliloquy in which Cassius talks of the devices by which he will "seduce" the credulous Brutus into joining the dastardly conspiracy against Cæsar.

The third scene opens upon the cowering figure of Casca, whose abject fear of the fearful tempest and the prodigies it has brought forth is thrown into relief by the philosophical and rather scornful calm of Cicero. Cassius is worked into a state of high excitement by the strange impatience of the heavens, and rashly dares them to do their worst with him. As far as Cæsar is concerned, this scene is chiefly interesting, apart from the development of the conspiracy, for the way in which Cassius likens him to the portents of the night. In Cassius's obsessed mind Cæsar is actually "prodigious grown;" and when, working upon Casca, he speaks of Cæsar as a tyrant, and, warming to his work, as a vile thing, we shall recognize again that he is giving himself away, not telling us anything about Cæsar. The storm serves another purpose as well: an Elizabethan audience would see it as an omen of Cæsar's approaching death. They would scarcely need Calphurnia's later warning: "The heavens themselves blaze forth the death of princes" (II. ii. 31).

Act II, Scene i, shows us the monstrous visage of the maturing conspiracy, and on stage or screen is full of excitement. In it we also learn much about Cæsar, from an honest man who is striving to be entirely fair-minded. Brutus knows no personal cause to spurn at

Cæsar, he says; but he has been whetted against him by Cassius, and has spent a night of sleepless torment trying to work out what course of action will be best for the welfare of the state.

> He would be crown'd:
> How that might change his nature, there's the question.
> ... Th' abuse of greatness is when it disjoins
> Remorse from power; and, *to speak truth of Cæsar,*
> *I have not known when his affections sway'd*
> *More than his reason.* (II. i. 12–21)

But, he goes on, it is a common experience that the ambitious man who has climbed to the top of the ladder scorns the lower steps—becomes a god and tyrannizes over those beneath him.

> So Cæsar *may;*
> Then lest he may, prevent. *And since the quarrel*
> *Will bear no colour for the thing he is,*
> *Fashion it thus:* that what he is, augmented,
> Would run to these and these extremities. (II. i. 27–31)

Brutus has never known Cæsar to be governed by his feelings rather than his judgement, yet in his agony of indecision he is willing to "fashion it thus", to make it look like this: that, like the common run of men, he will let kingly power go to his head. On a purely hypothetical assumption he resolves to slay his "best lover". He has persuaded himself that he is doing it for the good of Rome. He is not dishonest, merely blind. Though his reasoning is false, his motives are of the loftiest, and alone of the conspirators he will be a sacrificer, not a butcher.

In this scene we also learn from Decius (ll. 203–8) that Cæsar is susceptible to flattery. This is a weakness not uncommon in great men, and I do not think we need count it heavily against Cæsar.

Now (II. ii) we are taken to Cæsar's house on the morning of the assassination. Commentators have spoken of the superstitious fear and the vacillation of Cæsar in this scene. I see no sign of either. It has been a night of fearful prodigies. Calphurnia has had terrifying dreams and three times in her sleep has cried out, "Help, ho! they murther Cæsar!" The bravest man might be frightened. Not so Cæsar. There is to be an important meeting of the Senate, and he is determined to attend it in spite of Calphurnia's fears and pleas. He orders sacrifices to be made, as any prudent Roman would—"to know what should happen him that day", as Plutarch puts it; but when the omens are unfavourable, and he is warned by the augurs not to leave the house, he remains unshaken in his determination: "And Cæsar shall go forth." If there is anything of which we can disapprove in his conduct here, it is not his superstitious fear, but rather something approaching foolhardiness, and the too emphatic assertion of his fearlessness.

> Cowards die many times before their deaths;
> The valiant never taste of death but once,

he says, and this is a noble utterance, worthy of Cæsar at his greatest. But he goes on to speak of himself in inflated terms:

> Danger knows full well
> That Cæsar is more dangerous than he.
> We are two lions litter'd in one day,
> And I the elder and more terrible.

This is the thrasonical Cæsar,[1] whose "wisdom is consum'd in confidence", as Calphurnia tells him. His arrogance in assuming that he is too great to be liable to ordinary human fears is emphasized by his referring to himself in the third person, and a little later by the manner in which he bids Decius tell the greybeard senators that he "will not come" to the session.

Shakespeare has significantly modified Plutarch's account of this episode. According to Plutarch,[2] the violence and noise of the storm in the night awoke Cæsar, "and made him afraid when he saw such light: but more, when he heard his wife Calpurnia, being fast asleep, weep and sigh, and put forth many fumbling lamentable speeches . . . it seemed that Cæsar likewise did fear or suspect somewhat. . . But much more afterwards, when the soothsayers having sacrificed many beasts one after another, told him that none did like them." For all his boastfulness, he is a stronger man in Shakespeare than in Plutarch.

In spite of his firmly expressed intention of going to the Senate House, he does at length agree to stay at home, but only when Calphurnia has knelt before him with the most moving entreaties to do so. He is persuaded to feel ashamed of yielding to her fears when Decius gives an interpretation of her dream as rational as her own, and more flattering, and tells him that the Senate have decided to offer him the crown. Whatever we may think of his behaviour, it is scarcely fair to call it vacillation.

---

1. It is easy to lay too much stress on Cæsar's boastfulness. Where a modern play-goer might take Cæsar's claims to fearlessness merely as evidence of his vanity and vainglory, an Elizabethan, accustomed to the technique of "direct self-explanation" in drama, would also see in them Shakespeare's "handiest way of telling the audience that Cæsar *is* fearless." (See J. I. M. Stewart, 'Julius Cæsar and Macbeth', *Mod. Lang. Rev.*, XL (1945), pp. 166–71.)

2. Skeat, p. 98; Appendix, pp. 142–3.

We now have a picture of the courtly and gracious Cæsar. He has the right word of welcome for each of the conspirators, who have come to escort him to the Senate House, Cassius alone being absent. The scene closes with the irony of his courteous invitation:

Good friends, go in, and taste some wine with me;
And we, *like friends*, will straightway go together.   (II. ii. 126–7)

Brutus is the only one to feel the irony.

Shakespeare begins the assassination scene with another significant departure from Plutarch. Artemidorus presents his schedule, urging Cæsar to read it first, since it touches him more nearly than that proffered by Decius. In Plutarch,[1] "Cæsar took it of him, but could never read it, though he many times attempted it, for the number of people that did salute him." Shakespeare gives the incident a nobler turn. "What touches us ourself shall be last served," says Cæsar; and when Artemidorus becomes more pressing, he thrusts him aside with the words, "What, is the fellow mad?"

In the seventy lines or so that remain before the assassination, Shakespeare deliberately alienates some of the sympathy and admiration that his Cæsar has awakened in us. This is essential if we are not to feel that the stabbing is mere senseless butchery. It is that, of course, as we are very soon to realize, but for the moment we must not be allowed to feel so, or we shall lose the sense of dramatic conflict. Some balance of sympathy must be maintained, as it has hitherto been maintained by the shifting emphasis laid upon the faults and virtues both of the conspirators and of Cæsar. The envy and fanaticism of Cassius have been set off by the honest if misguided motives of Brutus, the arrogance of Cæsar by his nobility.

Now the arrogance takes the upper hand. For a few minutes we forget our admiration, as we are intended to do, and it is only the agony of his last cry, when he sees that Brutus too has betrayed him, that reawakens some of our sympathy.

What is now amiss
That Cæsar and his senate must redress?

So Cæsar begins, and as he repels the successive petitions presented on Publius Cimber's behalf with increasingly inflated expressions of his inflexibility, so we steadily harden our hearts against him. With the words, "Hence! Wilt thou lift up Olympus?" we feel that here is a monstrous pride that must have a fall, and are almost prepared to accept the justice of the conspirators' action.

1. Skeat, p. 99; Appendix, p. 147.

Almost prepared, and only for a moment. For assassination is no way in which to bring pride low, pride moreover that is not associated with any form of criminality. It is not many minutes before any sympathy that we may have felt with the conspirators is alienated more decisively and more permanently than that for Cæsar which we lost only temporarily. Henceforth, with Cæsar's person removed, we are to hear nothing but good of him, except in the inexplicable statement[1] of Brutus, during his quarrel with Cassius, that this foremost man of all the world was slain "but for supporting robbers" (IV. iii. 23). With Cæsar's dying words,

> *Et tu, Brute?*—Then fall Cæsar!

Brutus's treachery is fully brought home to us, though not to him; and the theatrical episode in which he and the other conspirators bathe their hands in Cæsar's blood merely disgusts us. We cannot, like him, see in this action a grand symbol of "peace, freedom, and liberty".

The interview, first with Antony's servant and then with Antony himself, emphasizes the superiority of Cæsar to all other Romans. The message brought by the servant begins with cautious and politic flattery, and with more than a touch of the irony that Antony is to develop so effectively in a few moments: "Brutus is noble, wise, valiant, and honest." But can we doubt the sincerity of the next line: "Cæsar was mighty, bold, royal, and loving"? Antony professes to love and honour Brutus; his behaviour both before and after the assassination shows how he "fear'd Cæsar, honour'd him, and lov'd him". When he comes into the presence of the conspirators and looks down on Cæsar's body, the reality and depth of his grief are unquestionable; but he is also emboldened by it to make the first steps towards vengeance. However, the means by which he brings the vengeance about belong to a later section.

As far as the presentation of Cæsar is concerned, we are reminded in Antony's speeches here of his "conquests, glories, triumphs, spoils"; we are told that he was the "heart" of the world (III. i. 208), and is now

> the ruins of the noblest man
> That ever lived in the tide of times;

1. Inexplicable, that is, as far as the play is concerned, for Cæsar's association with robbers has not been previously mentioned. However, if Shakespeare is careless in introducing a new motive for the assassination thus late, it is because at this point he is following Plutarch closely: "Brutus in contrary manner answered, that he should remember the Ides of March, at which time they slew Julius Cæsar, who neither pilled nor polled the country, but only was a favourer and suborner of all them that did rob and spoil, by his countenance and authority" (Skeat, p. 135; Appendix, p. 157).

and we hear the assassins justly described as "butchers" and "bloody men", whose

> foul deed shall smell above the earth
> With carrion men, groaning for burial.

Moreover, we see the spirit of Cæsar animating Antony to outwit alike the naïve Brutus and the shrewd Cassius, and we soon realize that he has entrusted his vengeance to safe hands. By the end of the assassination scene Cæsar has regained a great deal of the sympathy that he lost in the opening part, and the conspirators have forfeited all our respect.

In the Forum speeches of Brutus and Antony we are told by Brutus that Cæsar had to be killed because he was ambitious, but otherwise we hear nothing that is not to his credit. From both we learn that he was a loving friend; from Antony, that he was valorous, faithful and just to his friends, and generous and public-spirited in filling the general coffers with the ransoms of his captured foes and in making a will that benefited every single Roman citizen.

The second half of the play, as has often been pointed out, is dominated by Cæsar's spirit. Though his body has been slain, his spirit manifests itself in many ways, and he is never long absent from the thoughts of those who slew him. Brutus spoke more truly than he knew when, at the first meeting of the conspirators, he declared,

> We all stand up against the spirit of Cæsar, (II. i. 167)

for it was this spirit that rose up from the base of Pompey's statue to exact vengeance for bloody treason. Antony gave a new and ominous turn to the phrase in his prophecy over Cæsar's body:

> And Cæsar's spirit, ranging for revenge,
> With Ate by his side come hot from hell,
> Shall in these confines with a monarch's voice
> Cry havoc and let slip the dogs of war. (III. i. 270–3)

And Brutus, seeing in the death of Cassius a manifestation of the dead Cæsar's power, exclaimed:

> O Julius Cæsar, thou art mighty yet!
> Thy spirit walks abroad, and turns our swords
> In our own proper entrails. (v. iii. 94–6)

Cæsar is in the minds of Brutus and Cassius throughout their quarrel, as is shown by their significant references to him. That same night his ghost appears to Brutus, and we learn later (v. v.

17–19) that it visits him again on the eve of the battle at Philippi. This ghost, as Dowden says,[1] "serves as a kind of visible symbol of the vast posthumous power of the dictator". It works through the omens to dispirit the armies of Brutus and Cassius on the march to Philippi (v. i. 80–9), and clouds the judgement of Cassius during the battle.

Finally, both Brutus and Cassius die with Cæsar's name on their lips. Cassius turns upon himself the sword that ran through Cæsar's bowels, with the words,

> Cæsar, thou art reveng'd
> Even with the sword that killed thee.

Brutus dies with the knowledge that he has lost all that he held most dear, his wife, his best friends, and the cause for which he pledged himself to murder Cæsar. With a full realization of his failure, he apostrophizes Cæsar's spirit as he runs upon his sword:

> Cæsar, now be still;
> I kill'd not thee with half so good a will.

With the deaths of Brutus and Cassius, Cæsar's revenge is complete; though his body is dead, his spirit has triumphed. The play rightly bears his name.

Can it be doubted that Shakespeare wishes us to admire his Cæsar? He has wasted no words in formal panegyric; Cæsar's stature has been revealed in more subtle ways, and the final effect is all the more striking. "Cæsar's greatness is assumed throughout the play. It fills the mind of the dramatist and is communicated to the audience in phrases that fall from his pen whenever Cæsar is mentioned, even by his enemies."[2] Cæsar has some weaknesses, of course. He has ambition, if that be a weakness, and not rather an essential accompaniment of greatness; his was not the uncontrolled and wicked ambition of Macbeth. He has pride and vanity, but these are qualities that not infrequently fall to the share of the great. He has one or two physical disabilities, but these do not prevent us from remembering that he was one of the mightiest conquerors in the world's history—and we are reminded in the play that he was so. Cæsar's shortcomings give him concrete reality as a fallible human being like ourselves; it is actually necessary that they should be given some prominence if he is not to tower so far above the other characters as to destroy the dramatic balance of the tragedy. Without some apparent justification for the conspiracy

1. *Shakspere: His Mind and Art*, p. 288.
2. John Palmer, *Political Characters of Shakespeare*, p. 35.

against him, his assassination could not have been felt as anything more than wanton and motiveless butchery. By his treatment of Cæsar, Shakespeare has not only provided some intelligible motives for this almost incredible piece of criminal folly; he has also made the almost legendary figure of Cæsar himself come convincingly to life.

Marcus Brutus. Brutus is the dramatic hero of *Julius Cæsar.* He is the most prominent figure, and at almost every stage our interest is focused on his deliberations and decisions. Obviously Shakespeare was greatly interested by the mind of Brutus. As presented by Plutarch, he was a man of great probity and integrity, and of sound judgement backed by a philosophical training, and he was loved and esteemed by his compatriots. Yet he slew the one undoubted genius of his age, partly, we gather from Plutarch, because he was ambitious of succeeding him as leader of the state, partly because of some not clearly specified private quarrel, and partly because he was incensed against him by Cassius. His hatred of tyranny, which is mentioned almost in passing, made him the readier to listen to Cassius's promptings. We may suppose that Shakespeare found it difficult to reconcile the conspicuous wisdom and virtue of Plutarch's Brutus with the motives he was given for desiring Cæsar's death. At any rate, he modified his character in several ways, making him at the same time more obviously consistent in the purity of his intentions, and less amiable and less intelligent.

I cannot help feeling that the majority of past critics have been misled by Brutus's estimate of himself into regarding him as a more wholly admirable person than Shakespeare intended him to be. The dramatist, says MacCallum,[1] "reserves his chief enthusiasm for Brutus"; and "throughout the piece, it is the personality of Brutus that attracts our chief sympathy and concern."[2] The terms in which almost all other commentators discuss the character of Brutus are similarly those of admiration and approval.

In *Julius Cæsar* the virtue and nobility of Plutarch's Brutus are brought out, but beside them are set a number of faults for which there is little or no warrant in Plutarch. Shakespeare's Brutus is, with all his estimable qualities, pompous, opinionated and self-righteous. His judgement is not to be trusted. He is led by the nose by Cassius and gulled by Antony. At almost every crisis in his fortunes he makes decisions, against the advice of experienced men of the world, that contribute materially to the failure of his cause. He seems completely blind to reality, an ineffectual idealist whose

1. *Shakespeare's Roman Plays*, p. 215.   2. *Ibid.*, p. 212.

idealism cannot prevent him from committing a senseless and
terrible crime. We may respect the motives for which he spares
Antony's life, and later allows him to speak in Cæsar's funeral—if
not the reasoning by which he led himself to think Cæsar's death
necessary; but on both occasions his decisions are foolish blunders
as far as the success of the conspiracy is concerned.

The character of Cæsar is established by incidental phrases and
by implication rather than by statement or description. Of Brutus
we hear much more, both from other people and from himself. We
soon learn that he is greatly respected by all who know him. Cassius declares that he is noble (I. ii. 305), and adds that he is one of
those honourable men who, themselves innocent of guile, may
easily be "seduced" by less honourable but cleverer men. At the
end of the next scene Casca pays him a high tribute:

> O, he sits high in all the people's hearts:
> And that which would appear offence in us,
> His countenance, like richest alchemy,
> Will change to virtue and to worthiness. (I. iii. 157–60)

All the conspirators, even Cassius, defer to his opinions at their first
meeting. Caius Ligarius calls him "Soul of Rome", and pledges
himself to an unknown enterprise simply because Brutus leads him
on. Cæsar, too, loves Brutus dearly.

For the modern play-goer admiration is somewhat tempered by
the manner in which Brutus himself frequently stresses his sense of
his own disinterestedness and honour. In one of his very first
speeches he says:

> What is it that you would impart to me?
> If it be aught toward the general good,
> Set honour in one eye, and death i' th' other,
> And I will look on both indifferently;
> For let the gods so speed me as I love
> The name of honour more than I fear death. (I. ii. 83–8)

It should be remembered, however, that one of Shakespeare's sim-
plest—and habitual—methods of telling us what a person is really
like is to let that person himself tell us. We must be on our guard
against judging Brutus's estimate of himself according to modern
notions of how people should speak about themselves, and saying
that in this and similar utterances he is merely "talking big".
Nevertheless, his manner at various points in the play does not give
us as favourable an impression of him as his friends entertain.

Although he has been drawn into the conspiracy by Cassius, he
assumes the rôle of leader as his natural due, though it must be ad-

mitted that no one questions his right to the position. However, he takes advantage of it to veto every proposal put forward by any one else. Cassius wants the conspirators to bind themselves by an oath. No, says Brutus, conscious of his own integrity, the word of a Roman is inviolable; and he delivers a pompous little homily on the virtue of their enterprise and the sacredness of a Roman promise. Then Cassius, seconded by Casca, Cinna, and Metellus, suggests that Cicero be sounded about joining them, but Brutus firmly rejects the suggestion. Cassius points out the potential danger in sparing Antony's life, and urges that he should fall with Cæsar. And again Brutus knows better: Antony, he says, "can do no more than Cæsar's arm when Cæsar's head is off". It is not the moral rightness of his decision here that we question, but the immediate grounds on which he bases it, and his inability to see that, once committed to the monstrous conspiracy, he would be defeating its ends if he did not ensure its success by whatever means. Surely it is with deliberate irony that Shakespeare in the middle of this discussion makes Brutus say of another man,

> For he will never follow any thing
> That other men begin. (II. i. 151–2)

In much the same tone Brutus, after the death of Cæsar, overrides Cassius's prudent objection to letting Antony speak in Cæsar's funeral. Antony will be speaking with his gracious permission, and after he himself has given the people unanswerable reasons for Cæsar's death; and in any case he sees no cause to distrust Antony's professions. Throughout this episode he shows an almost ludicrous naïveté, yet at the end his self-esteem is probably higher than at any other time in the play—as of course Antony intended it should be.

It is during his quarrel with Cassius that Brutus shows to least advantage. No one who reads with care the first hundred lines of Act IV, Scene iii, could feel that Shakespeare meant us to have any sympathy with Brutus during this exchange. It is otherwise in later parts of the scene; but while the altercation is at its height, though we may grant that Brutus has right on his side in the main points at issue, his demeanour is intolerable. He adopts the tone of an Olympian god chiding an erring mortal, and at the same time lapses into the language of a squabbling schoolboy. Cæsar himself is no more arrogant than Brutus when he says, for example:

> There is no terror, Cassius, in your threats;
> For I am arm'd so strong in honesty
> That they pass by me as the idle wind,
> Which I respect not. (IV. iii. 66–9)

This aspect of Brutus is brought into prominence several times in later scenes. For instance, when Octavius says, "I was not born to die on Brutus' sword," Brutus replies,

> O, if thou wert the noblest of thy strain,
> Young man, thou could'st not die more honourable.
> (v. i. 59–60)

Later in the same scene he declares to Cassius:

> Think not, thou noble Roman,
> That ever Brutus will go bound to Rome;
> He bears too great a mind. (v. i. 111–13)

And finally, a few moments before he abjures his Stoic principles and takes his life, when the battle to which he has ill-advisedly committed the republican armies is lost, and all that he stands for is in ruins, he says:

> I shall have glory by this losing day
> More than Octavius and Mark Antony
> By this vile conquest shall attain unto. (v. v. 36–8)

However, as I have said, we must beware of hasty judgements. "All that he stands for is in ruins"; "this vile conquest": if we bear these words in mind we shall not put too harsh a construction on Brutus's speeches. Some of his "thrasonical" utterances must be put down to Shakespeare's technique of making his characters reveal their own qualities by direct reference to them; some, in the later scenes, to a species of unconscious compensation in Brutus for the defeat of all the high principles by which he had been governed in joining the conspiracy and in his subsequent actions. In Brutus Shakespeare gives us a very subtle portrait of a man divided against himself—"with himself at war", to use Brutus's own phrase. Even before his first encounter with Cassius he has been torn by conflicting passions: his admiration for Cæsar's high gifts and noble qualities and his fears of his ambition, his love for Cæsar as a personal friend and his sense of duty to the republic. Throughout the play he is to some degree accompanied by this internal conflict. It is this that leads him to justify and assert himself so positively, this that stands behind much of his demeanour to Cassius during the quarrel, this that causes him to kill himself with a better will than that with which he slew Cæsar. He is an entirely honourable man engaged in what he does not realize is a dishonourable cause, and associated with unscrupulous men whose lack of principle he does not see and would not understand. The sense of conflict in him is best seen in his soliloquy in his garden. The line of reasoning which here leads him to decide that Cæsar must die has already been discussed;[1] it should be added that the soliloquy is a wonderful exposition of the state of mind of a man who, with reasons that are very nearly right, reaches a conclusion that is entirely wrong.

It is impossible not to sympathize with Brutus in his agonizing dilemma; but it is even more impossible to sympathize with its outcome. For, having reached the wrong conclusion, Brutus goes no further. The other conspirators "did that they did in envy of great Cæsar"; all that mattered to them was that Cæsar should be got out of the way. Brutus thinks that he is acting from the purest patriotic motives; it does not occur to him that he is doing the state no service by robbing it of its head and making no provision for its safety thereafter—for so it appears in the play. When Cæsar has fallen the conspirators, including Brutus, are at a loss. Until Antony imposes on them a course of action for the following day, all they can think of doing, apart from bathing their hands in the murdered man's blood, is to walk about in a transport of republican enthusiasm, waving their bloody swords and shouting, "Peace, freedom, and liberty!" Within twenty-four hours of Cæsar's death, Antony is in charge of the city, not Brutus; he and Cassius have fled for their lives.

Cæsar grows in stature as the play proceeds; Brutus deteriorates. In his quarrel with Cassius he is irritable, undignified, and unjust; he is more intolerant of the meddlesome poet than Cassius; and though he vehemently disputes Cassius's claim to be the abler soldier, his reasons for engaging the enemy at Philippi are less convincing than those of Cassius for deferring the battle. It is impossible to reconcile Shakespeare's presentation of Brutus with the common Renaissance view of him as the great liberator and patriot, the second of his name to free the Romans from the tyrant's yoke.

He is shown at his most sympathetic in his intimate personal relationships. Hard upon the meeting of the conspirators comes the beautiful episode in which Portia insists on sharing his anxieties. Here he is seen as the tender and loving, and dearly loved, husband. The prelude to this encounter brings out his affectionate consideration for his serving-lad Lucius, and this is seen again at the end of the quarrel scene.

The loyal friendship that Brutus can inspire is well illustrated in the last scene of the play, when he and the poor remains of his supporters are resting from the battle which they now know to be lost. He asks them in turn to hold his sword while he runs upon it, and they shrink back from the request in horror. In this moment of de-

1. See pp. xxxii–xxxiii.

feat and humiliation their sorrow is all for him, not for themselves; and conscious of their love, Brutus is moved to say,

> My heart doth joy that yet in all my life
> I found no man but he was true to me.

If I seem to have emphasized Brutus's less admirable qualities at the expense of the many fine qualities with which Shakespeare endows him, it is not that I underrate the latter, but because the majority of commentators have brought out what is sympathetic in him to the virtual exclusion of the faults that Shakespeare must equally want us to see in him. Brutus seems to me to be a man whom we must respect, but for whom it is difficult to feel love. Shakespeare accentuates any weaknesses or errors for which there is the slightest warrant in Plutarch, and gives him what is in many respects a disagreeable personality—such a personality, indeed, as is not uncommon in perfectly upright men who cannot see beyond their own strict code of conduct. On the other hand, he makes him act from an entirely sincere belief that he is serving his country by killing Cæsar. He shows him struggling with a problem beyond his capacity to resolve, and in his perplexity coming to the wrong decision. A man who committed Brutus's crime could not be portrayed as a wholly sympathetic character; but Shakespeare shows him as blind, not evil. And finally he buries Brutus's crime in his virtues, and ends the play with Antony's tribute:

> This was the noblest Roman of them all.
> All the conspirators save only he
> Did that they did in envy of great Cæsar;
> He only, in a general honest thought
> And common good to all, made one of them.
> His life was gentle, and the elements
> So mix'd in him, that Nature might stand up
> And say to all the world, "This was a man!"

This is the impression of Brutus that Shakespeare leaves with us. He leaves us with the feeling, too, that the play, though it rightly bears Cæsar's name, is rather "The Death and Revenge of Julius Cæsar" than "The Tragedy of Julius Cæsar", for its tragedy is the tragedy of Marcus Brutus.

Caius Cassius. "But Cassius, being a choleric man, and hating Cæsar privately more than he did the tyranny openly, he incensed Brutus against him." These words from Plutarch[1] seem more than any others to have been the foundation upon which Shakespeare

1. Skeat, p. 111. See Appendix, p. 135.

built the character of his Cassius. In Plutarch he read too that Cassius, "even from his cradle, could not abide any manner of tyrants";[1] and that "men reputed him commonly to be very skilful in wars, but otherwise marvellous choleric and cruel, who sought to rule men by fear rather than with lenity."[2]

Cassius himself speaks of the "rash humour" that he inherited from his mother (IV. iii. 119); and a little earlier in the same scene Brutus—in words which, since he himself is in a towering rage, betray some irony on Shakespeare's part—taunts him with his "rash choler", his "testy humour", and his waspishness. Otherwise, apart from a certain irritability which shows in his denunciation of Cæsar in the second scene of the play, and again in the flyting of the generals before the battle of Philippi, Shakespeare makes little of this choler in Cassius. On the other hand, he develops with some thoroughness the envy and malice that he feels towards Cæsar ("hating Cæsar privately"), and his sense of inferiority to one who is so much more highly gifted than himself. Of these aspects of Cassius I have already spoken,[3] and there is little that needs to be added.

However, Shakespeare, as we have also seen, puts into the mouth of Cæsar a masterly character-sketch of Cassius (I. ii. 191 ff.) which brings out this side of him clearly, and which, for what else it tells us of him, is worthy of close study. Of course he has other qualities than those mentioned by Cæsar, most of which are displayed in the second half of the play: such things as courage in war and generalship, the ability to attract loyal followers, generous sympathy for an afflicted friend, and the magnanimity not to hold his leader's blunders against him. But in the earlier scenes Shakespeare is concerned to show him as the type of the scheming malcontent, a man whom we could easily visualize as plotting the murder of a great national leader; and in Cæsar's description of Cassius he has hit such a man to the life. Cadaverous and hungry-looking, much given to brooding ("he thinks too much"), and a great reader; a scorner of sports and light diversions, a very shrewd judge of human nature, and deeply envious of those who are greater than himself: such a man is Cassius, and he is a bitter and unhappy man. When he allows himself to smile at all, the way in which he smiles betrays his frustrated nature, and Cæsar has the insight to see that he is very dangerous.

At present he is obsessed by his hatred of Cæsar, and, as his first conversation with Brutus shows, not fully in control of his feelings. But Shakespeare depicts him as always inclined to be unstable. He

1. Skeat, p. 112. See Appendix, p. 135. 2. *Ibid.*, p. 129. See Appendix, p. 136
3. See p. xxx.

loses his nerve when Popilius Lena approaches Cæsar at the Senate House, and has to be reassured by Brutus; and after the assassination his changeability is shown in another way, when for a few moments his personal envy is replaced by an exalted enthusiasm for the principle of liberty. The omens which dispirit his soldiers on the march from Sardis to Philippi cause him to waver in the Epicurean beliefs which formerly he held so strongly (v. i. 77–89); and when things appear to be going badly in the battle, he does not wait for confirmation of Pindarus's report that Titinius has been captured on his reconnaissance, but in "mistrust of good success" prematurely takes his life. In his changeability as well as in his motives for plotting against Cæsar, he is an admirable foil to the steadfast Brutus, whose self-control breaks down only in the quarrel scene; here Cassius shows, if anything, the more restraint of the two.

Yet even in this portrait of an arch-conspirator Shakespeare compensates weakness with strength, evil qualities with good. As has already been pointed out, whenever critical decisions are to be taken, Cassius proves himself more clear-sighted than Brutus; and though he allows himself each time to be overborne by Brutus with a good enough grace, we are aware that, had his counsels prevailed, especially in regard to Antony, the republican cause would have had a much greater chance of success.

As though the death of the object of his hatred has liberated more generous instincts in him, Cassius becomes more likeable in the latter part of the play. There are no more vindictive outbursts such as that in which he whetted Brutus against Cæsar, and in the councils of the leaders he is just as calm as Brutus, and certainly more far-seeing. I have already suggested that in the quarrel he has more of our sympathy than Brutus, and it is he who makes the first moves towards reconciliation; moreover, while Brutus reviles the meddlesome poet, he treats him with good-humoured tolerance. He feels deeply for Brutus in the "insupportable and touching loss" of Portia; and he wholeheartedly joins with him in burying all their unkindness in a cup of wine:

> My heart is thirsty for that noble pledge.
> Fill, Lucius, till the wine o'erswell the cup.
> I cannot drink too much of Brutus' love. (IV. iii. 159–61)

The new spirit of mutual respect and affection that is born from this encounter remains unaffected by their difference of opinion about the best place for an encounter with the enemy, and is charmingly exemplified in the frank and friendly way in which they converse and bid each other farewell before the battle is engaged (v. i. 93–126).

Thus Shakespeare, expanding a few statements and hints in Plutarch, begins by depicting Cassius as a man of the breed of Dryden's Achitophel, "for close designs and crooked counsels fit"—and the parallel holds in other respects. Then, as if recognizing that no man is wholly bad, and that Cassius may, like Brutus, have acted from mistaken rather than evil motives, he somewhat softens and ennobles his character. And in the end he all but effaces the earlier impressions by adopting for Cassius's epitaph the valedictory words which in Plutarch Brutus speaks over the body of his friend, and adding to them a strong expression of Brutus's love:

> The last of all the Romans, fare thee well!
> It is impossible that ever Rome
> Should breed thy fellow. Friends, I owe moe tears
> To this dead man than you shall see me pay.
> I shall find time, Cassius, I shall find time.

Marcus Antonius. The development of Antony's character belongs largely to the last three acts. In the first two he is an unimportant figure, and appears little more than "a limb of Cæsar". By the end of the play he has, by the talents he has displayed as orator, statesman, and soldier, made himself the avenger of Cæsar and a "triple pillar of the world". He has shown that he possesses, as Moulton puts it,[1] "all the powers that belong both to the intellectual and practical life". I cannot, however, agree with Moulton when he says, as other critics also say, that Antony "has concentrated his whole nature in one aim, ... unmitigated self-seeking".

His first appearance is as one of the Lupercalian runners, anxious to please and serve Cæsar. Cæsar reminds him to touch Calphurnia in the holy chase, and he replies,

> I shall remember:
> When Cæsar says, "Do this," it is perform'd.

He speaks only three more lines before the assassination of Cæsar. In two of them he gives an estimate as mistaken as Cæsar's is correct of the character of Cassius, whom he describes as "well given" and not at all dangerous. But this is the last error of judgement he is to make.

Other things we hear about him do not render him any more impressive. Brutus speaks of his liveliness ("quick spirit"), says he is "given to sports, to wildness, and much company", and dismisses him as a mere tool of Cæsar, ineffectual without his master's guid-

1. *Shakespeare as a Dramatic Artist*, p. 182.

ance. Cæsar refers to his fondness for plays and for revelling long a-nights. This frivolous side of his nature is recalled for a moment later, when at Philippi Cassius taunts him with being "a masker and a reveller"; but the words can by then carry no sting, and Antony replies with good-humoured contempt, "Old Cassius still!" In the first two acts the only hints we have of his potential greatness are the fact that Cæsar has singled him out for his special regard, and the opinion of Cassius that he is a "shrewd contriver" who, with the means at his command, may well prove a danger if he is allowed to outlive Cæsar (II. i. 155–60).

When Cæsar is struck down, Antony flies to his house in stupefaction. But before the assassins have left the scene of their crime he has sent his servant with a tactfully worded request for an interview. His first object is to win the confidence of Brutus. Backed by the countenance of Brutus, he may be able to set in motion some plan of vengeance for Cæsar. In his message he makes no attempt to conceal his love and reverence for Cæsar; these emotions are genuine, but he is also aware that Brutus will respect him all the more for his loyalty to his dead friend. He plays upon the vanity of Brutus, and upon the magnanimity that he knows such a man will display towards one who comes to him as a suppliant; and he ends with an ambiguously worded promise that he will throw in his lot with Brutus if he can be satisfied that Cæsar deserved to die. Brutus is completely taken in. In the assurance that Antony will prove a good friend he promises him safe conduct, and as Cassius is voicing misgivings, Antony himself appears.

Though surrounded by men whose arms are red to the elbows with Cæsar's blood, Antony for the first few moments has eyes for nothing but the body at their feet. Then he turns to the murderers, and in words that are charged with irony expresses his readiness, if it so please them, to die by Cæsar's side, at the hands of "the choice and master spirits of this age". Brutus hastens to declare that they have nothing but "kind love, good thoughts, and reverence" for him; and Cassius too reassures him, though, being more worldly-wise, he appeals to his ambition and offers him an equal share with the conspirators "in the disposing of new dignities".

Antony has made a good start. From now on he is in command of the situation. With ironical flattery and professions of friendship for the conspirators, especially Brutus, he gains their esteem as well as their trust; and when Cassius interrupts him in one of the apostrophes to Cæsar with which he intersperses his appeals to their vanity and their generosity, he feels confident enough of their sympathy to be able to round on him:

> Pardon me, Caius Cassius:
> The enemies of Cæsar shall say this:
> Then, in a friend, it is cold modesty.

And Cassius can only reply,

> I blame you not for praising Cæsar so.

But Cassius is a realist. He asks what compact Antony is prepared to make with them. Antony is ready with his answer, and if it is a rather evasive answer, at least it satisfies the conspirators:

> Therefore I took your hands, but was indeed
> Sway'd from the point by looking down on Cæsar.
> Friends am I with you all, and love you all,
> Upon this hope, that you shall give me reasons
> Why, and wherein, Cæsar was dangerous.

Brutus promises to satisfy him, and Antony at last feels it safe to come to the real point of the interview he has sought.

He asks permission to take Cæsar's body to the market-place and to speak a funeral oration, as becomes a friend. Brutus at once consents, and brushes aside the objections that Cassius raises. Antony desires no more; he has won the first round.

Left alone with Cæsar's body, he shows his true feelings:

> O, pardon me, thou bleeding piece of earth,
> That I am meek and gentle with these butchers.
> Thou art the ruins of the noblest man
> That ever lived in the tide of times.
> Woe to the hand that shed this costly blood!

And he prophesies a period of fierce civil strife, blood, and destruction that shall end only when a terrible vengeance for the foul murder has been exacted. There is no dissembling in this speech of Antony. It is impossible to doubt here the depth and sincerity of his love and grief for Cæsar, or the fury and tenacity with which he will hound the murderers to their doom. As he is pronouncing this prophecy a servant enters with the news that an ally, in the person of Octavius Cæsar, is on the way to Rome, and the scene ends with Antony's resolution to try in his funeral oration how the people take "the cruel issue of these bloody men". He has shown himself a magnificently resourceful opportunist in his dealings with the conspirators; who knows what he may not accomplish with the populace at large on the morrow?

Shakespeare's Antony has been frequently censured as unstable, immoral, and dishonest. I have quoted Moulton's view that his

whole nature is concentrated in "unmitigated self-seeking". Mac-
Callum writes:[1] "Shakespeare conceives him as a man of genius
and feeling but not of principle, resourceful and daring, ambitious
of honour and power, but unscrupulous in his methods and a voluptuary in his life." More recently Professor Hereward Price has said:[2]
"Antony is the least Roman of the Romans. Where they are steadfast he is labile; where they keep their emotions under lock and key,
he will coin his heart for whatever gold it will bring him; where
they are virtuous, he is dissolute; where they are straightforward in
language, he loves to play with words, to tease and deceive by
double meanings, and he will even lie outright." Other critics who
see nothing but nobility in Brutus have come close to making Antony the villain of the piece.[3]

We may grant that he is unscrupulous in his methods; but is he
any more so than the men with whom he is dealing? Does he do
more than turn the methods of the conspirators upon themselves?
These blood-guilty men have secretly plotted the murder of the
greatest man of the age, have butchered the man whom of all men
he most deeply loved and admired, and he takes upon himself the
sacred duty of vengeance. The *virtuous* Brutus and his confederates
hid the monstrous visage of conspiracy in smiles and affability;[4]
Antony's dissimulation is certainly no worse than theirs. Cassius
whets Brutus against Cæsar; Antony will whet the Roman people
against Cassius and Brutus. Apart from Brutus, the conspirators
"did that they did in envy of great Cæsar"; envy and malice are
not nobler motives for the taking of life than the desire and duty to
avenge a murdered friend and national leader. Antony is no less
straightforward in his speech or honourable in his tactics than the
men to whom he truthfully says:

> You show'd your teeth like apes, and fawn'd like hounds,
> And bow'd like bondmen, kissing Cæsar's feet;
> Whilst damned Casca, like a cur, behind
> Struck Cæsar on the neck. (v. i. 41–4)

He is no whit less stable and steadfast than Cassius; no man could
be more single-hearted than he shows himself in planning and

1. *Shakespeare's Roman Plays*, pp. 289–90.

2. *Julius Cæsar*, ed. Hereward T. Price (Crofts Classics, New York, 1949),
Introduction, p. ix.

3. Perhaps the "conventional" estimate of Antony owes something to the way
in which he is presented in *Antony and Cleopatra*. In discussing one of Shakespeare's dramatic personages, the overriding consideration must be the contribution of that personage to the dramatic conflict of the play under discussion.

4. ii. i. 81–2, 224–7.

carrying through his vengeance on the assassins. I can see no signs whatever that he is seeking honour and power for himself in pursuing this aim; amongst other things, he ignores Cassius's offer to let him share the honour and power that the conspirators anticipate for themselves. Nor does he keep his emotions less securely under lock and key than Cassius in the second and third scenes of the play, or, for that matter, than Brutus when he is quarrelling with Cassius. In the earlier acts we are told that he is something of a voluptuary, which is not the same thing as saying that he is dissolute; we must suppose that with Cæsar's death he renounced the lighter pleasures of former days, for we hear no more of them except in a sneering remark of Cassius. Cæsar's death brings out all the strength and greatness of Antony, and his conduct rapidly effaces any impression we may have formed earlier that he is a trifler or a mere limb of Cæsar.

It is sometimes suggested that Antony shows a singular callousness and lack of principle in bartering his nephew's life for that of Lepidus's brother during the proscriptions (IV. i. 1–6). It is possible to interpret his conduct here as just and unsentimental; it is Lepidus who starts the bargaining, and Antony shows that he will not be swayed by family ties if Lepidus insists that Publius is a danger to the cause of the Triumvirs. What he says next reveals him in a more questionable light: he proposes to misappropriate to the use of his party some of the money bequeathed in Cæsar's will. But his proposal appears to have the full concurrence of his colleagues, and there is no suggestion that he is to gain personally from the affair. On the other hand, we have it on the authority of Brutus that Cassius, who belongs to the "honourable" party, is much condemned for selling and marting his offices for gold to undeservers (IV. iii. 9–12). Are we to believe that Shakespeare intends us to regard Antony as a man of baser motives and principles than Cassius and Casca? He is much cleverer at their own game than they are, and more amiable, and he has better justification for almost all his actions than they have. The only time that he is allowed to appear actively unamiable is in his contemptuous estimate of Lepidus (IV. i. 12–40); and the only occasions on which he is shown in any sense at a loss are those on which he matches his will against that of Octavius,[1] certainly not in his encounters with the conspirators. In the circumstances in which he is placed by Cæsar's murder he reveals what can only be called genius in exploiting every turn in a situation to the advantage of the cause to which he has dedicated himself.

1. e.g., V. 1. 14–20.

If we admire Antony's resource and daring when he faces the
conspirators in their moment of triumph—or rather what should
be triumph, but utterly fails to be—how are we to name the qualities he displays in the Forum on the following day? If ever Shakespeare wished to show genius at work, surely it was in Antony's
oration. By a magnanimous and calmly reasonable appeal to their
Roman sense of independence, Brutus has convinced an initially
uneasy crowd that Cæsar was an ambitious tyrant who had to be
slain for the good of Rome, and they are ready to shower every honour on him as their deliverer. Antony is there on sufferance; he is to
speak by the kind permission of the hero of the hour, and the crowd
he faces is actively hostile to Cæsar and likely to tear to pieces any
one who exalts Cæsar at the expense of Brutus. As on the previous
day, he must tread very warily; and he must pick his words even
more carefully than then, for the crowd, already wrought to a state
of high feeling, will be infinitely more suggestible and inflammable
than a small band of nobles. A mistake may cost him his life; the
exploitation of a single favourable current may carry him to where
Brutus now stands.

Antony begins circumspectly by disclaiming any intention of
praising Cæsar. There is a touch of his characteristic irony in what
he adds to the disclaimer: let Cæsar, he says, suffer the common fate
of being remembered solely for his bad qualities. He passes on to
the question of Cæsar's ambition, the grievous fault for which he
was slain, according to Brutus; and whenever he mentions Brutus
he is careful to couple expressions of respect with his name. He does
not try to prove that Cæsar was not ambitious. He merely speaks of
actions of Cæsar which were not ambitious; he can count on mob-
logic to do the rest. With the instinct of the natural orator he keeps
his line of thought simple, and uses catch-phrases to hammer home
his points. "Cæsar was ambitious"; "Brutus is an honourable man":
these are the phrases of which he makes his refrain.

> But Brutus says he was ambitious,
> And Brutus is an honourable man.

With each increasingly striking instance of Cæsar's lack of ambition the irony of this refrain becomes increasingly apparent, and
when Antony sees that it is beginning to penetrate the conscious-
ness of the crowd, he manufactures a pause:

> Bear with me.
> My heart is in the coffin there with Cæsar,
> And I must pause till it come back to me.

This is a telling stroke. The crowd are given time to put their heads together and carry the argument to the illogical conclusion that Cæsar was not ambitious, and that he has had great wrong; and they are also able to see Antony with a manly effort pull himself together to resume his speech.

Two minutes earlier Antony's hearers had been suspicious of him and hostile to Cæsar. Now he has won their sympathy both for himself and for Cæsar, and he can afford to remind them of Cæsar's might and renown, and of their own fickleness in forgetting them now he is dead:

> But yesterday the word of Cæsar might
> Have stood against the world; now lies he there,
> And none so poor to do him reverence.

But he has another important task to accomplish. Insidiously, under the pretext of deprecating violence, he sows in their minds the seeds of mutiny and rage against the honourable men who have killed Cæsar, and whom he can now begin to lash more openly. Better, he says, that Cæsar, and he, and his countrymen in general, should suffer wrong than such honourable men as Brutus. But he does not want the hint to be taken yet, not until he has stirred up such an implacable fury as can only be assuaged by blood. He produces another card. Here is Cæsar's will, he says; no, no, you must not hear it, for if you did, what a saint you would make of Cæsar. No, I must not read it.

> It is not meet you know how Cæsar lov'd you.
> ... It will inflame you, it will make you mad.
> 'Tis good you know not that you are his heirs;
> For if you should, O, what would come of it?

Naturally the crowd clamours to hear the will. But not yet.

> Will you be patient? Will you stay awhile?
> I have o'ershot myself to tell you of it.
> I fear I wrong the honourable men
> Whose daggers have stabb'd Cæsar; I do fear it.

One might expect Antony to be satisfied with the reception given this time to the catch-phrase, and to read the will at last. Even now he holds it back. Let his good friends but look on Cæsar's mantle, the mantle he first put on the day he won that glorious victory over the Nervii; let them see the rents made by the swords of his trusted friends, especially the well-beloved Brutus; let them see his body, hacked by traitors; then they will know what bloody treason has flourished over them.

Tears of pity fill the eyes of the beholders, succeeded by blind rage and lust for blood. Remorselessly Antony holds them back. The wise and honourable men who slew Cæsar, he says, no doubt had good private reasons for their deed; no doubt they will make fine speeches and justify it. For himself, he is no orator, has no glib powers of persuasion; he can only speak what is in his heart. Of course, an orator like Brutus would know how to ruffle up their spirits and rouse them to mutiny. With a roar the crowd take up the word "mutiny", and Antony can only just prevent them from rushing off to rend the traitors limb from limb by raising his voice above the clamour to gain silence for the will. And at last they hear that Cæsar has left a sum of money to every Roman citizen, and his private gardens to them all in common as pleasure-grounds.

Here was a royal Cæsar indeed! Nothing could hold them after this, and exultantly Antony watches them stream away, to burn the body in "the holy place", and to fire the traitors' houses with the brands.

> Now let it work. Mischief, thou art afoot,
> Take thou what course thou wilt!

Where the triumph of Cæsar's assassins fizzled out in vapouring speeches and irresolution, Antony's triumph is complete. It is a twofold triumph. Antony has roused mighty powers of mischief to vengeance for Cæsar; in a few minutes he hears with grim calmness that "Brutus and Cassius are rid like madmen through the gates of Rome." Just as important to him, he has vindicated Cæsar's good name, has indeed added new lustre to it. Insistently, throughout his oration, he has dinned Cæsar's name into the ears of his auditors, and, with increasing emphasis, Cæsar's greatness. When he began his speech, Cæsar was a lifeless clod, deservedly slain—so Brutus had persuaded the citizens—because he was an ambitious tyrant and a danger to the state. When he ended, Cæsar was a godlike conqueror and a royally munificent benefactor, the greatest of all Romans. There is nothing in the speech to suggest that Antony is seeking anything for himself; everything has been directed towards two ends, the extinction of Cæsar's murderers, and the re-establishment of Cæsar's name and fame. For himself he has gained only a long period of warfare and peril.

For the audience in the theatre, too, Antony's speech effaces the bad impression that Shakespeare has allowed Cæsar himself to make in his last few minutes of life. On their minds, as on those of the Roman citizens, it stamps the image of the "mightiest Julius" who was to be counted one of the Nine Worthies of the World.

Antony appears in four further scenes. The first of these (IV. i) I have already discussed. The second begins by revealing him at something of a disadvantage when he contests the opinion and will of Octavius (v. i. 1–20); but in a few moments he shows that he is still more than a match for Brutus and Cassius in the flyting of the generals (ll. 27–63). That he has, in the months that have passed since the assassination, been entirely steadfast in his pursuit of vengeance against Cæsar's murderers is evidenced by the way in which he retorts to their taunts by recalling their vile treachery to Cæsar (ll. 29–32; 36–44). Some words which Shakespeare puts into the mouth of Octavius might with equal appropriateness have been given to Antony:

> I draw a sword against conspirators.
> When think you that the sword goes up again?
> Never, till Cæsar's three and thirty wounds
> Be well aveng'd. (v. i. 51–4)

Antony's last two appearances are calculated to leave an entirely favourable impression. He shows a thorough appreciation of the devotion and loyalty of Lucilius, who has been captured while masquerading as Brutus, and who, in words which might well be his last, courageously asserts the nobility of Brutus. "Keep this man safe," says Antony; "give him all kindness. I had rather have such men my friends than enemies" (v. iv. 27–9). And in the penultimate speech of the play, Shakespeare brings out in Antony a full understanding of the essential integrity of Brutus, and in the epitaph he speaks over the body of his fallen enemy shows him capable of the highest magnanimity.

No more than any other of the major persons in the play has Antony a wholly attractive and sympathetic personality; but for what he does and what he stands for, he is intended, I think, to gain a generous measure of sympathy and admiration.

Minor Characters. All other persons in the play are so far overshadowed in the interest they provide by the four whom I have discussed as to require little more than passing mention.

Of the subsidiary conspirators Casca is the most fully drawn. Plutarch gives no details about the personality of Casca, merely the information that he was the first to strike Cæsar, from behind, and that when Cæsar turned and grappled with him, he cried out to his brother in Greek for help.[1] Shakespeare turns the mention of the Greek into a sour jest about his not understanding a pointed remark of Cicero concerning Cæsar's refusal of the crown because it was spoken in Greek (i. ii. 275–81). The stab in the back provides the

---

1. Skeat, pp. 100, 119; Appendix, pp. 148-9.

foundation for most of the other qualities he attributes to Casca.

It is in keeping with the character of the man who could strike this treacherous blow that he should be officious to serve the great man of the hour in his presence (I. ii. 1; 14), and a few minutes later should speak jeeringly of him behind his back. Like Cassius, Casca is a malcontent, jealous of Cæsar's supremacy. "He was quick mettle when he went to school" (I. ii. 293); but he has grown resentful of those who have outstripped him in the race for power, and bitter with himself that he has let himself be thus outstripped. Cassius assures Brutus that, despite his "tardy form", he is still quick mettle "in execution of any bold or noble enterprise"; but Shakespeare gives him no nobility. He hides his feelings of frustration beneath the affectation of a "sour fashion" of speech, and of a bluntness that passes for a cross-grained good-humour. This is illustrated in his description of the scene in the market-place when Cæsar was offered the crown:

> I can as well be hang'd as tell the manner of it: it was mere foolery; I did not mark it. I saw Mark Antony offer him a crown; yet 'twas not a crown neither, 'twas one of these coronets; and, as I told you, he put it by once; but for all that, to my thinking, he would fain have had it. . . (I. ii. 231 ff.)

He makes something of a parade of his honour and reliability when Cassius is sounding him as a potential member of the conspiracy:

> You speak to Casca, and to such a man
> That is no fleering tell-tale. Hold, my hand:
> Be factious for redress of all these griefs,
> And I will set this foot of mine as far
> As who goes furthest. (I. iii. 116–20)

A few minutes earlier this bold and dependable Casca has been cowering in superstitious terror in the prodigious storm, his fear thrown into relief by the cool scepticism of Cicero; and Cassius too has been a little contemptuous of his lack of "those sparks of life that should be in a Roman" (I. iii. 57–8).

The clear-sighted Antony sees Casca for what he is. He reserves for him his most bitterly ironical courtesy when he takes the conspirators' hands: "my valiant Casca", he calls him; and in his Forum speech he refers to him as "the envious Casca". While Brutus and Cassius are given eulogistic epitaphs, the last we hear of Casca is when Antony recalls how

> damned Casca, like a cur, behind
> Struck Cæsar on the neck. (V. i. 43–4)

The character of Decius Brutus is clearly established in half a dozen speeches. He is self-important, and proud of his diplomatic gifts. When Cassius suggests the possibility that Cæsar may not come to the Capitol after so terrifying a night, Decius confidently declares that he can bring him at the appointed time by a little judicious flattery:

> Let me work;
> For I can give his humour the true bent,
> And I will bring him to the Capitol. (II. i. 209–11)

And in fact, by his flattering interpretation of Calphurnia's dream and his insinuation that Cæsar will lay himself open to a mocking charge of cowardice if he is kept at home by his wife's superstitious fears, he does prevail on him to feel ashamed of listening to her entreaties. Like the other conspirators he hides his treacherous designs under smiles and affability, and under the appearance of solicitude for Cæsar's welfare:

> Pardon me, Cæsar; for my dear dear love
> To your proceeding bids me tell you this,
> And reason to my love is liable. (II. ii. 102–4)

With this betrayal he ceases to play any important part in the events of the play. The few words he speaks after the assassination show him still somewhat officious, as when we first encountered him. He suggests that Cassius as well as Brutus should address the populace, and he interrupts the theatrical raptures of Brutus and Cassius to bring them back to the business in hand.

Cicero is one of the most vividly drawn of the incidental figures—incidental in the sense that he has no place in the actual plot of the play, though his presence adds to the verisimilitude of the Roman and historical background. No doubt Shakespeare had read Plutarch's life of Cicero, and drew thence the main lines of his character; but apart from his vanity and his dislike of Cæsar, the Cicero of the play is essentially of Shakespeare's own creation. He speaks only in the third scene; but in the preceding scene a few telling lines give a sharp impression of his personality. When Cæsar returns from the market-place, in high dudgeon at the shouts of approval that greeted his refusal of the crown, Cicero, we are told,

> Looks with such ferret and such fiery eyes
> As we have seen him in the Capitol,
> Being cross'd in conference by some senators.

He cannot conceal his irritation and disgust at the "foolery" he has witnessed, and perhaps at Cæsar's ill-tempered acceptance of the set-back. Casca reports that when Cæsar recovered from his swoon and hastened to reassure himself of the favour of the commons, Cicero said something in Greek that made those who understood him smile at each other and shake their heads; we may presume that it was a sarcastic comment at the expense of Cæsar.

During the meeting of the conspirators at Brutus's house, Cassius, seconded by Casca and Cinna, suggests that Cicero might prove a valuable colleague, and Metellus agrees that his reputation for mature wisdom and his high standing in Rome will add countenance to their design:

> O, let us have him, for his silver hairs
> Will purchase us a good opinion,
> And buy men's voices to commend our deeds.
> It shall be said his judgment rul'd our hands;
> Our youths and wildness shall no whit appear,
> But all be buried in his gravity. (II. i. 144–9)

It is, somewhat ironically, Brutus who rules him out of court for his vanity and his unwillingness to play second fiddle in any enterprise:

> O, name him not; let us not break with him;
> For he will never follow anything
> That other men begin.

Cicero encounters the terrors of the storm in the third scene with philosophic calm. Quivering with fright, Casca speaks of the "tempest dropping fire" as a sign of civil war in heaven, or a prelude to the destruction of the world. "Why, saw you any thing more wonderful?" Cicero coolly asks. And when Casca describes the fearful prodigies he has seen and heard of, Cicero sceptically dismisses his interpretation of them, and goes on to speak of other things:

> Indeed, it is a strange-disposed time:
> But men may construe things, after their fashion,
> Clean from the purpose of the things themselves.
> Comes Cæsar to the Capitol to-morrow?

We hear no more of Cicero except that he perished by "the order of proscription" of the Triumvirs (IV. iii. 176–9); but we gain a memorable picture of him from the few episodes with which he is associated.

Portia figures more prominently; but she appears in only two scenes, and it is impossible not to wish that the exigencies of the play had allowed her to play a bigger part. With mounting anxiety she has observed Brutus's increasing preoccupation with some difficult and dangerous design, and its adverse effects on his health and

temper. She has endured with tact and forbearance his altered demeanour towards herself; but after the secret conclave of the conspirators she comes to him as dawn breaks and insists that she be
allowed to share the burden of grief by which he is weighed down.
Brutus at first resists her importunity, but she refuses to be put off,
and appeals to his love and to his sense of what is her due as his wife:

> No, my Brutus;
> You have some sick offence within your mind,
> Which, by the right and virtue of my place,
> I ought to know of; and upon my knees,
> I charm you, by my once commended beauty,
> By all your vows of love, and that great vow
> Which did incorporate and make us one,
> That you unfold to me, your self, your half,
> Why you are heavy. (II. i. 267–75)

She wrings from him the avowal:

> You are my true and honourable wife,
> As dear to me as are the ruddy drops
> That visit my sad heart.

But this is not all that Portia wants. "If this were true," she says,
"then should I know this secret": as the woman that Brutus chose
for his wife, and Cato's daughter, she declares, she is worthy to
share her husband's secrets and to support him in his anxieties. She
has proved her fortitude in bearing physical pain by wounding herself in the thigh, and she has the moral courage to participate in the
grief that oppresses Brutus. Brutus can no longer withstand her appeal. "O ye gods," he cries, "render me worthy of this noble wife!"
and he promises to disclose to her all the secrets of his heart. By her
love and constancy and dignity, Portia does indeed show herself a
wife of whom any man would wish to prove himself worthy.

However, we are not to be allowed to see Portia only as a personification of the virtues she has inherited from her Stoic father.
She is rendered more natural and lovable by the agitation she displays when Brutus has left her to go to the Capitol on the morning
of the ides of March. In her distraction she scarcely knows what she
is saying to Lucius, and has to make a great effort to control her
tongue.

> O constancy, be strong upon my side;
> Set a huge mountain 'tween my heart and tongue!
> I have a man's mind, but a woman's might.
> How hard it is for women to keep counsel. (II. iv. 6–9)

She imagines that she hears, from the direction of the Capitol, "a bustling rumour, like a fray", though Lucius can hear nothing; and when the Soothsayer enters, she again almost gives away the knowledge she has of the harm that is intended towards Cæsar. She has to go indoors to conceal her fears.

By this scene Shakespeare establishes Portia as a fully rounded character, endowed with a woman's heart as well as the constancy of Cato's daughter. When, some time after the assassination of Cæsar, she realizes that Brutus is fighting a hopeless battle in a lost cause, she falls distracted with grief, but retains the resolution to take her own life by swallowing burning coals (IV. iii. 151–5).

Calphurnia is more slightly sketched. She appears in the second scene of the play, but it is not until Act II, Scene ii, that she reveals anything of herself. She is terrified by the portents of the storm and her dreams about the murder of Cæsar, but terrified rather for Cæsar than herself. These prodigies, she knows, have been sent to foretell the death of some great man, and she is sure they point to the approaching death of her husband:

> When beggars die, there are no comets seen;
> The heavens themselves blaze forth the death of princes.

When Cæsar makes vaunting speeches about his unmatchable courage, her love gives her courage too, and she tells him that his "wisdom is consum'd in confidence." Most earnestly she entreats him not to court disaster by going to the Senate House. "Call it my fear that keeps you in the house, and not your own," she says, and at length she prevails on him to indulge her in this "humour". Her work is immediately undone by Decius; but in these few moments she has given striking testimony of her love for Cæsar and her strength of purpose. I do not agree with those who see in her nothing but feminine fear and weakness.

Lucius is another figure by whom the Roman *gravitas* of the play is somewhat softened. Unimportant in himself, he brings out the gentler side of Brutus's nature. In the midst of perplexities that make him forgetful of the feelings of his wife and friends, Brutus has nothing but consideration for his young page. Calling for attendance when the conspirators have left his house, he finds Lucius asleep and forbears to rouse him. Would that he himself could sleep with such carefree innocence!

> Boy! Lucius! Fast asleep? It is no matter;
> Enjoy the honey-heavy dew of slumber:
> Thou hast no figures nor no fantasies
> Which busy care draws in the brains of men;
> Therefore thou sleep'st so sound. (II. i. 229–33)

That Lucius is the object of Brutus's affectionate regard, and returns it, is again shown in their exchange a few minutes before
Cæsar's ghost appears (iv. iii. 238–71). Brutus feels remorse at over-
taxing the boy's strength, and Lucius shows that it gives him pleasure to serve and solace his lord.

Portia, Calphurnia, and Lucius bring an element of loyal and
tender love into a play which deals predominantly in dark intrigue
and sinister motives. They are more important than their small
part in the play might at first sight suggest.[1]

9. LANGUAGE AND IMAGERY

I have already in passing drawn attention to some of the most
impressive passages in *Julius Cæsar*. Cassius's tirade against Cæsar,
Cæsar's appraisal of Cassius, the descriptions of portents, Brutus's
tormented self-questioning and his Forum speech, Portia's appeal
to Brutus, Antony's hoodwinking of the conspirators, his Forum
speech, and his eulogy of Brutus: all these, and many other passages, are remarkable whether for their exposition of character and
background or for their fine poetic or rhetorical qualities. One does
not have to seek far to find speeches as memorable in their own way
as any that Shakespeare wrote. In their own way: Shakespeare
seems to have been trying in this play to fashion an atmosphere and
a diction in keeping with the gravity and dignity traditionally associated with the Roman character. He avoided the lyricism and
the humour that we find in, for instance, *Antony and Cleopatra*, and
wrote probably less purely descriptive poetry than in any other of
his mature plays. The strength of the most noteworthy speeches lies
in their clarity, directness, and simplicity. This is seen in, for example, Cassius's speech which begins:

> Why, man, he doth bestride the narrow world
> Like a Colossus; (i. ii. 133–59)

or in Cæsar's analysis of Cassius (i. ii. 195–211); or in Brutus's farewell to Cassius (v. i. 111–19); or in a score of other fine speeches.
The effectiveness of Antony's famous oration depends, not on its
use of imagery or obvious rhetorical tricks, but on its structure; Antony carries the crowd with him for the most part by a series of
short, direct statements, so arranged as to lead their thoughts and

---

1. Since this volume went to press, I have read Virgil K. Whitaker's *Shakespeare's Use of Learning*. I am interested to see how closely Professor Whitaker's
view of the main characters of *Julius Cæsar* approximates to that which I have
put forward.

their feelings in a particular direction. Brutus's oration is more obviously rhetorical, perhaps, with its studied parallelism and antithesis and its carefully wrought climaxes, but its diction is simple
and bare, and the total effect is that of the most lucid simplicity. Of
this oration Granville-Barker writes:[1] "I prefer it to Antony's. It
wears better. It is very noble prose."

As in all his mature plays, Shakespeare varies his language
according to the personality and cast of mind of the speakers. I cannot agree with Dr Ifor Evans when he says:[2] "For, unlike *Hamlet*,
where the diction varies with character and mood, and from soliloquy to public speech, here from public oration to the secret
thoughts of the lonely meditating mind all is gathered into one
cumulative surge of ordered and formal narration." There is a considerable difference between the twisted thought and comparatively complex imagery of Brutus's meditations in his orchard and
the clarity and bareness to which I have drawn attention in his prepared speech in the Forum. And neither passage can reasonably be
described as narration.

Brutus speaks a more metaphorical and rhetorical language than
any one else in the play. This is apparent already in some of his
earliest speeches:

> Nor construe any further my neglect,
> Than that poor Brutus, with himself at war,
> Forgets the shows of love to other men.

> Set honour in one eye, and death i' th' other,
> And I will look on both indifferently.

His habit of thinking in metaphors is strikingly illustrated in his
soliloquies in his orchard: not only by the serpent and the ladder
images of his first long speech, but also by the even more compli-
cated imagery of the later lines beginning, "Between the acting of a
dreadful thing. . ." (II. i. 63–9). In the meeting of the conspirators
that follows, while his associates make their proposals in simple and
straightforward terms, Brutus delivers his opinions and decisions
in an inflated and rhetorical manner. His wordiness reflects his
inner conflict, and emphasizes what we are to learn from his
conduct, that he is an unpractical and far from clear-headed
man; and it seems also to distract the minds of the other conspirators from seeing the essentials of whatever problem they are
discussing.

Throughout the play Brutus tends to talk in this way. After the

1. *Prefaces to Shakespeare: First Series*, p. 105.
2. B. Ifor Evans, *The Language of Shakespeare's Plays*, p. 164.

assassination of Cæsar, not having thought of the future, he can only call upon the Fates to know their pleasures (III. i. 98), and in a theatrical fashion suggest the ritual washing of hands in Cæsar's blood. In his quarrel with Cassius his resentment and self-righteousness find expression in high-flown metaphors; and the only extended image in the later acts comes from his lips when he is in one of his dictatorial moods—that of the "tide in the affairs of men" (IV. iii. 217–23). This and the previous speech of Brutus are in marked contrast with those of Cassius in this episode.

At times Cæsar too speaks in figurative language, but as a rule only when Shakespeare is developing the thrasonical side of his nature. When he feels that his courage may be in question he is ready with an elaborate boast:

> Danger knows full well
> That Cæsar is more dangerous than he.
> We are two lions litter'd in one day,
> And I the elder and more terrible.

In the speeches he utters just before he is stabbed he is intended to lose some of our sympathy, and Shakespeare again gives him an inflated and boastful manner of speech. In long-drawn similes he likens the suppliants to fawning curs, and himself to the unassailably constant northern star.

However, Cæsar has a more forceful character than Brutus, and for the most part he speaks directly and decisively. In his description of Cassius every word is to the point. When the Soothsayer bids him beware the ides of March, he says, "Set him before me; let me see his face" (I. ii. 20); and, when the warning is repeated, "He is a dreamer. Let us leave him. Pass." Similarly, when Artemidorus importunes him to read his schedule, he brushes him aside. "What, is the fellow mad?" he says (III. i. 10), and moves on to the Senate House. And though the portents of the storm bring out some boastfulness, he speaks simply and authoritatively when he calms Calphurnia's fears and declares his resolution to go to the Capitol.

The instability and irritability of Cassius are reflected in his manner of speech. As he begins to lose control of his feelings in his denunciation of Cæsar, his utterance becomes more and more disjointed and exclamatory:

> And when the fit was on him, I did mark
> How he did shake; 'tis true, this god did shake;
> His coward lips did from their colour fly,
> And that same eye whose bend doth awe the world
> Did lose his lustre; I did hear him groan;

> Ay, and that tongue of his, that bade the Romans
> Mark him and write his speeches in their books,
> Alas, it cried, "Give me some drink, Titinius,"
> As a sick girl. Ye gods, it doth amaze me...
> ...Now in the names of all the gods at once,
> Upon what meat doth this our Cæsar feed,
> That he is grown so great? Age, thou art sham'd!
>
> (I. ii. 119–48)

Similarly, in the quarrel scene, the difficulty with which he keeps his temper is reflected in his exclamatory manner: "Is't possible?" "O ye gods, ye gods! Must I endure all this?" "Is it come to this?" "What? durst not tempt him?"

But apart from these two episodes, the speeches in which he is sounding Casca (I. iii. 57–115), and one or two to which he is prompted by Brutus's exaltation after the death of Cæsar, Cassius is in full control of his tongue. He has the second largest part in the play, and most of the time his speeches are straightforward and uncomplicated by imagery. When practical measures are to be considered he speaks concisely and sensibly. In the meeting of the conspirators, the negotiations with Antony over Cæsar's funeral, and the council of the generals at Sardis, his directness and common sense reveal a grasp of practical realities such as Brutus never possessed.

Some of Antony's speeches have already been considered. He has every nuance of speech at his command. With a few subtle phrases he can at the same time bring out the greatness of Cæsar and whip Brutus with his scorn. In four beautifully balanced lines he both flatters Brutus and asserts the superiority of Cæsar:

> Brutus is noble, wise, valiant, and honest;
> Cæsar was mighty, bold, royal, and loving:
> Say I love Brutus, and I honour him;
> Say I fear'd Cæsar, honour'd him, and lov'd him.
>
> (III. i. 126–9)

In this scene, apart from the permission to speak in Cæsar's funeral, he asks for nothing from his enemies—neither mercy nor concessions; he manipulates them into a position where they are only too anxious to show him good will, and he presses home every advantage he gains. Brutus thinks more highly of him with every word he utters. When at last the long fight with the conspirators is won, Shakespeare puts into his mouth, in his epitaph on Brutus, a speech of the most noble simplicity.

Caroline Spurgeon, whose investigation of Shakespeare's imagery has led to many interesting conclusions, finds little to hold her in *Julius Cæsar*. After drawing attention to the relative scarcity of extended images, she goes on to say:[1]

There is no leading or floating image in the play; one feels it was not written under the particular stress of emotion or excitement which gives rise to a dominating image. There is, however, a certain persistence in the comparison of the characters to animals: Cæsar is a wolf, a lion, a falcon, a serpent's egg, an adder, a stricken deer; the Romans are sheep and hinds and bees; the conspirators are apes and hounds; Brutus is a lamb; Lepidus is an ass, a horse; Metellus and Casca are curs; Cassius is a showy, mettlesome steed which fails at the moment of trial; and Octavius and Antony are bears tied to the stake. But this animal imagery is not nearly so marked as in either *King Lear* or *Othello*, and entirely lacks consistency of character, so that it fails to produce the cumulative effect so strongly felt in both those plays.

Now it is true that there is no single dominating image, such as Professor Spurgeon found in *Romeo and Juliet*, for example, or *Othello*; but there are several that recur often enough to be worthy of remark.

Up to the assassination of Cæsar the play is to a large degree concerned with conflicts within and between individuals: Brutus's tormented communings with himself, Cassius's notion of himself as a rival to Cæsar, Portia's and Calphurnia's struggles to wrest secrets or concessions from their husbands. After the assassination there is outward, physical conflict, which develops into actual war: Antony pits himself against the conspirators, first as an individual, and then in association with Octavius as a leader of great armies at war with the armies of Brutus and Cassius. In the first half a persistent image of civil warfare, in the mind of Brutus and in the heavens, reflects the discord represented by the plot against Cæsar, and prefigures the "domestic fury and fierce civil strife" which form the background of the second half of the play.

When Cassius shows concern at Brutus's recent lack of friendliness, Brutus admits that he has been vexed "with passions of some difference"; the reason for his apparent coldness, he says, is that

> poor Brutus, with himself at war,
> Forgets the shows of love to other men. (i. ii. 45–6)

Later, when he is meditating alone in his garden, he again likens the turbulence in his soul, the hideous nightmare of doubt that comes "between the acting of a dreadful thing and the first motion", to a civil uprising:

1. Caroline F. E. Spurgeon, *Shakespeare's Imagery*, pp. 346–7.

> the state of man,
> Like to a little kingdom, suffers then
> The nature of an insurrection. (II. i. 67–9)

Like other Elizabethans, Shakespeare often draws a correspond·
ence between man and the state.

But there is also a correspondence between the microcosm, man,
and the macrocosm, the universe; and the civil war metaphor is
given much greater force when it is extended to the storm, that
great upheaval of the elements which gives a forewarning of
Cæsar's death, and at the same time symbolizes what is going on in
the minds of the human figures of the play—reflects on the universal scale the conflicts at the human level. To Casca the storm means
either that "there is a civil strife in heaven," or that the angry gods
are punishing their disobedient subjects on the earth (I. iii. 11–13).
Cæsar declares that "nor heaven nor earth have been at peace to-
night" (II. ii. 1); and Calphurnia reports that, among the "most
horrid sights" seen during the night,

> Fierce fiery warriors fight upon the clouds
> In ranks and squadrons and right form of war,
> ... The noise of battle hurtled in the air. (II. ii. 19–22)

Allied with this imagery of civil warfare is Cassius's way of looking on Cæsar and himself as contestants for some kind of supremacy.
He describes how he and Cæsar strove, "with hearts of controversy"
to outswim each other in the swollen Tiber; and it infuriates him
that Cæsar should have outstripped him and all other competitors
in the struggle for power in the state:

> Ye gods, it doth amaze me
> A man of such a feeble temper should
> So get the start of the majestic world,
> And bear the palm alone. (I. ii. 127–30)

It is Cassius's rankling sense of inferiority, his knowledge that Cæsar
will beat him in any contest for power, that makes him organize the
conspiracy. If he had really had patriotic motives for doing so, he
would have thought about what was to replace Cæsar's rule. He
was too intelligent to have forgotten this consideration, except
under the stress of his obsessing hatred.

The image of strife is used once more. Portia, in her violent agitation of mind after Brutus has gone to the Capitol, imagines that
she hears "a bustling rumour, like a fray", though Lucius can hear
nothing.

After Antony's speech to the citizens there is actual mutiny in
Rome, and Italy is plunged into the bloody discord which he fore-

told over Cæsar's murdered body. There is no longer any need for Shakespeare to use as an image what is one of the principal themes of the play.

Mr John Crow has drawn my attention to another recurrent image in which the characters are seen in terms of metals; in which contrasts are brought out or implied between the sharpness and bluntness of metal objects, between liveliness and dullness, between preciousness and baseness. In his first full speech in the play Brutus says,

> I am not gamesome: I do lack some part
> Of that quick spirit that is in Antony. (I. ii. 27–8)

Thus Brutus himself brings to our notice a contrast which is to be most glaringly exemplified in Act III, Scene 1, where the nimble-witted Antony leads him by the nose, and makes him look a very dullard. When Brutus and Cassius part after their first interview, Cassius declares that Brutus's "honourable mettle may be wrought from that it is dispos'd". There is a play here on the two meanings of the word *mettle*, "disposition" and "metal" (as it is nowadays spelt when used in this sense). Cassius, amongst other feelings about Brutus, regards him as a piece of precious metal which he can fashion into a tool that will suit his own purposes; there is also the implication that he will turn him into base metal by "seducing" him. The same metaphor occurs at the end of the following scene, when Casca says that the "countenance" of Brutus, "like richest alchemy", will make the baseness of the other conspirators appear to be worthiness.

The image of a tool that has been edged by a craftsman is put into the mouth of Brutus when, soliloquizing in his garden, he says,

> Since Cassius first did *whet* me against Cæsar,
> I have not slept. (II. i. 61–2)

It is present again in Antony's words:

> I am no orator, as Brutus is,
> But (as you know me all) a plain *blunt* man.
> (III. ii. 219–20)

The ironical implication is that Brutus is "a sharp fellow", who has stolen away the hearts of the citizens by the glib arts of the practised orator.

This line of imagery would, of course, gain extra point if we could be sure that Shakespeare was consciously punning on Brutus's name in using it. It is improbable that Shakespeare would not know the meaning of the Latin word *brutus*, which in Lewis and

Short's dictionary is given thus: "I. Lit., *heavy, unwieldy, immovable.*
II. Trop., *dull, stupid, insensible, unreasonable.*" He would perhaps
also know Livy's or Ovid's account of how the word *brutus* became
the cognomen of the family from which Marcus Brutus claimed
descent; and Plutarch refers briefly to the legend. According to
Livy,[1] Lucius Junius Brutus, the great liberator who "did from
the streets of Rome the Tarquin drive", feigned stupidity to save
himself when Tarquinius Superbus was massacring all potential
rivals. He "kept up the appearance and conduct of an idiot", and
"did not even protest against his nickname of 'Brutus' ". Now
Shakespeare's Brutus has, over and above the fine qualities that he
derives from his model in Plutarch, others which give us some justification for regarding him as dull and unreasonable; and it is tempt-
ing to think that Shakespeare, unable to believe that a man as wise
and virtuous as Plutarch's Brutus could associate himself with the
wicked and senseless murder of Cæsar, took a hint from Brutus's
name in providing him with less estimable traits.

The same imagery is once or twice applied to Casca. Brutus says
of him:

> What a blunt fellow is this grown to be!
> He was quick mettle when he went to school. (I. ii. 292–3)

Cassius defends him on this occasion, and explains that this "tardy
form" is a pose; but in the next scene, wishing to whet him too
against Cæsar, he tells him that he is "dull", and wanting in "those
sparks of life that should be in a Roman" (I. iii. 57–8).

There are other less obvious instances of the use of this and kindred metaphors: where, for example, Brutus undertakes to "fashion"
Ligarius (II. i. 220); or where Flavius speaks of the "basest mettle"
(in a double sense) of the citizens (I. i. 61). And when Brutus says,
"To you our swords have leaden points, Mark Antony" (III. i. 173),
it is possible to see an implied contrast between the leaden dullness
of Brutus in this scene and the quicksilver brilliance of Antony.

Professor Spurgeon has perhaps done less than justice to the consistency and interest of the imagery in *Julius Cæsar.* As in his other
mature plays, Shakespeare has used the imagery to reinforce the
impressions that characters give of themselves by their speech and
conduct. He has also used it to heighten atmosphere. I must content myself with citing two instances of this. Blood and destruction
play an important part in the action of the play; blood plays an important part in the imagery as well. Then on three occasions a certain theatricality, whether in character or incident, is emphasized

I. I. 56 ff.

by imagery connected with the theatre: when Cæsar has a fit while he is being offered the crown, when Brutus gives his final exhortation to the conspirators in the garden, and when Brutus and Cassius are swept away by their exalted but purposeless enthusiasm after they have stabbed Cæsar.

Finally, Professor Price has drawn attention[1] to the importance of the word *love* as a key-word of the play. "There is this love of Brutus for Cæsar and of Cæsar for Brutus, the love of Brutus and Cassius, Brutus and Portia, the mutual love between Brutus and Lucius and all his servants. Brutus is a center of love wherever he goes. There is the love of Antony for Cæsar, which drives him to destroy the conspirators. There is the ominous absence of love around Octavius. Love violated and betrayed, the man who lives for love violating himself, these are among the most moving *motifs* of the play."[2]

10. THE PRESENT TEXT

General Procedure. As I have elsewhere indicated, this text is based on that of the First Folio. Spelling and punctuation have been brought into line with modern usage. However, in accordance with the principles of the Arden series, archaic variants have been retained where they are Elizabethan alternatives in the form, not merely in the spelling of the words: examples are *swound, murther, disgest, vildly, strucken, Y'have* (="You've"), *where* (="whether"). Incorrect forms which are obviously no more than misprints have been silently corrected; a few examples of these will be found in footnote 2 on page xxiii. I have drawn attention to any departures from the Folio lineation in the apparatus criticus.

All the stage-directions of the Folio have been reproduced, unless emendation has seemed necessary, in which case the fact has been noted; and as a rule they appear in their original positions. If at times it may seem to the modern reader that they occur rather early, this is because on the Elizabethan stage a person might come on at some distance from persons already on the stage, and a few moments before he might be supposed to be within speaking distance of them. Sometimes, too, stage-directions appear to have been marked early by the prompter so that they caught his eye in good time. Whenever I have changed the position of a Folio stage-direc-

1. *Julius Cæsar*, ed. Hereward T. Price, Introduction, p. xii.
2. For a perceptive study of the place of *Julius Cæsar* in the development of Shakespeare's style and dramatic technique, see H. Granville-Barker, *From Henry V to Hamlet* (British Academy Shakespeare Lecture, 1925).

tion, whether to prevent confusion in the mind of the reader or producer or for any other reason, I have noted the change in the apparatus criticus, and if it seemed necessary have explained it in a note.[1] All stage-directions that have been introduced by editors since the Folio, and all additions to its stage-directions, have been enclosed in square brackets. I have retained the Folio convention of using *Enter* each time a character comes on, whether it is his first entry in a scene or a re-entry.

Act- and scene-division. In the Folio the first act is headed *Actus Primus. Scæna Prima.* Later acts are headed *Actus Secundus, Actus Tertius,* etc. There is no formal scene-division. Rowe numbered the scenes, and indicated their locality. I have followed the now conventional numbering, with one small departure. What are traditionally presented as the second and third scenes of Act IV are in fact a single scene, as, among other things, the Folio stage-direction *Manet Brutus and Cassius* makes clear. Presumably Brutus and Cassius would move from outside Brutus's tent to inside by moving to another part of the stage. Or perhaps they would enter one of the structures known as "houses" or "mansions" which seem often to have been used on the Elizabethan stage to represent tents and the like.[2] To have broken the tradition and run the two scenes together as one, as seems desirable, would have caused awkwardness in cross-reference and in the use of dictionaries and other reference works. I have therefore compromised by changing the conventional central scene-heading to a less conspicuous heading moved to the left (thus in effect making the scene continuous), and retaining the conventional line-numbering.

Apparatus criticus. In the apparatus criticus I have tried to record all departures from the Folio text—apart of course from those that are due to the modernization of spelling and punctuation and to the correction of obvious misprints. Since the later Folios are mere derivative texts, and have no authority, I have ignored them in the collation except on the rare occasions when their readings have added point to an annotation,[3] or have corrected manifest errors in the First Folio. I have noted also what seem to me to be the most interesting or significant attempts at emendation by previous editors, even where I have not followed them. I have not myself collated all the editions to which reference is made; I have depended to a large extent on the collations of the editors of the old *Cambridge*

1. e.g., IV. iii. 230.
2. See Leslie Hotson, 'Shakespeare's Arena' (*Sewanee Review,* July 1953).
3. e.g., II. i. 83; III. ii. 223; IV. iii. 5.

Shakespeare (vol. vii, 1865) and the Furness Variorum *Julius Cæsar* (1913), checking where I suspected errors.

Proper names. I have been conventional rather than consistent. In several instances proper names appear in the Folio in forms that are un-Roman, or that differ from those used by North. The practice of previous editors has been generally to give these names as they appear in North, and in this I have followed them. Thus I have given the *Murellus* (or *Murrellus*) of the Folio in its accepted form *Marullus*. Similarly the Folio forms *Antonio, Octavio, Varrus, Claudio, Labio,* and *Flavio* are replaced—where they are used, for the Folio is not consistent—by *Antonius, Octavius, Varro, Claudius, Labeo,* and *Flavius,* and attention is drawn to the changes in the apparatus criticus.

For complete consistency the Folio forms *Portia, Lena,* and *Dardanius* should have been changed to North's *Porcia, Laena* and *Dardanus;* but they have now become traditional, and I have followed my predecessors in keeping them. However, in common with several recent editors, I have left the tradition to give *Calphurnia.* This form is invariable in the Folio; North uses both *Calpurnia* and *Calphurnia* (as well as *Calphurnius* for the masculine equivalent), and the form with *h* is used also in *Cæsar's Revenge,* and in the *Caius Iulius Cæsar* in *A Mirror for Magistrates.*

North misread or mistook the name of the historical Decimus Brutus as *Decius Brutus,* and was followed by Shakespeare. The mistaken form is traditionally accepted in editions of *Julius Cæsar.*

I have not standardized the form in which names appear in stage directions, since the Folio variants (*Cæsar: Julius Cæsar; Antony: Mark Antony,* etc.) nowhere cause confusion.

References. The text used for illustrative quotations from the works of Shakespeare, apart from the present play, is that of the Oxford Shakespeare, edited by W. J. Craig. Where Malone Society editions of plays by other Elizabethan dramatists exist I have used them for quotations and references; otherwise I have gone to such standard editions as Herford and Simpson's *Ben Jonson,* McKerrow's *Nashe,* and the like. I have named any unusual editions from which I quote.

II. FURTHER READING

I have not tried in this Introduction to deal with all the topics that have interested commentators on *Julius Cæsar.* Among many helpful studies of the play I recommend particularly those which appear in the following works:

Edward Dowden, *Shakspere: His Mind and Art* (8th edn.), London, 1886.

Richard G. Moulton, *Shakespeare as a Dramatic Artist* (2nd edn.), Oxford, 1888.

M. W. MacCallum, *Shakespeare's Roman Plays*, London, 1910.

Harley Granville-Barker, *Prefaces to Shakespeare, First Series*, London, 1933.

Harley Granville-Barker, *From Henry V to Hamlet* (British Academy Shakespeare Lecture, 1925).

John Palmer, *Political Characters of Shakespeare*, London, 1945.

J. I. M. Stewart, ' "Julius Cæsar" and "Macbeth": Two Notes on Shakespearean Technique' (*Mod. Lang. Rev.*, XL, 1945, pp. 166–71).

Virgil K. Whitaker, *Shakespeare's Use of Learning: An Inquiry into the Growth of his Mind and Art*, San Marino, California: The Huntington Library, 1953 (Chap. x).

Furness's Variorum edition of *Julius Cæsar* gives numerous extracts from the writings of earlier critics touching on aspects of the play that I have not dealt with.

12. ACKNOWLEDGEMENTS

Every modern editor of Shakespeare owes unconscious debts to many generations of scholars whose work has laid the foundations on which his own edition must be based; and even when he is aware of special obligations he cannot always record them in his annotations without making these seem inordinately long. I should like to acknowledge here some of my own most substantial debts. Previous editions of *Julius Cæsar* that I have found especially helpful in matters of interpretation are those of William Aldis Wright, G. L. Kittredge, and the Furness Variorum *Shakespeare*; and more often than I have noted, I have taken over the sense, and at times some of the wording, of annotations made by my predecessor in the Arden series, Michael Macmillan.

I also owe much to the general editors of the new Arden series, Professor Una Ellis-Fermor and Dr Harold Brooks. Dr Brooks, in particular, has been most generous with advice and constructive criticism; he has helped me with textual difficulties and has provided, among other things, the material on *A Mirror for Magistrates* of which I have made use in this Introduction and elsewhere in the volume. Mr John Crow has at various stages of the work made valuable and stimulating comments, and deserves more thanks than he gets in my annotations. I am grateful, too, to Miss Mary Beare, Mr E. Honigmann, and others, who have answered questions or made suggestions. If I have sometimes been wilful and disregarded advice offered to me, I am aware that I have done so at my peril; and I am none the less grateful to those who have shown so much kindness in offering it.

13. ABBREVIATIONS

The abbreviated titles of Shakespeare's works are those of Dr Onions in his *Shakespeare Glossary*.

F indicates the First Folio; *F1* is used only when the First has to be distinguished from the later Folios, *F2*, *F3*, and *F4*.

The following abbreviations are used for editions of Shakespeare's works, or of *Julius Cæsar*:

Rowe	*The Works*, ed. Nicholas Rowe, 1709 (3rd edn., 1714).
Pope	*The Works*, ed. Alexander Pope, 1723.
Theobald	*The Works*, ed. Lewis Theobald, 1733.
Hanmer	*The Works*, ed. Sir Thomas Hanmer, 1744.
Warburton	*The Works*, ed. William Warburton, 1747.
Johnson	*The Plays*, ed. Samuel Johnson, 1765.
Capell	*The Comedies, Histories and Tragedies*, ed. Edward Capell [1768].
Variorum 1773	*The Plays*, ed. Samuel Johnson and George Steevens, 1773.
Malone	*The Plays and Poems*, ed. Edmond Malone, 1790.
Steevens	*The Works*, ed. George Steevens, 1793.
Singer	*The Works*, ed. S. W. Singer, 1826.
Knight	*The Pictorial Shakespeare*, ed. Charles Knight [1841].
Collier	*The Works*, ed. John Payne Collier, 1842.
Staunton	*The Works*, ed. Howard Staunton, 1860.
Grant White	*The Works*, ed. R. Grant White, 1861.
Keightley	*The Plays*, ed. T. Keightley, 1864.
Cambridge	*The Cambridge Shakespeare*, ed. W. G. Clark and W. A. Wright, 1863–6.
Hudson	*The Harvard Shakespeare*, ed. H. N. Hudson, 1881.
Wright	*Julius Cæsar*, ed. William Aldis Wright (*Clarendon Press Series*), 1869.
Hunter	*Julius Cæsar*, ed. Mark Hunter (*College Classics*), 1900.
Macmillan	*Julius Cæsar*, ed. Michael Macmillan (*The Arden Shakespeare*), 1902.
Furness	*Julius Cæsar*, ed. Horace Howard Furness, Jr. (*The Variorum Shakespeare*), 1913.
Kittredge	*Julius Cæsar*, ed. George Lyman Kittredge, 1939.
Dover Wilson	*Julius Cæsar*, ed. John Dover Wilson (*New Cambridge Shakespeare*), 1949.
Collier MS.	Manuscript annotations (allegedly of the seventeenth century, but actually forgeries) in J. P. Collier's copy of the Second Folio.

Other abbreviations used are as follows:

Abbott	E. A. Abbott, *A Shakespearian Grammar* (3rd edn), London, 1870.
Bibl. Soc.	The Bibliographical Society.
Bulloch	John Bulloch, *Studies on the Text of Shakespeare*, London, 1878.
Cartwright	Robert Cartwright, *New Readings in Shakspere*, London, 1866.
Craik	G. L. Craik, *The English of Shakespeare*, London, 1856.
Daniel	P. A. Daniel, *Notes and Conjectural Emendations of Certain Doubtful Passages in Shakespeare's Plays*, London, 1870.
E.E.T.S.	The Early English Text Society.
Farmer	Richard Farmer, *An Essay on the Learning of Shakespeare*, London, 1767.
Herr	J. G. Herr, *Scattered Notes on the Text of Shakespeare*, Philadelphia, 1879.
Mal. Soc.	The Malone Society.
Mason	J. M. Mason, *Comments on the Last Edition of Shakespeare's Plays* [*Variorum, 1778*], London, 1785.
Mod. Lang. Rev.	*The Modern Language Review.*
N. & Q.	*Notes and Queries.*
O.E.	Old English.
O.E.D.	*A New English Dictionary on Historical Principles*, Oxford, 1884–1928.
Onions	C. T. Onions, *A Shakespeare Glossary* (2nd edn), Oxford, 1919.
Sk.	Walter W. Skeat, *Shakespeare's Plutarch*, London, 1875.
Tilley	M. P. Tilley, *A Dictionary of the Proverbs in England in the Sixteenth and Seventeenth Centuries*, University of Michigan, 1950.

THE TRAGEDY OF
JULIUS CÆSAR

DRAMATIS PERSONÆ[1]

JULIUS CÆSAR.

OCTAVIUS CÆSAR,
MARCUS ANTONIUS, } *Triumvirs after the death of Julius Cæsar.*
M. ÆMILIUS LEPIDUS,

CICERO,
PUBLIUS, } *Senators.*
POPILIUS LENA,

MARCUS BRUTUS,
CASSIUS,
CASCA,
TREBONIUS,
LIGARIUS, } *Conspirators against Julius Cæsar.*
DECIUS BRUTUS,
METELLUS CIMBER,
CINNA,

FLAVIUS *and* MARULLUS, *Tribunes.*

ARTEMIDORUS, *a Sophist of Cnidos.*

A Soothsayer.

CINNA, *a Poet.*

Another Poet.

LUCILIUS, TITINIUS, MESSALA, YOUNG CATO, *and* VOLUMNIUS, *Friends to Brutus and Cassius.*

VARRO, CLITUS, CLAUDIUS, STRATO, LUCIUS, DARDANIUS, *Servants or Officers to Brutus.*

PINDARUS, *Servant to Cassius.*

A Cobbler, a Carpenter, and other Plebeians.

A Servant to Cæsar; to Antony; to Octavius.

CALPHURNIA, *Wife to Cæsar.*

PORTIA, *Wife to Brutus.*

The Ghost of Cæsar.

Senators, Guards, Attendants, etc.

SCENE: *During a great part of the Play, at Rome; afterwards near Sardis, and near Philippi.*

1. The *dramatis personæ* were first, but incompletely, listed by Rowe. The present form of the list is substantially that of Theobald.

For the forms of some of the names see Introduction, p. lxxi.

THE TRAGEDY OF
JULIUS CÆSAR

ACT I

SCENE I.[—*Rome. A Street.*]

Enter FLAVIUS, MARULLUS, *and certain Commoners
over the stage.*

Flav. Hence! home, you idle creatures, get you home:
Is this a holiday? What, know you not,
Being mechanical, you ought not walk
Upon a labouring day without the sign
Of your profession? Speak, what trade art thou?   5
Carpenter. Why, sir, a carpenter.
Mar. Where is thy leather apron, and thy rule?
What dost thou with thy best apparel on?
You, sir, what trade are you?

Scene I

S.D. *Marullus*] *Theobald; Murellus* F.
out scene).

7. *Mar.*] *Theobald; Mur.* F (*so throughout scene*).

3. *mechanical*] being handicraftsmen, artisans. Cf. *2 H 4*, v. v. 39, "Hal'd thither / By most mechanical and dirty hand"; North's *Plutarch* (Sk., p. 113), "Thinkest thou that they be cobblers, tapsters, or suchlike base mechanical people, that write these bills and scrolls which are found daily in thy praetor's chair?" As substantive, cf. the "rude mechanicals" of *MND*.

ought not walk] The only example I have found in Shakespeare of the infinitive used after *ought* without the preposition *to*. See Abbott, ¶ 349.

4–5. *without . . . profession*] There is no need to follow those who have searched for laws, Roman or Elizabethan, requiring artisans to dress in a particular fashion. Flavius merely refers to such things as the *leather apron* and the *rule* of l. 7, which the commoners have discarded on taking a holiday for Cæsar's triumph, and put their *best apparel* on. Contrast Cleopatra's picture of such an occasion, *Ant.*, v. ii. 210, "Mechanic slaves / With greasy aprons, rules, and hammers, shall / Uplift us to the view."

3

Cobbler. Truly, sir, in respect of a fine workman, I am but,   10
   as you would say, a cobbler.

Mar. But what trade art thou? Answer me directly.

Cob. A trade, sir, that I hope I may use with a safe con-
   science; which is, indeed, sir, a mender of bad soles.

Mar. What trade, thou knave? thou naughty knave,
   what trade?   15

Cob. Nay, I beseech you, sir, be not out with me: yet, if
   you be out, sir, I can mend you.

Mar. What meanest thou by that? Mend me, thou saucy
   fellow?

Cob. Why, sir, cobble you.

Flav. Thou art a cobbler, art thou?   20

Cob. Truly, sir, all that I live by is with the awl: I meddle

14. soles] soules *F1;* soals *F4.*   15. *Mar.*] *Mur. Capell; Fla. F.*   15.] *As verse
this edn; as prose F.*   18.] *As verse this edn.; as prose F.*   meanest] *This edn.;*
mean'st *F.*

10. *in respect of*] in comparison with.
Cf. *AYL.,* III. ii. 69, "Most shallow
man! thou worms-meat, in respect of a
good piece of flesh, indeed!" Cf. also
Ado, III. iv. 19, and *LLL.,* v. ii. 636.

11. *a cobbler*] The Cobbler is play-
ing on two meanings of the word *cobbler,* "mender of shoes" and "bung-
ler".

12. *directly*] straightforwardly, plainly. Cf. III. iii. 9.

14. *soles*] The Folio spelling *soules*
emphasizes the pun. Cf. *Rom.,* I. iv. 15;
and *Mer.V.,* IV. i. 123 (F. spelling),
"Not on thy soale: but on thy soule
harsh Iew / Thou mak'st thy knife
keene."

15. *What trade . . . trade?*] The Folio
gives this speech to Flavius. Capell
was surely right in taking it as part of
the exchange between Marullus and
the Cobbler. The Folio also prints the
line as prose. Perhaps the compositor
was misled by its length combined
with its position between the Cobbler's prose speeches.

naughty] good-for-nothing, worthless.

16. *out with*] angry with. Cf. *Mer.
V.,* v. iii. 34, "Launcelot and I are

out." In l. 17 *out* is "out at heels, worn
out". Cf. *Meas.,* II. i. 59, "out at elbow", a phrase still in use.

18. *What meanest . . . fellow?*] Like
l. 15, printed as prose in the Folio,
presumably for the same reasons. The
appearance on the written page of
these two lines, and of ll. 12 and 20,
all sandwiched between the Cobbler's
prose, would not indicate clearly to
the compositor's eye that the Tribunes are intended to speak in verse.
The emendation of the Folio *mean'st* to
meanest seems necessary on metrical
grounds; nowhere else do the Tribunes speak unmetrically. The change
produces an alexandrine.

21–3. *I meddle . . . old shoes*] No emendation is necessary in this passage.
In l. 23 *withal* has the normal enough
Shakesperian sense of "yet", "at the
same time", and the pun ("with awl")
is implicit. Malone was almost certainly right in suspecting some equivocal meaning in the phrase *women's
matters.* Cf. John Heywood, *The Foure
PP,* ed. Manly (*Spec. of Pre-Shak.
Drama,* I, p. 492), l. 279, "Let womens
maters passe, and marke myne."
Also *Ham.,* III. ii. 124, "country mat-

with no tradesman's matters, nor women's matters;
but withal I am, indeed, sir, a surgeon to old shoes:
when they are in great danger I recover them. As
proper men as ever trod upon neat's leather have   25
gone upon my handiwork.

Flav. But wherefore art not in thy shop to-day?
Why dost thou lead these men about the streets?

Cob. Truly, sir, to wear out their shoes, to get myself into
more work. But indeed, sir, we make holiday to see   30
Cæsar, and to rejoice in his triumph.

Mar. Wherefore rejoice? What conquest brings he
home?
What tributaries follow him to Rome,

---

22. tradesman's] Tradesmans *F;* tradesmen's *Warburton;* trade,—man's
Farmer; trades, man's *Staunton conj.*   women's] womens *F;* woman's *Rowe.*
23. withal I] *F;* with all. I *Capell;* with awl. I *Farmer.*   32.] As *Rowe;* Wherefore reioyce? / . . . home? / *F.*

---

ters". It is just possible that Shakespeare's audiences saw in the passage
also a slightly satirical topical allusion.
Dekker's play *The Shoemaker's Holiday*
was being performed in 1599 by the
Admiral's Men, and is referred to in
Henslowe's *Diary* as early as 15 July,
whereas the earliest reference to *Julius
Cæsar* that can be dated is Platter's
statement that he saw it acted on 21
Sept. 1599. In *The Shoemaker's Holiday*
the master shoemaker Simon Eyre
does meddle with *tradesman's matters*
and *women's matters*. He deals in merchandise, and in fact owes his riches,
and hence his election as Lord Mayor,
to the profit he makes by buying and
selling the cargo of a ship; and at the
end of the play he asks of the king that
"your Grace would vouchsafe some
priuilege to my new Leden hall, that
it may be lawfull for vs to buy and sell
leather there two dayes a weeke" (ed.
Bowers, v. v. 153–5). He meddles with
women's matters in the help he gives
to Jane and Rose. Shakespeare's Cobbler may possibly be echoing words
spoken by Dekker's cobbler Firk in
The Shoemaker's Holiday, v. ii. 156,
"Yes sir, shoomakers dare stand in a

womans quarrel I warrant you, as
deepe as another, and deeper too."
(See Norman Nathan, in *Mod. Lang.
Rev.,* XLVIII, 2, Apr. 1953).

24. *recover*] Another pun: "restore
to health" and "patch".

24–5. *As proper . . . neat's leather*] as
fine men as ever walked in shoes. A
proverbial expression: cf. *Tp.,* II. ii.
73, "He's a present for any emperor
that ever trod on neat's leather"; Porter, *Two Angry Women of Abington*
(Mal. Soc.), ll. 2318–20, "as good a
man . . . as ere went on Neats leather".
Neat is still a provincial term for cattle,
especially in the north of England.

31. *triumph*] Cæsar defeated Gnaeus
and Sextus, sons of Pompey the Great,
at Munda in Spain in March, 45 B.C.,
and his triumph took place at the beginning of October in the same year.
Plutarch says it was resented because
it celebrated a victory over "the sons
of the noblest man of Rome, whom
fortune had overthrown". See note on
l. 67 below.

33. *tributaries*] payers of tribute. Cf.
Ham., v. ii. 39; and *Ant.,* III. xi. 96,
"Were't twenty of the greatest tribu-
taries / That do acknowledge Cæsar".

To grace in captive bonds his chariot wheels?
You blocks, you stones, you worse than senseless things!
O you hard hearts, you cruel men of Rome,   36
Knew you not Pompey? Many a time and oft
Have you climb'd up to walls and battlements,
To towers and windows, yea, to chimney-tops,
Your infants in your arms, and there have sat   40
The livelong day, with patient expectation,
To see great Pompey pass the streets of Rome:
And when you saw his chariot but appear,
Have you not made an universal shout,
That Tiber trembled underneath her banks   45
To hear the replication of your sounds
Made in her concave shores?
And do you now put on your best attire?
And do you now cull out a holiday?
And do you now strew flowers in his way,   50
That comes in triumph over Pompey's blood?
Be gone!
Run to your houses, fall upon your knees,
Pray to the gods to intermit the plague
That needs must light on this ingratitude.   55
Flav. Go, go, good countrymen, and for this fault

37. Pompey? Many . . . oft] *Rowe; Pompey* many . . . oft? *F.*   39. windows,
yea,] *Rowe;* Windowes? Yea, *F.*

34. *captive bonds*] the fetters of cap-
tives.

37–9. *Knew you not . . . chimney-tops*]
Question-marks several times go astray
in the Folio, and Rowe's punctuation
must be accepted here. (See apparatus criticus.)

42. *pass the streets*] pass through the
streets. Cf. Gosson, *School of Abuse* (ed.
Arber), p. 36, "Beeing so knowen that
they are the bywoordes of euery mans
mouth, and pointed at commonly as
they passe the streetes." The omission
of prepositions with verbs of motion is
not uncommon; cf. i. ii. 109, "But ere
we could arrive the point propos'd".

45–7. *her banks . . . her concave shores*]
The feminine possessive adjective
sounds strange when applied to the

Tiber, which seems to have been regarded by the Romans as an essentially masculine river. Cf. Horace,
Odes, i. ii, where Ilia, or Rhea Silvia,
is spoken of as the wife of the Tiber,
uxorius amnis, whom she urges to
avenge the assassination of Julius
Cæsar, her descendant.

46. *replication*] reverberation, echo.

47. *concave shores*] overhanging
banks, which catch and reflect the
noise.

49. *cull out a holiday*] pick this out as
a holiday. Note how *cull* leads on to
flowers in the next line.

51. *Pompey's blood*] Pompey's kindred, i.e., his sons. The blood that has
been shed is implied as well.

54. *intermit*] delay, put off.

Assemble all the poor men of your sort;
Draw them to Tiber banks, and weep your tears
Into the channel, till the lowest stream
Do kiss the most exalted shores of all.   60

[Exeunt all the Commoners.

See where their basest mettle be not mov'd;
They vanish tongue-tied in their guiltiness.
Go you down that way towards the Capitol;
This way will I. Disrobe the images,
If you do find them deck'd with ceremonies.   65

Mar. May we do so?
You know it is the feast of Lupercal.

Flav. It is no matter; let no images
Be hung with Cæsar's trophies. I'll about
And drive away the vulgar from the streets;   70
So do you too, where you perceive them thick.
These growing feathers pluck'd from Cæsar's wing

61. where] *F;* whe're *Theobald;* whe'r *Hanmer;* whether *Cambridge.*

58. *Tiber banks*] Cf. *Cor.*, I. viii. 8, "Corioli walls"; and *Ham.*, I. v. 33, "Lethe wharf".

60. *the most exalted shores*] the highest banks.

61. *where*] whether. This form occurs several times in Shakespeare: cf. v. iv. 30, "And see where Brutus be alive or dead." It is sometimes printed "whe'r" in modern editions.

mettle] spirit, disposition. *Mettle* and *metal* are interchangeable spellings in Shakespeare. The idea of "base metal" is picked up by *guiltiness* in the next line, with a pun ("gilt") suggested.

64. *Disrobe the images*] Plutarch tells how the two tribunes, Flavius and Marullus, pulled down the images of Cæsar set up in the city, "with diadems upon their heads like kings".

65. *ceremonies*] symbols of state. Cf. *H 5*, IV. i. 110, "His [i.e., the king's] ceremonies laid by, in his nakedness he appears but a man." Here presumably the diadems mentioned by Plutarch, though perhaps Shakespeare is merely thinking of any kind of festal adorn-

ment, since at I. ii. 282 Casca says that "Marullus and Flavius, for pulling *scarfs* off Cæsar's images, are put to silence."

67. *the feast of Lupercal*] The Lupercalia, a festival of expiation and purification held in Rome on 15 February in honour of Lupercus, an ancient Italian deity worshipped by shepherds as protector of their flocks, and sometimes identified by the Romans with the Arcadian Pan. Cæsar's triumph celebrating his victory over Pompey's sons had been held in the previous October, but for dramatic effect Shakespeare has combined it with the Lupercalia. Plutarch describes the celebrations separately.

69. *trophies*] ornaments in honour of Cæsar, such as scarves, not the spoils of conquest, as in the normal modern sense of the word. In *Ham.*, IV. vii. 173, Ophelia's *coronet weeds* are the same as her *weedy trophies* two lines later.

70. *the vulgar*] the common people, as normally in Shakespeare.

72–3. *These growing feathers . . . ordinary pitch*] the plucking of these

Will make him fly an ordinary pitch,
Who else would soar above the view of men
And keep us all in servile fearfulness.   [*Exeunt.*   75

[SCENE II.—*The Same. A public Place.*]

Enter CÆSAR, ANTONY *for the course,* CALPHURNIA, PORTIA,
DECIUS, CICERO, BRUTUS, CASSIUS, CASCA, *a Soothsayer,*
[*and a great crowd;*] *after them* MARULLUS *and* FLAVIUS.

Cæs. Calphurnia.
Casca.   Peace, ho! Cæsar speaks.
Cæs.   Calphurnia.
Cal. Here, my lord.
Cæs. Stand you directly in Antonius' way
    When he doth run his course. Antonius.
Ant. Cæsar, my lord?   5
Cæs. Forget not, in your speed, Antonius,
    To touch Calphurnia; for our elders say,
    The barren, touched in this holy chase,
    Shake off their sterile curse.
Ant.   I shall remember:
    When Cæsar says, "Do this," it is perform'd.   10
Cæs. Set on, and leave no ceremony out.
Sooth. Cæsar!

Scene II

S.D. *Enter . . . Flavius.*] F; *Enter in solemn procession, with Musick &c., Cæsar . . .
Flavius.* | *Rowe; Enter in solemn procession, with music, Cæsar, reclining in his litter . . .* |
Dover Wilson.   1. speaks.] F; speaks. [*Music ceases.* | *Capell et al.*   3. Antonius']
Pope; Antonio's F.   4, 6. Antonius] *Pope; Antonio F.*   11. out.] F; out. [*Music.*|
Capell et al.

growing feathers from Cæsar's wing
will make him fly at an ordinary
height. *Pitch,* a term from falconry,
means the height to which a falcon
soars before stooping, i.e., swooping
down on its prey. Shakespeare uses it
both literally and, as here, in metaphor; cf. *R 2,* I. i. 109, "How high a
pitch his resolution soars."

74. *above the view of men*] beyond
human sight—like the gods.

Scene II

4–9. *his course . . .*] See Appendix,
pp. 138–9, for Plutarch's description of
this *holy chase* ("holy course" in North),
which was part of the celebration of
the Lupercalia, and in which barren
women hoped to *shake off their sterile
curse,* i.e., the curse of barrenness, by
allowing themselves to be struck with
the leather thongs carried by the
runners.

Cæs. Ha! Who calls?

Casca. Bid every noise be still; peace yet again!

Cæs. Who is it in the press that calls on me?   15

  I hear a tongue shriller than all the music

  Cry "Cæsar!" Speak. Cæsar is turn'd to hear.

Sooth. Beware the ides of March.

Cæs.   What man is that?

Bru. A soothsayer bids you beware the ides of March.

Cæs. Set him before me; let me see his face.   20

Cas. Fellow, come from the throng; look upon Cæsar.

Cæs. What say'st thou to me now? Speak once again.

Sooth. Beware the ides of March.

Cæs. He is a dreamer. Let us leave him. Pass.

                    [*Sennet. Exeunt. Manent Brutus and Cassius.*

Cas. Will you go see the order of the course?   25

Bru. Not I.

Cas.   I pray you, do.

Bru. I am not gamesome: I do lack some part

  Of that quick spirit that is in Antony.

  Let me not hinder, Cassius, your desires;

  I'll leave you.   30

Cas. Brutus, I do observe you now of late:

  I have not from your eyes that gentleness

  And show of love as I was wont to have.

---

14. again!] *F; again!* [*Music ceases. | Capell et al.*   24. S.D. *Manent] F2;*
Manet F1.

15. *press*] throng. Cf. *H 8*, iv. i. 78; and the Authorized Version of the Bible—e.g., *Mark*, ii. 4 and v. 30.

17. *Cæsar is turn'd to hear*] Cæsar is deaf in one ear: see l. 210. In his arrogance he speaks of himself in the third person.

18. *Beware the ides of March*] In Plutarch the Soothsayer "had given Cæsar warning long time afore, to take heed of the day of the Ides of March (which is the fifteenth of the month), for on that day he should be in great danger." Suetonius gives his name as Spurinna.

24. S.D. Sennet] a flourish of trumpets.

25. *the order of the course*] how the

race goes. Cf. *2 H 4*, iv. iv. 100, "The manner and true order of the fight".

27–8. *gamesome . . . quick spirit*] Brutus speaks rather scornfully. *Gamesome* is probably intended to imply both Antony's fondness for sport and his frivolous disposition, as *quick* could suggest both his speed and his liveliness.

32–3. *I have not . . . wont to have*] Plutarch mentions an estrangement between Brutus and Cassius which arose from Cæsar's granting to Brutus the praetorship, for which Cassius was the rival claimant. Shakespeare makes Brutus's private worries the reason for his apparent coolness.

You bear too stubborn and too strange a hand
Over your friend that loves you.

Bru.   Cassius,   35
Be not deceiv'd: if I have veil'd my look,
I turn the trouble of my countenance
Merely upon myself. Vexed I am
Of late with passions of some difference,
Conceptions only proper to myself,   40
Which give some soil, perhaps, to my behaviours;
But let not therefore my good friends be griev'd
(Among which number, Cassius, be you one)
Nor construe any further my neglect,
Than that poor Brutus, with himself at war,   45
Forgets the shows of love to other men.

Cas. Then, Brutus, I have much mistook your passion;
By means whereof this breast of mine hath buried
Thoughts of great value, worthy cogitations.
Tell me, good Brutus, can you see your face?   50

Bru. No, Cassius; for the eye sees not itself
But by reflection, by some other things.

Cas. 'Tis just;

51–2.] *As Rowe;* No *Cassius:* / . . . reflection, / . . . things. / *F.*

34–5. *You bear . . . loves you*] A metaphor from horsemanship. Cf. *Lr.*, III. i.
27, "Or the hard rein which both of
them have borne / Against the old kind
king". *Stubborn* suggests firm control,
riding on the curb: cf. *H 8*, v. iii. 21,
"for those that tame wild horses / Pace
'em not in their hands to make 'em
gentle, / But stop their mouths with
stubborn bits."

34. *strange*] estranged, almost hostile.

36–8. *if I have . . . upon myself*] if my
face has been clouded, I myself am the
man on whom my frowns have been
turned. *Merely*, as often, means "entirely, purely". At II. i. 307 Brutus says
to Portia, who likewise complains of
his changed demeanour. "All my
engagements I will construe to
thee, / All the charactery of my sad
brows."

39. *passions of some difference*] con-
tending emotions. Brutus is at war
with himself (l. 45) because his love for
Cæsar conflicts with his love of freedom.

40. *Conceptions . . . myself*] thoughts
that concern myself alone.

41. *soil*] blemish, stain.

44. *Nor construe . . . my neglect*] nor
read any more into my neglect.

47. *passion*] feelings.

48. *By means . . . buried*] and because
of my mistake I have kept to myself . . .

49. *worthy*] important.

51–2. *the eye . . . other things*] Cf.
Troil., III. iii. 105–11; also Robert
Cawdray, *A Treasurie or Store-House of
Similes* (1600), "As our eyes . . . doo not
see themselues, but looking in a Glasse
. . . they perfectly see themselues."

53. *'Tis just*] 'Tis true—as often in
Shakespeare.

And it is very much lamented, Brutus,
That you have no such mirrors as will turn   55
Your hidden worthiness into your eye,
That you might see your shadow. I have heard,
Where many of the best respect in Rome
(Except immortal Cæsar), speaking of Brutus,
And groaning underneath this age's yoke,   60
Have wish'd that noble Brutus had his eyes.
Bru. Into what dangers would you lead me, Cassius,
That you would have me seek into myself
For that which is not in me?
Cas. Therefore, good Brutus, be prepar'd to hear; 65
And since you know you cannot see yourself
So well as by reflection, I, your glass,
Will modestly discover to yourself
That of yourself which you yet know not of.
And be not jealous on me, gentle Brutus: 70
Were I a common laughter, or did use

57.] *As Rowe;* That . . . shadow: / . . . heard, / *F.*   62.] *As Rowe;* Into . . . you/
. . . Cassius? / *F.*   71. laughter] *F, Dover Wilson (N.C.S. text); lover conj. Herr,*
Hudson, Dover Wilson (N.C.S. Notes); laugher Rowe et al.

57. *shadow*] reflection. Cf. *John*, II. i.
498, "The shadow of myself form'd in
her eye"; *Ven.*, 161, "Narcissus so himself himself forsook, / And died to kiss
his shadow in the brook." In the present passage *shadow* also implies "out
of the sun", referring to Brutus's veiled
looks.

58. *of the best respect*] of the highest
repute.

59. *immortal Cæsar*] Cassius's first
mention of Cæsar, as an immortal
exalted high above those of the highest
repute in Rome, is bitterly ironical.

61. *had his eyes*] were not blind, i.e.,
saw the yoke beneath which the age
was groaning.

65. *Therefore*] Perhaps, as most editors suggest, Cassius, impatient to
come to the point, or deliberately
brushing aside Brutus's self-doubts, is
merely carrying on with what he has
been saying. But it seems more natural
to let *therefore* refer to the question itself: "As to that, good Brutus, you

must be prepared to hear me." For
therefore in the sense of "in respect of
that", "as to that", cf. *R 3*, IV. iv. 479,
"*K. Rich.* . . . Thou wilt revolt and fly
to him, I fear. / *Stan.* No, my good
lord; therefore mistrust me not." Cf.
also *2 H 6*, I. iv. 3.

68. *modestly*] moderately, without
exaggeration. Cf. *Troil.*, IV. v. 221,
"and modestly I think, / The fall of
every Phrygian stone will cost / A drop
of Grecian blood."

70. *jealous*] suspicious.

71. *laughter*] The Folio reading. If
retained, as I think it should be, it
must mean "laughing-stock, a person
not to be taken seriously". Cf. IV. iii.
49, "I'll use you for my mirth, yea, for
my laughter"; cf. also IV. iii. 113. But
Rowe, Pope, and almost all later editors, emend to *laugher*, i.e., "jester".
Dover Wilson (N.C.S. edn.) has another suggestion: "But the context has
solely to do with (pretended) loving,
and 'lover' (conj. Herr, ap. Furness,

To stale with ordinary oaths my love
To every new protester; if you know
That I do fawn on men and hug them hard,
And after scandal them; or if you know   75
That I profess myself in banqueting
To all the rout, then hold me dangerous.

[Flourish and shout.

Bru. What means this shouting? I do fear the people
    Choose Cæsar for their king.

Cas.   Ay, do you fear it?
    Then must I think you would not have it so.   80

Bru. I would not, Cassius; yet I love him well.
    But wherefore do you hold me here so long?
    What is it that you would impart to me?
    If it be aught toward the general good,

78–9.] *As Rowe;* What . . . Showting? | . . . *Cæsar* | . . . King. | . . . feare it? | F

and Hudson) would fit exactly; i.e., 'everyone's friend,' Cass. would imply, 'is no one's friend'. Perhaps 'loffer' in the copy (fr. 'loff', obs. form of both 'love' and 'laugh') was misinterpreted." However, in the Introduction to his *Facsimile of the First Folio Text of Julius Cæsar* Wilson himself reminds us that "there can be no doubt at all that the 'copy' for *Julius Cæsar* presented Jaggard's compositors with an unusually easy task"; and the rarity of other misinterpretations or misreadings of this magnitude makes me suspicious of the suggestion. Had the compositor found *loffer*, he might conceivably have changed it to either *laugher* or *lover*, but scarcely to *laughter*. But there is no dictionary warrant for such a form as *loffer* in Shakespeare's time. *Laughter*, "one who is not to be taken seriously", fits well into Cassius's description of the sort of man that he is not.

72–3. *To stale . . . new protester*] Usually explained thus: "With commonplace oaths to make stale, or cheap, my love to every newcomer who professes a strong affection for me". I think, however, that *ordinary* implies two stronger meanings than "commonplace": (i) "customary oaths,

ritual oaths"—cf. *Ludus Coventriae* (ed. Block, E.E.T.S.), p. 79, l. 217, ". . . to obey the ordenaryes of the temple echon"; and (ii) "tavern oaths"—cf. Powell, *Tom of All Trades* (ed. Furnivall, New Shak. Soc.), l. 141, "The unwholsome ayre of an Eightpenny Ordinarie". The latter sense is picked up in *banqueting* in l. 76.

75. *after scandal them*] afterwards defame them.

76. *profess myself*] make professions of friendship. Cf. *Wint.*, I. ii. 455, "dishonour'd by a man which ever | Profess'd to him". The intransitive use of *profess* in this parallel is perhaps supported by the omission of *myself* here in the later Folios, though this omission may be due to a slip in the second Folio.

77. *all the rout*] all the common herd. Cf. *Shr.*, III. ii. 184, "after me . . . the rout is coming."

84–8. *If it be . . . fear death*] "If it is anything that concerns the public welfare, I will contemplate both death and honour quite impartially; for heaven knows I value an honourable reputation even more than I fear death." Honour requires him to promote the welfare of his fellows, and he will not be deterred from doing so even

Set honour in one eye, and death i' th' other,   85
And I will look on both indifferently;
For let the gods so speed me as I love
The name of honour more than I fear death.
Cas. I know that virtue to be in you, Brutus,
As well as I do know your outward favour.   90
Well, honour is the subject of my story.
I cannot tell what you and other men
Think of this life; but for my single self,
I had as lief not be as live to be
In awe of such a thing as I myself.   95
I was born free as Cæsar; so were you;
We both have fed as well, and we can both
Endure the winter's cold as well as he:
For once, upon a raw and gusty day,
The troubled Tiber chafing with her shores,   100
Cæsar said to me, "Dar'st thou, Cassius, now
Leap in with me into this angry flood,
And swim to yonder point?" Upon the word,

86. both] *F;* death *Warburton, Theobald, Hanmer.*

by the fear of losing his life in the cause. In l. 86 Theobald and Warburton unnecessarily emended *both* to *death.* For *indifferently* in the sense of "impartially" cf. *Cor.,* II. ii. 19, "If he did not care whether he had their love or no, he waved indifferently 'twixt doing them neither good nor harm."

87. *speed*] prosper, favour. Cf. *Wiv.,* III. iv. 12, "Heaven so speed me", and the expression, "God speed the plough."

90. *outward favour*] outward appearance.

94. *had as lief not be*] would as soon not live.

95. *such a thing as I myself*] i.e., Cæsar, a man, like himself.

99–114. *For once . . . tired Cæsar*] Shakespeare seems to have invented this anecdote to suit Cassius's purpose of belittling Cæsar. Actually Cæsar was a strong swimmer. Both Plutarch and Suetonius (*Jul. Cæs.,* 64) relate how in the harbour of Alexandria he

escaped from the Egyptians by swimming some distance, almost a quarter of a mile, according to Suetonius, at the same time holding up "divers books" to keep them dry. Plutarch adds that his enemies "made towards him with their oars on every side", and "shot marvellously at him", and Suetonius that he drew "his rich coate armour after him by the teeth, because the enemie should not have it as a spoyle." Sir Thomas Elyot, in *The Gouernour,* I. xvii, follows Suetonius's account of this episode fairly closely in his discussion of swimming as one of the "Exercises wherby shulde growe both recreation and profite".

100. *chafing with her shores*] i.e., raging at them for their restraint. Cf. *Wint.,* III. iii. 89, "I would you did but see how it chafes, how it rages." The other sense of *chafe,* "rub against", is also implied: cf. *Lr..* IV. vi. 21, "The murmuring surge / That on the unnumber'd idle pebbles chafes".

Accoutred as I was, I plunged in
And bade him follow; so indeed he did.   105
The torrent roar'd, and we did buffet it
With lusty sinews, throwing it aside
And stemming it with hearts of controversy.
But ere we could arrive the point propos'd,
Cæsar cried, "Help me, Cassius, or I sink."   110
I, as Æneas, our great ancestor,
Did from the flames of Troy upon his shoulder
The old Anchises bear, so from the waves of Tiber
Did I the tired Cæsar. And this man
Is now become a god, and Cassius is   115
A wretched creature, and must bend his body
If Cæsar carelessly but nod on him.
He had a fever when he was in Spain,
And when the fit was on him, I did mark
How he did shake; 'tis true, this god did shake;   120
His coward lips did from their colour fly,
And that same eye whose bend doth awe the world
Did lose his lustre; I did hear him groan;
Ay, and that tongue of his, that bade the Romans

122. bend] *F;* beam *Daniel.*

108. *hearts of controversy*] Implies both the struggle with the torrent and the rivalry of the two men.

109. *arrive*] land at. Cf. *3 H 6*, v. iii. 8, "those powers . . . have arrived our coast"; *Par. L.*, ii. 409, "ere he arrive / The happy Ile". See note on I. i. 42.

111. *Æneas . . . ancestor*] This story is told by Virgil, *Æn.*, II. 721 ff. Shakespeare uses the comparison also in *2 H 6*, v. ii. 63. Æneas, as progenitor of the Roman nation, is "*our* great ancestor".

116. *bend his body*] bow.

118. *a fever*] Cassius is determined to show Cæsar as a man of *feeble temper* (l. 128). Shakespeare took a hint for this incident from Plutarch: "He was lean, white, and soft-skinned, and often subject to headache, and otherwhile to the falling sickness: (the which took him the first time, as it is reported, in Corduba, a city of Spain)." But Plutarch goes on to say with what endurance and courage he always fought his weakness.

121. *His coward lips . . . fly*] Shakespeare intensifies the notion of cowardice by the inversion, which calls up a comparison with a soldier deserting his colours.

122. *bend*] inclination, i.e., look, glance. Shakespeare elsewhere associates the verb *bend* with the eyes in the sense of "incline, direct": e.g., *1 H 4*, II. iii. 45, "Why dost thou bend thine eyes upon the earth . . . ?"; and *Ham.*, II. i. 100, "And to the last bended their light on me."

123. *his*] The neuter possessive pronoun, according to the normal usage of Shakespeare. The form *its* is not pre-Elizabethan, and is comparatively rare in Shakespeare.

Mark him and write his speeches in their books,   125
Alas, it cried, "Give me some drink, Titinius,"
As a sick girl. Ye gods, it doth amaze me
A man of such a feeble temper should
So get the start of the majestic world,
And bear the palm alone.   [*Shout. Flourish.*
Bru.   Another general shout?   130
I do believe that these applauses are
For some new honours that are heap'd on Cæsar.
Cas. Why, man, he doth bestride the narrow world
Like a Colossus, and we petty men
Walk under his huge legs, and peep about   135
To find ourselves dishonourable graves.
Men at some time are masters of their fates:
The fault, dear Brutus, is not in our stars,

125. *books*] writing tablets. Plutarch compares Cæsar favourably with Cicero as an orator.

126. *Alas*] The Folio uses no quotation marks when a speaker quotes the words of another. Many editors enclose *Alas* in quotation marks as part of Cæsar's cry of distress. It seems more effective without them as another example of Cassius's irony.

Titinius] Plutarch mentions Titinius as "one of Cassius' chiefest friends", as he is shown to be at the end of the play.

127. *amaze*] stupefy. The Shakespearian sense is stronger than the modern. Cf. *John*, IV. iii. 140.

128. *temper*] constitution, temperament—the normal Elizabethan sense of the word.

129. *get the start of*] outstrip, and carry off the palm of victory (in the contest for power and honour). Cf. *Wiv.*, V. v. 170, "You have the start of me."

130. S.D. Shout. Flourish] Note the timing of this stage direction.

134. *Colossus*] The most celebrated of the colossal statues of antiquity was the bronze statue of Apollo as the sun-god, which, under the name of "The Colossus of Rhodes", was one of the

seven wonders of the world. It was more than 100 feet high, and the Elder Pliny (*H.N.*, xxxiv. 18), presumably repeating the account of one who had seen it after its fall, gives an interesting description. The Rhodian sculptor Chares executed it between 292 and 280 B.C., and it was overthrown by an earthquake in 224. Though there is no authority for the belief, long-standing tradition says that its legs spanned the harbour of Rhodes. Shakespeare no doubt had this colossus in mind in Cassius's picture of petty men like himself walking under Cæsar's legs, which dwarfed the world they bestrode.

136. *dishonourable graves*] "Cæsar's supremacy has closed every career of honourable ambition. There is nothing for us to seek except our own graves; and even those will be dishonourable, for they will not be the graves of freemen" (Kittredge).

137. *Men at some time . . . fates*] Cf. IV. iii. 217-20, "There is a tide in the affairs of men ..."

138. *our stars*] A reference to the belief, on which the science of astrology was built, that a man's constitution and conduct are determined by the relative positions of the planets at his birth. Cf. *Lr.*, IV. iii. 34, "It is the

But in ourselves, that we are underlings.
Brutus and Cæsar: what should be in that "Cæsar"?   140
Why should that name be sounded more than yours?
Write them together, yours is as fair a name;
Sound them, it doth become the mouth as well;
Weigh them, it is as heavy; conjure with 'em,
"Brutus" will start a spirit as soon as "Cæsar".   145
Now in the names of all the gods at once,
Upon what meat doth this our Cæsar feed,
That he is grown so great? Age, thou art sham'd!
Rome, thou hast lost the breed of noble bloods!
When went there by an age, since the great flood,   150
But it was fam'd with more than with one man?
When could they say, till now, that talk'd of Rome,
That her wide walks encompass'd but one man?
Now is it Rome indeed, and room enough,

153. walks] *F* (Walkes), *Rowe 1, 2 (1709)*, *Malone, Steevens, Singer, Hudson, Macmillan;* walls *Rowe (1714), et al.*

stars, / The stars above us, govern our conditions." With Cassius's repudiation of this doctrine cf. that of Edmund, *Lr.*, i. ii. 128, "This is the excellent foppery of the world, that, when we are sick in fortune (often the surfeit of our own behaviour) we make guilty of our disasters the sun, the moon, and the stars."

138–9. *The fault . . . underlings*] Cf. *A Mirror for Magistrates* (ed. L. B. Campbell, p. 130), the narrative of *Owen Glendower*, l. 238, "For they be faultes that foyle men, not their fates"; *ibid.*, p. 172, *Jack Cade*, ll. 34–5, "For sure this hap if it be rightly knowen, / Cummeth of our selves, and so the blame our owne." I am indebted to Dr Harold Brooks for these parallels.

141. *be sounded more*] be more re-sounding in fame. Cf. *Shr.*, ii. i. 193, "thy beauty sounded".

144. *conjure with 'em*] use them as names with which to conjure up spirits.

149. *bloods*] men of spirit.

150. *great flood*] When Zeus resolved to destroy degenerate mankind by a deluge, Deucalion, son of Prometheus

and King of Phthia, and his wife, Pyrrha, were on account of their piety the only mortals saved. Shakespeare uses this legend also in *Cor.*, ii. i. 102, "Yet you must be saying Marcius is proud; who, in a cheap estimation, is worth all your predecessors since Deucalion."

151. *fam'd with*] made famous by celebrated for.

153. *walks*] The Folio *Walkes* was emended to *walls* by Rowe in his 1714 edition, and most editors have accepted the change. The word *encompass'd* perhaps suggests walls rather than walks; but *wide* seems much more appropriate if *walks* is retained.

154. *Rome . . . room*] Cf. *John*, iii. i. 180, "O, lawful let it be / That I have room with Rome to curse awhile." In *Lucr.*, 715 and 1851, *Rome* is rhymed with *doom*, and at l. 1644 with *groom*. Probably Antony is making the same play on words at iii. i. 289, "Here is a mourning Rome, a dangerous Rome, / No Rome of safety for Octavius yet." Of the present passage Kittredge remarks: "Here (as often) the pun ex-

When there is in it but one only man.   155
O, you and I have heard our fathers say,
There was a Brutus once that would have brook'd
Th' eternal devil to keep his state in Rome
As easily as a king.
Bru. That you do love me, I am nothing jealous; 160
What you would work me to, I have some aim:
How I have thought of this, and of these times,
I shall recount hereafter. For this present,
I would not (so with love I might entreat you)
Be any further mov'd. What you have said 165
I will consider; what you have to say
I will with patience hear, and find a time
Both meet to hear and answer such high things.
Till then, my noble friend, chew upon this:
Brutus had rather be a villager 170
Than to repute himself a son of Rome
Under these hard conditions as this time
Is like to lay upon us.
Cas.   I am glad
That my weak words have struck but thus much show
Of fire from Brutus.   175

Enter CÆSAR *and his Train.*

Bru. The games are done and Cæsar is returning.
Cas. As they pass by, pluck Casca by the sleeve,

155. When . . . man.] *F; in margin* Pope, Hanmer. 158. eternal] *F;* infernal
conj. Johnson. 164. not (so with] *Theobald;* not so (with *F.* 173–5. I . . .
Brutus] *As* Walker; I . . . glad that . . . words / . . . shew of . . . Brutus. / *F.*

presses contempt: 'Rome! ay, it is
rightly named *Room*, for there's only
one MAN in it!'"

 157. *a Brutus once*] Lucius Junius
Brutus played a leading part in the
expulsion of the Tarquins from Rome,
and he and Tarquinius Collatinus became the first consuls. Plutarch tells us
that Marcus Brutus claimed descent
from this Brutus.
 brook'd] tolerated.
 158. *Th' eternal devil*] Johnson felt
that this should read *the infernal devil.*

More probably Shakespeare here uses
eternal as a term of strong reprobation,
as in *Oth.*, IV. ii. 130, "eternal villain".
 to keep his state] to maintain his court.
 160. *nothing jealous*] not at all doubtful.
 161. *aim*] conjecture.
 164. *so with love . . . entreat*] if I may
as a friend entreat.
 165. *mov'd*] urged.
 169. *chew*] ponder.
 170. *villager*] i.e., a villager rather
than a proud Roman citizen.

And he will (after his sour fashion) tell you
What hath proceeded worthy note to-day.
Bru. I will do so. But look you, Cassius,   180
The angry spot doth glow on Cæsar's brow,
And all the rest look like a chidden train:
Calphurnia's cheek is pale, and Cicero
Looks with such ferret and such fiery eyes
As we have seen him in the Capitol,   185
Being cross'd in conference by some senators.
Cas. Casca will tell us what the matter is.
Cæs. Antonius.
Ant.   Cæsar?
Cæs. Let me have men about me that are fat,
Sleek-headed men, and such as sleep a-nights.   190
Yond Cassius has a lean and hungry look;
He thinks too much: such men are dangerous.
Ant. Fear him not, Cæsar, he's not dangerous.
He is a noble Roman, and well given.
Cæs. Would he were fatter! But I fear him not: 195
Yet if my name were liable to fear,
I do not know the man I should avoid
So soon as that spare Cassius. He reads much,
He is a great observer, and he looks
Quite through the deeds of men. He loves no
    plays,   200

188. Antonius] Pope; *Antonio F.*

179. *worthy note*] Shakespeare often
uses *worthy of*, as at II. i. 303, "Render
me worthy of this noble wife." But the
omission of the preposition is also
common: cf. II. i. 317, "Any exploit
worthy the name of honour"; *All's W.*,
III. v. 104, "I will bestow some pre-
cepts of this virgin / Worthy the note";
Wiv., v. v. 64, "'Tis fit, / Worthy the
owner".

184. *ferret . . . fiery eyes*] A ferret's
eyes are red. Cicero's eyes are blood-
shot in his fiery resentment. Cf. Henry
More, *Psychozoia* (1642), II. 85, "Strait
Graculo with eyes as fierce as Ferrit
Reply'd".

186. *conference*] debate.

189–92. *Let me . . . are dangerous*]
Shakespeare derived these sentiments
of Cæsar from Plutarch: see Appendix,
p. 140. Cf. Jonson, *Bartholomew Fair*,
II. iii. 22, "Come, there's no malice in
these fat folkes, I neuer feare thee, and
I can scape thy leane Moonecalfe
heere."

194. *well given*] well disposed. Plutarch tells us that Cassius was "Brutus'
familiar friend, but not so well given,
and conditioned as he."

196. *my name*] A periphrasis for *I*; it
emphasizes Cæsar's arrogance.

199–200. *looks . . . deeds of men*]
i.e., sees right through to their
motives.

As thou dost, Antony; he hears no music.
Seldom he smiles, and smiles in such a sort
As if he mock'd himself, and scorn'd his spirit
That could be mov'd to smile at any thing.
Such men as he be never at heart's ease   205
Whiles they behold a greater than themselves,
And therefore are they very dangerous.
I rather tell thee what is to be fear'd
Than what I fear; for always I am Cæsar.
Come on my right hand, for this ear is deaf,   210
And tell me truly what thou think'st of him.
                    [*Sennet. Exeunt Cæsar and his Train.*
Casca. You pull'd me by the cloak. Would you speak with me?
Bru. Ay, Casca. Tell us what hath chanc'd to-day,
          That Cæsar looks so sad.
Casca. Why, you were with him, were you not?   215
Bru. I should not then ask Casca what had chanc'd.
Casca. Why, there was a crown offer'd him; and, being
          offer'd him, he put it by with the back of his hand,
          thus; and then the people fell a-shouting.
Bru. What was the second noise for?   220
Casca. Why, for that too.
Cas. They shouted thrice: what was the last cry for?
Casca. Why, for that too.
Bru. Was the crown offer'd him thrice?
Casca. Ay, marry, was't, and he put it by thrice, every   225

201. *he hears no music*] Contrast Brutus in IV. iii. For the implication cf. *Mer.V.*, v. v. 183, "The man that hath no music in himself, / Nor is not moved with concord of sweet sounds, / Is fit for treasons, stratagems, and spoils." As for Antony, to whom Cæsar speaks these words, we read of his pleasure-loving disposition in Plutarch.

202. *sort*] manner.

209. *always I am Cæsar*] Plutarch tells how Cornelius Balbus prevented Cæsar from rising before the senate: "What, do you not remember that you are Cæsar, and will you not let them reverence you, and do their duties?"

210. *this ear is deaf*] Plutarch says nothing of this deafness. It is "significantly introduced to us immediately after Cæsar has referred to himself as almost divine" (Dover Wilson). The words are, of course, spoken for the information of the audience, for Antony would know of any such infirmity.

212. *pull'd me by the cloak*] Cf. l. 177, "Pluck Casca by the sleeve". Actually the Roman toga had no sleeves.

214. *sad*] serious, perhaps even sullen. Cf. *R 2*, v. v. 70, "that sad dog / That brings me food".

217. *a crown*] In Plutarch it was a "laurel crown . . . having a royal band or diadem wreathed about it".

time gentler than other; and at every putting-by
mine honest neighbours shouted.

Cas. Who offered him the crown?

Casca. Why, Antony.

Bru. Tell us the manner of it, gentle Casca.   230

Casca. I can as well be hang'd as tell the manner of it:
it was mere foolery; I did not mark it. I saw Mark
Antony offer him a crown; yet 'twas not a crown
neither, 'twas one of these coronets; and, as I told
you, he put it by once; but for all that, to my think-   235
ing, he would fain have had it. Then he offered it to
him again; then he put it by again; but to my thinking, he was very loath to lay his fingers off it. And
then he offered it the third time. He put it the third
time by; and still as he refus'd it, the rabblement   240
hooted, and clapp'd their chopt hands, and threw
up their sweaty night-caps, and uttered such a deal
of stinking breath because Cæsar refus'd the crown,
that it had, almost, choked Cæsar; for he swounded, and fell down at it. And for mine own part,   245
I durst not laugh, for fear of opening my lips and
receiving the bad air.

Cas. But soft, I pray you; what, did Cæsar swound?

Casca. He fell down in the market-place, and foam'd at
mouth, and was speechless.   250

241. hooted] *Johnson;* howted *F;* shouted *Hanmer, Collier, Staunton, Macmillan.*
244–5. swounded] *Cambridge;* swoonded *F;* swooned *Rowe et al.*   248. swound]
F; swoon *Rowe et al.*

226. *gentler than other*] more gently
than the previous time. Abbott, in his
Shakespearian Grammar, ¶1, gives many
examples of adjectives used adverbi-
ally. Cf. III. ii. 116, "some will dear
abide it."

230. *gentle Casca*] Contrast l. 292,
"What a blunt fellow is this grown to
be!" And indeed Casca's bluntness is
his most striking quality in this dia-
logue, though one may contrast with it
his apparent obsequiousness in Cæsar's
presence at the beginning of the scene.

241. *hooted*] Hanmer emended the
Folio *howted* to *shouted*, influenced by

l. 227,"mine honest neighbours shouted." But Johnson's reading, or rather
modernized spelling, *hooted*, must be
right: cf. I. iii. 28, where the Folio
howting refers to the owl's cry. *Hooted* is
much the more colourful word—cf.
LLL., IV. ii. 61, "the people fall a-
hooting." It emphasizes Casca's contempt for the *rabblement*.

chopt] chapped, roughened with
toil.

244–5. *swounded*] swooned. The
Folio has *swoonded* here, and *swound* at
l. 248. Other Shakespearian variants
are *swoun, swown, sound*.

Bru. 'Tis very like; he hath the falling-sickness.
Cas. No, Cæsar hath it not; but you, and I,
     And honest Casca, we have the falling-sickness.
Casca. I know not what you mean by that, but I am sure
     Cæsar fell down. If the tag-rag people did not clap   255
     him and hiss him, according as he pleas'd and dis-
     pleas'd them, as they use to do the players in the
     theatre, I am no true man.
Bru. What said he when he came unto himself?
Casca. Marry, before he fell down, when he perceiv'd   260
     the common herd was glad he refus'd the crown, he
     pluck'd me ope his doublet, and offer'd them his
     throat to cut. And I had been a man of any occupa-
     tion, if I would not have taken him at a word, I
     would I might go to hell among the rogues. And so   265
     he fell. When he came to himself again, he said, if he
     had done or said anything amiss, he desir'd their

251. like; he] *Theobald;* like he *F, Collier, Macmillan;* like, he *Rowe.*

251. '*Tis very like . . . falling-sickness*]
On Cæsar's falling-sickness, or epi-
lepsy, see note on l. 118. In the Folio
there is no stop between *like* and *he.*
Theobald and most later editors provide a colon or semi-colon, and surely
this gives better sense. Brutus must
have known that Cæsar was an epileptic, since he was his friend, and in any
case it was common knowledge; he
would not state it merely as a probability. In the next line Cassius wilfully
misunderstands him, and declares that
he and his friends have the falling-
sickness in that they have fallen to being underlings. *Like* here means "likely", as often in Shakespeare: cf. *Cym.,*
v. v. 260, "Most like I did."
     255. *the tag-rag people*] In *Cor.,* III. i.
248, the rabble are called *the tag.* Cf.
Whetstone, *2 Promos and Cassandra,* IV.
i, "As lewde personnes, tagge, and
ragge". The origin of the phrase, and
of the word *tag,* is unknown. It occurs
in this sense as early as 1553, in Bale's
Vocation (Harl. Misc. VI. 423), "all the
Rable of the Shippe, hag, tag, and rag".

262. *pluck'd me . . . doublet*] In North's
account of this episode the word used is
gown (Amyot, *robe,* Plutarch, ἱμάτιον).
But in describing another occasion,
when Cæsar had offended the Senate
and people by disdaining to rise before
a senatorial deputation, and returning
home with his friends had offered his
bare throat for "any man that would
come and cut it", North speaks of his
"doublet collar"; and this doubtless
suggested the *doublet* of the present
passage, though it is an anachronism,
like Casca's *sleeve* in l. 177. For the use
of the ethic dative *me* cf. III. iii. 18.
     263. *And*] if. Frequent in Shake-
speare, with its variants, *an* and *an if,*
as the conditional conjunction. Cf.
l. 278 below.
     263-4. *a man of any occupation*] This
might mean either "a man of action",
or "a tradesman", like those to whom
Cæsar offered his throat to cut: cf.
Cor., IV. vi. 97, where "the voice of
occupation" means "the vote of working men". Perhaps both senses may be
implied.

worships to think it was his infirmity. Three or four
wenches, where I stood, cried, "Alas, good soul,"
and forgave him with all their hearts; but there's no   270
heed to be taken of them; if Cæsar had stabb'd their
mothers, they would have done no less.

Bru. And after that, he came thus sad away?

Casca. Ay.

Cas. Did Cicero say anything?   275

Casca. Ay, he spoke Greek.

Cas. To what effect?

Casca. Nay, and I tell you that, I'll ne'er look you i' th'
face again. But those that understood him smil'd at
one another, and shook their heads; but for mine   280
own part, it was Greek to me. I could tell you more
news too: Marullus and Flavius, for pulling scarfs
off Cæsar's images, are put to silence. Fare you well.
There was more foolery yet, if I could remember it.

Cas. Will you sup with me to-night, Casca?   285

Casca. No, I am promis'd forth.

Cas. Will you dine with me to-morrow?

Casca. Ay, if I be alive, and your mind hold, and your
dinner worth the eating.

Cas. Good. I will expect you.   290

Casca. Do so. Farewell, both.   [*Exit.*

Bru. What a blunt fellow is this grown to be!
He was quick mettle when he went to school.

Cas. So is he now in execution
Of any bold or noble enterprise,   295

282. Marullus] *Theobald; Murrellus F.*

268. *infirmity*] i.e., the falling-sickness.

276. *he spoke Greek*] Plutarch says in his *Cicero* that the people "commonly called him the Graecian".

278. *and*] if. Cf. l. 263 above.

281. *it was Greek to me*] I couldn't make head or tail of it. Cf. Gascoigne, *Supposes*, I. i, "This geare is Greeke to mee"; Greene, *James IV* (Mal. Soc.), l. 1575, "'Tis Greeke to mee, my Lord." The historical Casca was not

unfamiliar with Greek; Plutarch says that when he struck Cæsar in the neck, and Cæsar caught hold of his sword, Casca cried out "in Greek to his brother, Brother, help me". But the expression is in character with Shakespeare's Casca.

282. *scarfs*] See note on I. i. 65.

293. *quick mettle*] of lively disposition. See note on I. i. 61, and cf. l. 306 below. *Blunt* in the previous line fits in well with the mettle (=metal) image.

However he puts on this tardy form.
This rudeness is a sauce to his good wit,
Which gives men stomach to disgest his words
With better appetite.
Bru. And so it is. For this time I will leave you.   300
To-morrow, if you please to speak with me,
I will come home to you; or if you will,
Come home to me, and I will wait for you.
Cas. I will do so: till then, think of the world.   [*Exit Brutus.*
Well, Brutus, thou art noble; yet I see   305
Thy honourable mettle may be wrought
From that it is dispos'd: therefore 'tis meet
That noble minds keep ever with their likes;
For who so firm that cannot be seduc'd?
Cæsar doth bear me hard; but he loves Brutus.   310
If I were Brutus now, and he were Cassius,
He should not humour me. I will this night,
In several hands, in at his windows throw,
As if they came from several citizens,
Writings, all tending to the great opinion   315

307. 'tis] *F2* (tis); it is *F1*.

296. *However*] notwithstanding that.
tardy form] affectation of slowness.
297. *rudeness*] rough manner.
good wit] intelligence. Note the sequence: *sauce, stomach, disgest, appetite*.
298. *disgest*] A common variant of *digest*, which is used at IV. iii. 47. Cf. *disgest* (F. spelling) in *Ant.,* II. ii. 179; Porter, *The Two Angry Women of Abington* (Mal. Soc.), l. 1107, "Iests bitter to disgest".
304. *the world*] Probably, the present state of affairs. Cf. V. v. 22, "Thou seest the world, Volumnius, how it goes."
306. *honourable mettle*] honourable disposition, spirit. Again *mettle* (metal) is associated with an appropriate word, *wrought*. Cf. notes on l. 243 above, and on I. i. 61.
307. *From ... dispos'd*] away from its natural inclination.

310. *bear me hard*] has a grudge against me, bears me ill will. Cf. II. i. 215; III. i. 157, and Latin *aegre ferre.* Plutarch says that "Cæsar also had Cassius in great jealousy, and suspected him much."
311–12. *If I ... humour me*] now if I were Brutus, and he were I, he would not be able to work on me (as I am working on him). This soliloquy first brings out clearly the contrast between the honourable, disinterested, unsuspicious nature of Brutus, and the lack of scruple of the scheming Cassius.
312. *humour*] "to influence (a person) by observing his humours or inclinations" (Onions). Cf. *Ado,* II. i. 399, "I will teach you how to humour your cousin, that she shall fall in love with Benedick."
313. *hands*] handwriting. Cf *Ham.,* IV. vii. 51, "Know you the hand? ... 'Tis Hamlet's character."

That Rome holds of his name; wherein obscurely
Cæsar's ambition shall be glanced at.
And after this, let Cæsar seat him sure,
For we will shake him, or worse days endure.   [*Exit.*

[SCENE III.—*The Same. A Street.*]

Thunder and lightning. Enter CASCA *and* CICERO [*,meeting*].

Cic. Good even, Casca: brought you Cæsar home?
          Why are you breathless? and why stare you so?
Casca. Are you not mov'd, when all the sway of earth
          Shakes like a thing unfirm? O Cicero,
          I have seen tempests, when the scolding winds   5
          Have riv'd the knotty oaks; and I have seen
          Th' ambitious ocean swell and rage and foam,
          To be exalted with the threat'ning clouds:
          But never till to-night, never till now,
          Did I go through a tempest dropping fire.   10
          Either there is a civil strife in heaven,
          Or else the world, too saucy with the gods,
          Incenses them to send destruction.

Scene III

10. tempest dropping fire] *Rowe;* Tempest-dropping-fire *F.*

318–19. *And after . . . days endure*] Mr
John Crow has drawn my attention to
a reminiscence of these lines in Massinger (?) in *The Tragedy of Sir John
Van Olden Barnavelt* (ed. Frijlinck),
ll. 748–9, "and let this *Prince of Orange*
seat him sure, / or he shall fall, when
he is most secure."

318. *seat him*] seat himself. See
Abbott, *Shakespearian Grammar,* ¶223,
for other examples of this usage.

319. *worse days endure*] have to put up
with worse times as Cæsar grows more
and more despotic; or possibly, as
Macmillan suggests, "because, as was
generally recognized, the failure of a
plot against a tyrant made his rule
more tyrannical."

Scene III

3. *all the sway of earth*] Various inter-
pretations have been offered: e.g.,
"the whole weight or momentum of
this globe" (Johnson); "the balanced
swing of earth" (Craik); "equable
motion, or settled order" (Onions);
"government, dominion" (Dover Wilson, N.C.S. Glossary). I incline to
something like the last interpretation,
which involves no straining of a normal Shakespearian usage: "the whole
realm of earth shakes like something
unsteady."

6. *riv'd*] split. Cf. *Troil.,* I. iii. 316,
"Blunt wedges rive hard knots."

12. *saucy*] insolent—a stronger sense
than that of today.

Cic. Why, saw you any thing more wonderful?
Casca. A common slave, you know him well by sight,   15
    Held up his left hand, which did flame and burn
    Like twenty torches join'd; and yet his hand,
    Not sensible of fire, remain'd unscorch'd.
    Besides (I ha' not since put up my sword)
    Against the Capitol I met a lion,   20
    Who glaz'd upon me, and went surly by,
    Without annoying me. And there were drawn
    Upon a heap a hundred ghastly women,
    Transformed with their fear, who swore they saw
    Men, all in fire, walk up and down the streets.   25
    And yesterday the bird of night did sit,
    Even at noon-day, upon the market-place,
    Hooting and shrieking. When these prodigies
    Do so conjointly meet, let not men say,
    "These are their reasons, they are natural";   30
    For I believe, they are portentous things
    Unto the climate that they point upon.

21. glaz'd] *F*; gaz'd *conj. Johnson;* glar'd *Rowe.*   28. Hooting] *Johnson;*
Howting *F*.

14. *any thing more wonderful*] Craik
suggests, "anything more that was
awe-inspiring"; but more probably,
"anything that was more awe-
inspiring", since Cicero does not seem
greatly discomposed by the storm that
Casca describes.
    15–28. *A common slave . . . and shriek-
ing*] For the portents that preceded
Cæsar's death see Appendix, p. 142.
Plutarch does not mention the lion or
the "hundred ghastly women". Dover
Wilson compares with the prodigies
described here, and in II. ii. 17 ff,
Nashe's account of the omens that
preceded the fall of Jerusalem (Nashe,
ed. McKerrow, II. 60–2), and Marlowe, *Lucan*, I. 554–82.
    18. *Not sensible of fire*] not sensitive
to the fire.
    21. *glaz'd*] Rowe and many later
editors emend to *glar'd*, and Malone,
following a suggestion of Johnson, to
gaz'd. But no change is necessary. Both

O.E.D. and the *Eng. Dialect Dict.*
support *glaz'd* in the sense of "gazed
fixedly, stared"; and various editors
quote passages that give it much the
same meaning as "glared": e.g.,
Clyomon and Clamydes (Mal. Soc.), l.
1983, "But not long did that glasing
starre, giue light vnto mine eyes."
    22. *annoying*] injuring. Cf. II. i. 160.
    22–3. *drawn Upon a heap*] "huddled
into a crowd" (Dover Wilson). Cf.
H 5, IV. v. 18, "Let us on heaps go
offer up our lives."
    26. *bird of night*] the screech-owl,
like the raven a bird of ill omen. Cf.
Tit., II. iii. 96, "Here nothing breeds, /
Unless the nightly owl or fatal raven."
    28. *Hooting*] See note on I. ii. 241.
    29. *conjointly meet*] coincide.
    30. *These are . . . natural*] Such and
such are their reasons; they are merely
natural phenomena.
    31. *portentous*] ominous.
    32. *climate*] region, the commonest

Cic. Indeed, it is a strange-disposed time:
    But men may construe things, after their fashion,
    Clean from the purpose of the things themselves.   35
    Comes Cæsar to the Capitol to-morrow?
Casca. He doth; for he did bid Antonius
    Send word to you he would be there to-morrow.
Cic. Good night then, Casca: this disturbed sky
    Is not to walk in.
Casca.   Farewell, Cicero.   [*Exit Cicero.* 40

Enter CASSIUS.

Cas. Who's there?
Casca.   A Roman.
Cas.   Casca, by yóur voice.
Casca. Your ear is good. Cassius, what night is this!
Cas. A very pleasing night to honest men.
Casca. Who ever knew the heavens menace so?
Cas. Those that have known the earth so full of faults.   45
    For my part, I have walk'd about the streets,
    Submitting me unto the perilous night,
    And, thus unbraced, Casca, as you see,
    Have bar'd my bosom to the thunder-stone;
    And when the cross blue lightning seem'd to open   50
    The breast of heaven, I did present myself
    Even in the aim and very flash of it.
Casca. But wherefore did you so much tempt the heavens?
    It is the part of men to fear and tremble

---

37. Antonius] *Pope; Antonio F.*   39–40. Good night . . . in.] *As Rowe;*
Good-night . . . *Caska:* / . . . in. / *F.*   42.] *As Rowe;* Your . . . good. / . . .
this? / *F.*

sense of the word in Shakespeare's day.
Cf. *R 2,* IV. i. 30, "a Christian climate".
    34. *after their fashion*] in their own
way.
    35. *Clean from . . . themselves*] in a way
completely different from their real
meaning. For *from* meaning "diverg-
ing from, alien to" cf. l. 64 below.
    48. *thus unbraced*] with his doublet
unbuttoned. See note on *doublet* at
I. ii. 262, and cf. II. i. 262.

    49. *thunder-stone*] thunderbolt. Cf.
Cym., IV. ii. 271, "the all-dreaded
thunder-stone".
    50. *cross*] forked, zig-zag. Cf. *Lr.,*
IV. vii. 35, "the most terrible and
nimble stroke / Of quick cross lightning".
    52. *Even in the aim*] at the very point
at which it was aimed.
    53. *tempt*] try, i.e., take liberties
with.

When the most mighty gods by tokens send   55
Such dreadful heralds to astonish us.
Cas. You are dull, Casca, and those sparks of life
That should be in a Roman you do want,
Or else you use not. You look pale, and gaze,
And put on fear, and cast yourself in wonder,   60
To see the strange impatience of the heavens;
But if you would consider the true cause
Why all these fires, why all these gliding ghosts,
Why birds and beasts from quality and kind,
Why old men, fools, and children calculate,   65
Why all these things change from their ordinance,
Their natures, and pre-formed faculties,
To monstrous quality, why, you shall find
That heaven hath infus'd them with these spirits
To make them instruments of fear and warning   70
Unto some monstrous state.

57–60.] *As Rowe;* You . . . Caska: / . . . Roman, / . . . not. / . . . feare, /
. . . wonder, / *F.*   71–3.] *As F;* Unto . . . state. Now . . . Casca. / . . . man,
most . . . night, / *Hanmer, Capell, Malone, et al.*

56. *astonish*] stun, dismay—a much stronger sense than that of today.

57. *dull*] obtuse, stupid, as often in Shakespeare. Cassius uses the word to rouse Casca; we have seen that he does not really think Casca stupid.

58. *want*] lack.

60. *in wonder*] into a state of wonder.

64. *Why birds . . . and kind*] Dover Wilson suggests, "Poss. a line is lost after this"; and Johnson felt that the line should be placed after that which follows it, so that *change* (l. 66) would stand with *from quality and kind* as well as with *from their ordinance.* But Cassius is excited, and is speaking in an elliptical and disjointed manner, as the broken lines, 71 and 73, also indicate. The meaning of the lines is clear enough: "But if you consider the true reason why all these fires and these ghosts appear, why birds and beasts change their natures, why old men, fools and children can prophesy . . ."

quality and kind] Both words mean

"nature". Perhaps we can paraphrase: "their character and nature". For *from* meaning "alien to" cf. l. 35 above; and *Oth.*, I. i. 132, "from the sense of all civility".

65. *Why old men . . . calculate*] In his *Dictionary of the Proverbs in England in the 16th and 17th Centuries*, M. P. Tilley gives several parallels: e.g., *Misogonus* (in *Early Plays from the Italian*, ed. R. W. Bond), I. i. 185, "Children and fooles they say cannot ly"; Delamothe, *The Treasure of the French Toung* (1596), "Fooles and children often do prophesie." *Fools* means of course "natural fools, born idiots". *Calculate* means "prophesy" (originally by astrological or mathematical methods).

66. *ordinance*] normal practice, as ordained by providence.

67. *pre-formed faculties*] faculties or qualities with which they were originally endowed.

71. *monstrous state*] unnatural, abnormal state of affairs.

Now could I, Casca, name to thee a man
Most like this dreadful night,
That thunders, lightens, opens graves, and roars
As doth the lion in the Capitol;   75
A man no mightier than thyself, or me,
In personal action, yet prodigious grown,
And fearful, as these strange eruptions are.

Casca. 'Tis Cæsar that you mean, is it not, Cassius?

Cas. Let it be who it is: for Romans now   80
Have thews and limbs like to their ancestors;
But, woe the while! our fathers' minds are dead,
And we are govern'd with our mothers' spirits;
Our yoke and sufferance show us womanish.

Casca. Indeed, they say the senators to-morrow   85
Mean to establish Cæsar as a king;
And he shall wear his crown by sea and land,
In every place, save here in Italy.

Cas. I know where I will wear this dagger then;
Cassius from bondage will deliver Cassius: 90

79.] *As Rowe;* 'Tis . . . meane: / . . . *Cassius?* / F.

75. *the lion in the Capitol*] See l. 20.
Aldis Wright suggests that Shakespeare may have had in mind the lions
kept in the Tower which were one of
the sights of London, and to which
there are many contemporary references. Indeed, "to see the lions" became a proverbial expression for seeing the sights of London. Cf. Greene,
Never Too Late (ed. Grosart, vol. VIII,
p. 68), "To use the old prouerb, he had
scarce seene the lions"; Jonson, *Cynthia's Revels,* v. iv. 112, "Nor to be
frighted with a face, Signior! I haue
seene the lions."

77. *prodigious*] ominous, supernatur-
ally threatening.

78. *fearful*] Common in Shakespeare
in both the subjective sense of "timor-
ous", and the objective sense of "terrible", as here.

eruptions] outbreaks of nature. Cf.
Ham., I. i. 69, "This bodes some
strange eruption to our state."

79. *'Tis Cæsar . . . Cassius?*] "The

studied simplicity of Casca's question
is to be noted. It accords with his pose
of slowness of wit—the 'tardy form'
that he 'puts on'" (Kittredge).

81. *thews*] sinews.

82. *woe the while*] alas for these
times! Cf. *H 5,* IV. vii. 79; and *Tp.,*
I. ii. 15, "woe the day"; and Cicero's
"O tempora, o mores!"

84. *Our yoke and sufferance*] our servi-
tude and the patience with which we
endure it.

85–8. *Indeed . . . in Italy*] In Plutarch
Decimus Brutus urged Cæsar to go to
the Senate on the day of his assassination, among other reasons because
they were ready willingly "to proclaim him king of all the provinces of
the Empire of Rome out of Italy, and
that he should wear his diadem in
all other places, both by sea and
land".

89. *I know . . . dagger then*] Cf. *Rom.,*
v. iii. 170, "O happy dagger! / This is
thy sheath. [*Stabs herself.*]"

Therein, ye gods, you make the weak most strong;
Therein, ye gods, you tyrants do defeat.
Nor stony tower, nor walls of beaten brass,
Nor airless dungeon, nor strong links of iron,
Can be retentive to the strength of spirit;   95
But life, being weary of these worldly bars,
Never lacks power to dismiss itself.
If I know this, know all the world besides,
That part of tyranny that I do bear
I can shake off at pleasure.   [*Thunder still.*
Casca.   So can I: 100
So every bondman in his own hand bears
The power to cancel his captivity.
Cas. And why should Cæsar be a tyrant then?
Poor man! I know he would not be a wolf,
But that he sees the Romans are but sheep;   105
He were no lion, were not Romans hinds.
Those that with haste will make a mighty fire
Begin it with weak straws. What trash is Rome,
What rubbish, and what offal, when it serves
For the base matter to illuminate   110
So vile a thing as Cæsar! But, O grief,
Where hast thou led me? I, perhaps, speak this

91. *Therein*] i.e., in the use of the dagger.

95. *Can be . . . spirit*] can confine a resolute spirit—even though the body be imprisoned.

102. *cancel*] A legal term, meaning to annul a deed or bond. Its use here was perhaps suggested by *bondman* in the previous line, which shows the other normal sense of *bond*, i.e. "fetter". Shakespeare uses the expression "to cancel a bond" figuratively several times: e.g. *Mac.*, III. ii. 49; *Cym.*, v. iv. 28; and *R 3*, IV. iv. 77, "Cancel his bond of life".

104–5. *I know . . . but sheep*] Cf. Davies, *Vpon English Prouerbes*, 55, "If men become sheepe, the wolfe will devoure them."

106. *hinds*] deer. We can also read into it the other common

sense, "servants, menials".

108–9. *trash . . . offal*] Both have much the same figurative sense as *rubbish*, i.e., "refuse, dregs, scum, dross". Shakespeare seems to be using them also in something like their original senses. *Trash* means "broken or torn pieces, as twigs, splinters, 'cuttings from a hedge, small wood from a copse'" (*O.E.D.*); *offal* (from *off fall*) means "that which is thrown off, as chips in dressing wood" (*O.E.D.*)—in other words, both suggest material very suitable for making a *mighty fire* to *illuminate* Cæsar. *Rubbish* too would fit this context in its non-figurative sense of "waste or refuse material . . . such as results from the decay or repair of buildings . . . debris, litter, refuse" (*O.E.D.*).

111. *vile*] worthless.

Before a willing bondman; then I know
My answer must be made. But I am arm'd,
And dangers are to me indifferent.   115
Casca. You speak to Casca, and to such a man
That is no fleering tell-tale. Hold, my hand:
Be factious for redress of all these griefs,
And I will set this foot of mine as far
As who goes furthest.
Cas.   There's a bargain made.   120
Now know you, Casca, I have mov'd already
Some certain of the noblest-minded Romans
To undergo with me an enterprise
Of honourable-dangerous consequence;
And I do know, by this they stay for me   125
In Pompey's porch: for now, this fearful night,
There is no stir or walking in the streets;
And the complexion of the element
In favour's like the work we have in hand,

---

124. honourable-dangerous] *Capell;* honourable dangerous *F.*   129. In favour's like] *Q 1691;* In favour's, like *Johnson;* Is Fauors, like *F;* Is feav'rous, like *Rowe, Pope, Theobald;* Is favour'd like *Capell, Malone;* It favours like *Steevens.*

---

114. *My answer ... made*] I shall have to answer for my words.

117. *fleering*] sneering, gibing. Cf. *Rom.,* I. v. 61, "To fleer and scorn at our solemnity"; *Ado,* v. i. 58, "never fleer and jest at me."

my hand] here is my hand on it.

118. *Be factious . . . these griefs*] form a faction for redress of all these grievances. Cf. *the faction* (II. i. 77), Brutus's word for the conspirators.

123. *undergo*] undertake.

126. *Pompey's porch*] The portico of the theatre built by Pompey in 55 B.C. Plutarch makes this the scene of Cæsar's assassination, which Shakespeare places in the Capitol.

128. *the complexion of the element*] the condition of the sky (as it may be judged from its appearance). Cf. *R 2,* III. ii. 194, "Men judge by the complexion of the sky / The state and inclination of the day." *Complexion* originally denoted the physical constitu-

tion, hence also the disposition, of a person, determined by the relative proportions of the four "humours" in the body; later it assumed something like the modern meaning, the outward manifestation of this or that state of the humours, the facial appearance. *Element* is the generic name for the four primary substances, earth, water, air, and fire, of which, in ancient and medieval philosophy, all material things were compounded. Shakespeare sometimes uses the word in the restricted sense of "atmosphere", or "sky". Cf. *Tw.N.,* I. i. 26, "The element itself, till seven years' heat, / Shall not behold her face at ample view."

129. *In favour's like*] in appearance is like. The two lines may be rendered: "The ominous disposition of the sky gives it the same appearance as the conspiracy we have undertaken, most bloody, fiery, and terrible"—though

Most bloody, fiery, and most terrible.   130

Enter CINNA.

Casca. Stand close awhile, for here comes one in haste.
Cas. 'Tis Cinna. I do know him by his gait.
  He is a friend. Cinna, where haste you so?
Cin. To find out you. Who's that? Metellus Cimber?
Cas. No, it is Casca, one incorporate   135
  To our attempts. Am I not stay'd for, Cinna?
Cin. I am glad on 't. What a fearful night is this!
  There's two or three of us have seen strange sights.
Cas. Am I not stay'd for? Tell me.
Cin.   Yes, you are.
  O Cassius, if you could   140
  But win the noble Brutus to our party—
Cas. Be you content. Good Cinna, take this paper,
  And look you lay it in the prætor's chair,
  Where Brutus may but find it; and throw this
  In at his window; set this up with wax   145
  Upon old Brutus' statue: all this done,
  Repair to Pompey's porch, where you shall find us.
  Is Decius Brutus and Trebonius there?
Cin. All but Metellus Cimber, and he's gone
  To seek you at your house. Well, I will hie,   150

137.] *As Rowe;* I . . . on't. / . . . this? / *F.* 139–41. Yes, . . . party—] *As Walker;* Yes, . . . *Cassius,* / . . . *Brutus* / . . . party— / *F.*

of course Cassius does not accept the prodigies as portents. See the apparatus criticus for various suggested emendations of the Folio reading, *Is Fauors, like.* Johnson's seems the most reasonable, and is accepted by modern editors. It was partly the mistaken belief that *complexion* and *favour* were synonyms that led some earlier editors to emend the Folio *Fauors.*

 131. *Stand close*] stand out of sight.
 134. *Metellus Cimber*] Thus in Plutarch's *Julius Cæsar;* in the *Brutus* he is called Tullius Cimber. His proper name was L. Tillius Cimber. He had been a friend of Cæsar, but joined the conspiracy against him.

135–6. *incorporate To*] bound up with, united with. Cf. *Cor.,* I. i. 136, "my incorporate friends".

 137. *I am glad on't*] i.e., glad to hear that Casca has joined the confederacy.

 142. *content*] easy in mind.

 143. *prætor's chair*] The *sella curulis,* from which Brutus as prætor would settle disputes brought before him.

 144. *Where Brutus may but find it*] where only Brutus may find it. Cf. *Tp.,* I. ii. 169, "Would I might / But ever see that man!" Cf. also ll. 140–1 above.

 148. *Decius Brutus*] Actually Decimus. North follows Amyot's error.

And so bestow these papers as you bade me.

Cas. That done, repair to Pompey's theatre.   [*Exit Cinna.*
Come, Casca, you and I will yet ere day
See Brutus at his house: three parts of him
Is ours already, and the man entire   155
Upon the next encounter yields him ours.

Casca. O, he sits high in all the people's hearts:
And that which would appear offence in us,
His countenance, like richest alchemy,
Will change to virtue and to worthiness.   160

Cas. Him and his worth and our great need of him
You have right well conceited. Let us go,
For it is after midnight; and ere day
We will awake him and be sure of him.   [*Exeunt.*

159. *His countenance . . . alchemy*] The favour, or approval, of Brutus is likened to alchemy, by which it was hoped that base metals could be transmuted into rich gold. It is a finely appropriate image for one of the central ideas of the play, especially as alchemy had never succeeded in working the miracle.

162. *conceited*] conceived, judged. Cf. III. i. 192, "one of two bad ways you must conceit me".

ACT II

[SCENE I.—*Rome.*]

Enter BRUTUS *in his Orchard.*

Bru. What, Lucius, ho!
I cannot, by the progress of the stars,
Give guess how near to day. Lucius, I say!
I would it were my fault to sleep so soundly.
When, Lucius, when? Awake, I say! What, Lucius!   5

Enter LUCIUS.

Luc. Call'd you, my lord?
Bru. Get me a taper in my study, Lucius:
When it is lighted, come and call me here.
Luc. I will, my lord.   [*Exit.*
Bru. It must be by his death: and for my part,   10

ACT II

Scene 1

S.D. Orchard] garden. In Shakespeare's day the word did not necessarily have its restricted modern meaning. It is derived from O.E. *ortgeard* (later *orceard*), "enclosed piece of ground for the purposes of horticulture" (*O.E.D.*).

5. *When*] Sometimes used by Shakespeare as an impatient exclamation. Cf. *Tp.*, 1. ii. 316, "Come, thou tortoise! When?" *What* is used in the same way in this line and in l. 1.

7. *taper*] candle.

10–34. *It must be by his death,* ff.] Dover Wilson, in his Introduction, pp. xxx–xxxi, gives a sensible elucidation of this soliloquy, which other critics have found "perplexing", or

"confused", or "a marvel of fanatical self-deception". "Brutus's theme," says Wilson, "is the effect of power upon character, and his conclusion is that to crown Cæsar would endow him with . . . absolute power. . . So far, Brutus admits, Cæsar had not shown himself the tyrant; but then he has not yet attained 'the upmost round' of the ladder. Once thus high he will scorn 'the base degrees by which he did ascend'. Once crowned, all barriers will be down; and, human nature being what it is, 'the bright day will bring forth the adder', since absolute rulers have no use for mercy ('remorse')." In answer to the charge of "fanatical self-deception", it may be observed

33

I know no personal cause to spurn at him,
But for the general. He would be crown'd:
How that might change his nature, there's the question.
It is the bright day that brings forth the adder,
And that craves wary walking. Crown him?—that;— 15
And then, I grant, we put a sting in him,
That at his will he may do danger with.
Th' abuse of greatness is when it disjoins
Remorse from power; and, to speak truth of Cæsar,
I have not known when his affections sway'd   20
More than his reason. But 'tis a common proof,
That lowliness is young ambition's ladder,

15. Crown him?—that;—] *Steevens;* Crowne him that, *F.*

that Brutus is clear-headed enough to draw an important distinction. On *personal* grounds he recoils from the murder of Cæsar, who is his friend, an eminently reasonable man (ll. 20–1), and "the foremost man of all this world"; for the *general* good he must be ready to use violent measures against one in whose mounting ambition he sees a threat to the liberty of his fellows. But he is in a terrible dilemma, and he has not slept since Cassius first whetted him against Cæsar (l. 61).

11. *spurn*] A stronger meaning than it has today; it means literally "kick". Cf. *1 H 6*, I. iv. 52, "So great fear of my name 'mongst them was spread, / That they suppos'd I could rend bars of steel / And spurn in pieces posts of adamant."

12. *for the general*] for the public weal.

14. *bright day . . . adder*] A good thing can bring forth evil. If we crown Cæsar, we put a sting in him, i.e., turn him into an adder capable of doing us mischief.

15. *craves*] demands.

17. *do danger*] work mischief. Cf. *Rom.*, V. ii. 20, "the neglecting it / May do much danger."

18–31. *Th' abuse . . . extremities*] Structurally a parenthesis. Ll. 32–4 ("And therefore think . . . mischievous") are a logical development of

the snake image of ll. 14–17. It is at least possible that the intervening passage was added later by Shakespeare as an afterthought.

18–19. *Th' abuse . . . power*] greatness is misused when the power it confers is divorced from pity. *Remorse* is normally used in the sense of "pity" or "compassion" in Shakespeare. Cf. *John*, IV. iii. 50, "the tears of soft remorse"; *Mac.*, I. v. 44.

20–1. *when his affections . . . reason*] when his feelings ruled him more than his judgement. "Affections" normally has a wider sense in Elizabethan than in modern English.

21. *a common proof*] a matter of general experience. Cf. *Tw.N.*, III. i. 135, "For 'tis a vulgar proof, / That very oft we pity enemies."

22. *That lowliness . . . ladder*] that the affectation of humility is the means by which the ambitious man rises (by ingratiating himself with the common people). Compare Bolingbroke's conduct as described in *Richard II*. Already as a young man, Plutarch tells us, Cæsar knew how to win men's hearts: "The people loved him marvellously also, because of the courteous manner he had to speak to every man, and to use them gently, being more ceremonious therein than was looked for in one of his years" (Sk., p. 45); and his ambition is more pointedly sug-

Whereto the climber-upward turns his face;
But when he once attains the upmost round,
He then unto the ladder turns his back,   25
Looks in the clouds, scorning the base degrees
By which he did ascend. So Cæsar may;
Then lest he may, prevent. And since the quarrel
Will bear no colour for the thing he is,
Fashion it thus: that what he is, augmented,   30
Would run to these and these extremities;
And therefore think him as a serpent's egg,
Which, hatch'd, would, as his kind, grow mischievous,
And kill him in the shell.

Enter LUCIUS.

Luc. The taper burneth in your closet, sir.   35
Searching the window for a flint, I found
This paper, thus seal'd up; and I am sure
It did not lie there when I went to bed.
                                  [*Gives him the letter.*
Bru. Get you to bed again; it is not day.
Is not to-morrow, boy, the ides of March?   40

23. climber-upward] *Warburton;* Climber upward *F.*   40. ides] *Theobald;* first *F.*

gested in the account of the triumphs he celebrated for his African conquests: "After these three triumphs ended, he very liberally rewarded his soldiers; and to curry favour with the people, he made great feasts and common sports" (Sk., p. 90).

23, 25. *turns his face . . . turns his back*] An effectively-placed antithesis.

26. *base degrees*] low steps—perhaps with the sense of "mean grades of office" implied. The ambitious man, having gained his object, discards his earlier humility (*lowliness*, l. 22).

28. *prevent*] anticipate, forestall by taking the right action. Cf. ll. 85 and 160.

28-9. *since the quarrel . . . thing he is*] since the cause of complaint (Latin *querela*) is not plausible, considering what he is now. *Colour*, in the sense of

"excuse, pretext", is common in Elizabethan English. Cf. *Ant.,* I. iii. 32, "seek no colour for your going".

30. *Fashion it thus*] make it look like this, put it this way.

31. *these and these extremities*] such and such extremes of severity, or tyranny. Cf. *R 3*, I. i. 65, "'tis she / That tempers him to this extremity."

33. *as his kind*] as is its nature.

40. *ides of March*] Followed by most editors, Theobald reads thus for the Folio *first of March*, suggesting that "*Ides* in the MS. was written jˢ and thus confused by the compositors with the old symbol for Ist." Or possibly Shakespeare made a slip, recalling a passage in North's Plutarch (Sk., p. 113) in which Cassius asked Brutus "if he were determined to be in the Senate-house the first day of the month

Luc. I know not, sir.

Bru. Look in the calendar, and bring me word.

Luc. I will, sir.   [*Exit.*

Bru. The exhalations whizzing in the air

     Give so much light that I may read by them.   45

                 [*Opens the letter, and reads.*

     Brutus, thou sleep'st; awake, and see thyself.

     Shall Rome, etc. Speak, strike, redress!

     "Brutus, thou sleep'st; awake!"

     Such instigations have been often dropp'd

     Where I have took them up.   50

     "Shall Rome, etc." Thus must I piece it out:

     Shall Rome stand under one man's awe? What, Rome?

     My ancestors did from the streets of Rome

     The Tarquin drive, when he was call'd a king.

     "Speak, strike, redress!" Am I entreated   55

     To speak, and strike? O Rome, I make thee promise,

     If the redress will follow, thou receivest

     Thy full petition at the hand of Brutus.

Enter LUCIUS.

Luc. Sir, March is wasted fifteen days.   [*Knock within.*

---

52. What, Rome?] *Rowe;* What Rome? *F.*   59. fifteen] *F;* fourteen *Theobald et al.*

of March, because he heard say that Cæsar's friends should move the council that day, that Cæsar should be called king by the Senate". That *ides* is meant here is made clear by Lucius in l. 59, "Sir, March is wasted fifteen days", and by the events of the day that is just beginning.

44. *exhalations*] meteors. The sun was thought to produce meteors by drawing up vapours from the earth. Cf. *Rom.*, III. v. 13, "It is some meteor that the sun exhales."

whizzing] rushing along with a hissing noise. Cf. Harington, *Orlando Furioso*, IX. lxix, "The shot . . . Doth whiz, and sing"; *Troil.* (Q), v. i. 24, "whissing lungs" (= wheezing lungs).

52. *under one man's awe*] in awe of one

man. This use of the genitive is not infrequent in Shakespeare.

53. *ancestors*] See note on I. ii. 157.

56. *I make thee promise*] I promise thee. This seems to be the moment at which Brutus makes up his mind that there is no alternative to Cæsar's death.

57–8. *thou receivest . . . of Brutus*] thou wilt receive from Brutus all that thou dost ask. If he can be sure that the redress will follow, that his action will indeed bring relief from the evil he fears, Brutus is prepared to speak and strike.

59. *fifteen days*] Some editors emend to *fourteen*. But it is the dawn of the fifteenth day, which Lucius includes in his reckoning.

Bru. 'Tis good. Go to the gate; somebody knocks.   60
                                        [*Exit Lucius.*]
Since Cassius first did whet me against Cæsar,
I have not slept.
Between the acting of a dreadful thing
And the first motion, all the interim is
Like a phantasma, or a hideous dream: 65
The genius and the mortal instruments
Are then in council; and the state of man,
Like to a little kingdom, suffers then
The nature of an insurrection.

Enter LUCIUS.

Luc. Sir, 'tis your brother Cassius at the door,   70

60. S.D. *Exit Lucius.*] *Theobald; not in F.*   67. of man] *F2, Rowe et al.; of a man*
F1, Malone, Knight, Collier.

64. *the first motion*] the first promptings, or impulse.
65. *phantasma*] nightmare.
66–7. *The genius . . . in council*] Vari-
ously explained. I think that *genius*
may be taken in its normal Shakespearian sense of the attendant or
guardian spirit allotted to every man
at his birth, the *demon* of *Ant.*, II. iii. 19,
"Thy demon—that thy spirit which
keeps thee". I take the *mortal instruments* to be the bodily powers, which
are *mortal* in that they die with the
body, whereas the *genius* is immortal.
They are the same as the *offic'd Instrument* of *Oth.*, I. iii. 271 (Q, *actiue Instruments*), and the *corporal agents* of *Mac.*,
I. vii. 80, "bend up / Each corporal
agent to this terrible feat." Macbeth
in that scene is in just the same stage of
dilemma as Brutus here. *Are then in
council*, and the lines that follow, imply
the battle of debate rather than the
calm discussion and wise conclusion;
the *genius* is the chairman, and the
mortal instruments the unwilling doers of
the deed—cf. ll. 175–6. Ll. 61–9 give,
in nine lines, the core of *Hamlet*.
67. *state of man*] This reading seems
preferable to that of the Folio, *state of a*

man, and is generally adopted. The
Folio reading makes less clear Brutus's
parallel between the human organism
and the body politic, which is here the
leading idea. Cf. *Mac.*, I. iii. 140, "My
thought, whose murther yet is but fan-
tastical, / Shakes so my single state of
man . . ." Brutus, like Macbeth, is
thinking particularly of his own individual human organism; but he is also
generalizing, from his own experience,
about the characteristic effect of a particular kind of suspense on the mind.
The Folio error, as it appears to be,
may have come about through an
unconscious association in the compositor's mind with the parallel
phrase in the following line, *a little
kingdom*.
68. *Like to a little kingdom*] The correspondence of the human body (*microcosm*) with the universe (*macrocosm*),
or with the state, is a commonplace in
medieval and Renaissance literature.
70. *your brother Cassius*] brother-in-
law, we should say. "They were allied
together: for Cassius had married
Junia, Brutus' sister" (Plutarch,
Brutus). Shakespeare has not mentioned this relationship earlier.

Who doth desire to see you.

Bru.   Is he alone?

Luc. No, sir, there are moe with him.

Bru.   Do you know them?

Luc. No, sir, their hats are pluck'd about their ears,
And half their faces buried in their cloaks,
That by no means I may discover them   75
By any mark of favour.

Bru.   Let 'em enter.   [*Exit Lucius.*]
They are the faction. O conspiracy,
Sham'st thou to show thy dangerous brow by night,
When evils are most free? O, then by day
Where wilt thou find a cavern dark enough   80
To mask thy monstrous visage? Seek none, conspiracy;
Hide it in smiles and affability:
For if thou path, thy native semblance on,

---

73. hats] *F; omitted Pope, with blank space in text.*   74. cloaks] *F1;* Cloath(e)s
Ff2, 3, 4, Rowe, Pope.   76. S.D. *Exit Lucius.] Not in F.*   83. path, thy] *F2;*
path thy *F1;* march, thy *Pope;* put thy *Coleridge;* pass thy *Cartwright; and
other conj.*

72. *moe*] Fairly frequent as a variant
of *more* (in number).

73. *their hats*] Pope, outraged at the
thought of Romans wearing hats, left
a blank in his text: "their   are pluckt
about their ears." He need not have
been so gravely concerned about the
anachronism, since the Romans did
use headgear of various kinds: the
petasus, a broad-brimmed travelling
hat or cap, the *pilleus*, a close-fitting,
brimless felt hat or cap, worn at entertainments and festivals, and the
cucullus, a cap or hood fastened to a
garment. In *Cor.*, II. iii. 95, 164, Pope
is similarly unwilling to accept *hat*, and
emends to *cap*.

76. *favour*] appearance. Cf. I. ii. 90.

79. *When evils are most free*] when
evil things range most freely.

82. *smiles and affability*] Plutarch
(*Brutus*, Sk., p. 115): "he did so frame
and fashion his countenance and looks
that no man could discern he had anything to trouble his mind." For the
thought cf. *Err.*, III. ii. 13, "Bear a fair

presence, though your heart be taint-
ed"; Dekker, *Old Fortunatus* (ed.
Bowers), I. i. 277, "The fairest cheeke
hath oftentimes a soule / Leaprous as
sinne itself"; Jonson, *E.M.I.*, IV. iii.
95, "I haue knowne fayre hides haue
foule hartes eare now, I can tell you."

83. *if thou path, thy native semblance on*]
As the apparatus criticus shows,
several emendations have been suggested. But as a principle, and in view
of the general reliability of the Folio
text, emendation should be avoided
unless there is clear evidence of corruption. The *O.E.D.* gives six other
examples of *path* as a verb, meaning
"to go along or tread (a way)", four of
them from Shakespeare's period; in
five the verb is used transitively, and
in the other reflexively, and editors
have been unwilling to accept the present passage as evidence that it could
be intransitive. But Kittredge provides a parallel from *A Gorgious Gallery
of Gallant Inventions*, 1578: "Their pleasant course straung traces hath, / On

Not Erebus itself were dim enough
To hide thee from prevention.   85

Enter the Conspirators, CASSIUS, CASCA, DECIUS,
CINNA, METELLUS [CIMBER], *and* TREBONIUS.

Cas. I think we are too bold upon your rest:
Good morrow, Brutus. Do we trouble you?
Bru. I have been up this hour, awake all night.
Know I these men that come along with you?
Cas. Yes, every man of them; and no man here   90
But honours you; and every one doth wish
You had but that opinion of yourself
Which every noble Roman bears of you.
This is Trebonius.
Bru.   He is welcome hither.
Cas. This, Decius Brutus.
Bru.   He is welcome too.   95
Cas. This, Casca; this, Cinna; and this, Metellus Cimber.
Bru. They are all welcome.
What watchful cares do interpose themselves
Betwixt your eyes and night?
Cas. Shall I entreat a word?   [*They whisper.* 100
Dec. Here lies the east: doth not the day break here?
Casca. No.
Cin. O, pardon, sir, it doth; and yon grey lines
That fret the clouds are messengers of day.

tops of trees that groundles path"—
i.e., "who take their course on the tops
of trees without setting foot on the
earth". Moreover, the Second Folio,
in providing the comma omitted in the
other three Folios, shows willingness to
accept an intransitive use of the verb;
and no change seems necessary. The
line may be rendered: "for if thou pur-
sue thy course, showing thyself as thou
really art . . ."

84. *Erebus*] The dark and gloomy
place beneath the earth through
which the shades pass on their way to
Hades.

85. *from prevention*] from being forestalled and thwarted.

86. *upon your rest*] in breaking in
upon your rest.

98. *watchful cares*] cares that keep
you awake.

101–11. *Here lies . . . directly here*]
Not only does this realistic little discussion "cover" the whispered consultation of Brutus and Cassius, but it illustrates admirably how men will conceal pent-up feelings by talking of
trivial things.

104. *fret*] interlace, adorn (Old
French *freter*). Cf. *Ham.*, II. ii. 305,
"this majestical roof fretted with gold-
en fire". In architecture the word
means "to adorn (ceiling, vault, etc.)
with carved or embossed work." Cf.

Casca. You shall confess that you are both deceiv'd.   105
    Here, as I point my sword, the sun arises,
    Which is a great way growing on the south,
    Weighing the youthful season of the year.
    Some two months hence, up higher toward the north
    He first presents his fire; and the high east   110
    Stands, as the Capitol, directly here.
Bru. Give me your hands all over, one by one.
Cas. And let us swear our resolution.
Bru. No, not an oath. If not the face of men,
    The sufferance of our souls, the time's abuse—   115
    If these be motives weak, break off betimes,
    And every man hence to his idle bed.
    So let high-sighted tyranny range on,
    Till each man drop by lottery. But if these,
    As I am sure they do, bear fire enough   120
    To kindle cowards and to steel with valour
    The melting spirits of women, then, countrymen,
    What need we any spur but our own cause

114. not the face] *F;* that the face *Theobald;* that the fate *Warburton;* not the faiths *conj. Malone;* not the faith *conj. Mason.*   115. abuse—] *Theobald;* abuse; *F.*

Cym., II. iv. 88, "The roof o' the chamber / With golden cherubins is fretted"; and Gray's *Elegy,* "The long drawn aisle and fretted vault". The verb *fret* in the sense of "consume" or "wear away", used figuratively in modern English, comes from the Old English *fretan,* "to devour": cf. *Lr.,* I. iv. 309; and *R2,* III. iii. 167, where Richard talks of dropping tears "still upon one place, / Till they have fretted us a pair of graves".

    107. *growing on*] encroaching on.
    108. *Weighing*] considering.
    114. *the face of men*] Dover Wilson comments: "Almost certainly a corruption of 'faith' (Mason, conj. *ap.* Camb.), Plut.'s word"—referring to a marginal heading in North: "The wonderful faith and secrecy of the conspirators of Cæsar's death." Though this heading stands by a section in which Plutarch tells us that the conspirators had "never taken oaths

together", it is difficult to see how the Folio compositor could have misread the word in this way—and, indeed, how *the faith of men* could be regarded as a *motive.* I think that *face* may reasonably stand; the prevalent evils (*the time's abuse*) would give many men anxious or sorrowful faces.

    115. *sufferance*] suffering, distress— as several times in Shakespeare.

    117. *idle bed*] A transferred epithet of a kind common in Shakespeare. Cf. *watchful cares* in l. 98 above.

    118. *high-sighted tyranny*] tyranny with its power of seeing from a great height—a metaphor from falconry: cf. I. i. 72–4. The bird of prey will soar (*range*) above "an ordinary pitch", almost "above the view of men", select its prey, and swoop on it.

    119. *by lottery*] by chance, i.e., as the tyrant's gaze chances to light on him. Brutus suggests that Cæsar will dispose of his opponents as caprice directs him.

To prick us to redress? what other bond
Than secret Romans, that have spoke the word,   125
And will not palter? and what other oath
Than honesty to honesty engag'd,
That this shall be, or we will fall for it?
Swear priests and cowards, and men cautelous,
Old feeble carrions, and such suffering souls   130
That welcome wrongs; unto bad causes swear
Such creatures as men doubt; but do not stain
The even virtue of our enterprise,
Nor th' insuppressive mettle of our spirits,
To think that or our cause or our performance   135
Did need an oath; when every drop of blood
That every Roman bears, and nobly bears,
Is guilty of a several bastardy,
If he do break the smallest particle
Of any promise that hath pass'd from him.   140

Cas. But what of Cicero? Shall we sound him?
I think he will stand very strong with us.

Casca. Let us not leave him out.

Cin.   No, by no means.

Met. O, let us have him, for his silver hairs
Will purchase us a good opinion,   145
And buy men's voices to commend our deeds.
It shall be said his judgment rul'd our hands;
Our youths and wildness shall no whit appear,

124. *prick*] spur, incite. Cf. *Mac.*, I. vii. 25, "I have no spur / To prick the sides of my intent."

125. *Than secret... the word*] than the fact that we are Romans, who, having pledged ourselves, will not blab.

126. *palter*] use deceit, equivocate. Cf. *Mac.*, v. viii. 20, "And be those juggling fiends no more believed / That palter with us in a double sense."

127. *honesty to honesty engag'd*] pledges of honour interchanged.

129. *cautelous*] crafty, deceitful. Cf. *Cor.*, IV. i. 33, "caught / With cautelous baits and practice".

130. *carrions*] Used contemptuously for men who are little better than corpses. Cf. *H 5*, IV. ii. 39, "yon island carrions".

133. *even*] uniform, steadfast. Cf. *H 8*, III. i. 37, "I know my life so even".

134. *insuppressive*] insuppressible, indomitable. Abbott, ¶3, gives other examples of Shakespeare's use of the *-ive* suffix where *-ible* is normal usage: e.g., *plausive, incomprehensive, unexpressive*.

138. *guilty ... bastardy*] guilty of an act that shows it is not pure Roman blood.

144–6. *silver ... purchase ... buy*] As Wright points out, the word *silver* perhaps suggested to Shakespeare the use of *purchase* and *buy*.

But all be buried in his gravity.

Bru. O, name him not; let us not break with him;   150
For he will never follow any thing
That other men begin.

Cas.   Then leave him out.

Casca. Indeed he is not fit.

Dec. Shall no man else be touch'd but only Cæsar?

Cas. Decius, well urg'd. I think it is not meet,   155
Mark Antony, so well belov'd of Cæsar,
Should outlive Cæsar: we shall find of him
A shrewd contriver; and you know, his means,
If he improve them, may well stretch so far
As to annoy us all; which to prevent,   160
Let Antony and Cæsar fall together.

Bru. Our course will seem too bloody, Caius Cassius,
To cut the head off and then hack the limbs,
Like wrath in death and envy afterwards;
For Antony is but a limb of Cæsar.   165
Let's be sacrificers, but not butchers, Caius.
We all stand up against the spirit of Cæsar,

150. *break with him*] let him into the
secret—as often in Shakespeare. Cf.
Gent., III. i. 59, "I am to break with
thee of some affairs."

151-2. *never follow . . . begin*] Plutarch's reason for the omission of
Cicero from the conspiracy is that he
was "a coward by nature", and that
age had "increased his fear", though
in another passage he mentions his
ambition and vanity. See Appendix,
p. 144.

153. *is not fit*] Contrast Casca's advice in l. 143. We have something of
the same inconsistency in I. ii, where
he is servile in Cæsar's presence, and
contemptuous about him behind his
back.

158. *shrewd contriver*] mischievous
plotter. *Shrewd* is fairly common in
Shakespeare in the sense of "malicious,
mischievous." Cf. *1 H 6*, I. ii. 123,
"shrewd tempters"; *All's W.*, III. v. 68,
"do her / A shrewd turn"; *MND.*, II.
i. 33, "shrewd and knavish sprite".

159. *improve*] turn to advantage.

160. *annoy*] harm, injure. *Prevent*, as
already noted, means "anticipate,
forestall".

164. *Like wrath . . . afterwards*] Such
a course, says Brutus, would make it
look as if, in killing Cæsar, the conspirators were prompted by personal
malice against him and his supporters,
whereas he himself regards them as
sacrificers. *Envy* = "malice, hatred"
(Latin *invidia*).

165. *a limb of Cæsar*] a mere depen-
dant, or derivative, of Cæsar. Cf. Dryden on Fletcher in the Preface to his
Troilus and Cressida (1679), "To conclude all, he was a limb of Shakespeare." Brutus's words have a slightly
contemptuous implication: cf. "a limb
of Satan", or *H 8*, v. iv. 68, "Limbs of
Limehouse".

166. *Let's be sacrificers*] Cf. *Oth.*, v. ii.
64, "mak'st me call what I intend to
do / A murder, which I thought a sacrifice".

And in the spirit of men there is no blood.
O, that we then could come by Cæsar's spirit,
And not dismember Cæsar! But, alas,   170
Cæsar must bleed for it. And, gentle friends,
Let's kill him boldly, but not wrathfully;
Let's carve him as a dish fit for the gods,
Not hew him as a carcass fit for hounds.
And let our hearts, as subtle masters do,   175
Stir up their servants to an act of rage,
And after seem to chide 'em. This shall make
Our purpose necessary, and not envious;
Which so appearing to the common eyes,
We shall be call'd purgers, not murderers.   180
And for Mark Antony, think not of him;
For he can do no more than Cæsar's arm
When Cæsar's head is off.

Cas.   Yet I fear him;
For in the ingrafted love he bears to Cæsar—

Bru. Alas, good Cassius, do not think of him: 185
If he love Cæsar, all that he can do
Is to himself: take thought, and die for Cæsar.
And that were much he should; for he is given
To sports, to wildness, and much company.

Treb. There is no fear in him; let him not die;   190

184. Cæsar—] *Rowe; Cæsar. F.*

169. *come by*] get possession of. Cf. l. 259; and *Tp.,* II. i. 292, "As thou got'st Milan / I'll come by Naples."

171. *gentle*] noble. See note on v. v. 73. Some irony on Shakespeare's part.

173. *carve*] "Mr. Justice Madden in his *Diary of Master William Silence* finds in this passage an allusion to the practice of hunters, with whom it was an article of faith that 'the carcase of the hart should not be thrown rudely to the hounds as the fox, the marten, or the gray, but should be reverently disposed of.' The ceremonious cutting up of the deer [is] here expressed by the verb 'carve', as opposed to 'hew'" (Macmillan).

176. *their servants*] the passions, the *mortal instruments* of l. 66.

177–8. *This shall . . . envious*] This will make it evident that our action was necessary, not malicious. For *envious* see note on *envy* (l. 164).

180. *purgers*] healers.

184. *ingrafted*] deeply rooted.

187. *take thought*] give way to melancholy. Cf. *Ham.,*III. i. 85, where melancholy is characterized as "the pale cast of thought" in contrast to "the native hue of resolution". Cf. also *Ant.,* IV. vi. 36, "thought will do't, I feel"; and *Ant.,* III. xiii. 1, "Think, and die".

188. *much he should*] too much for him to do. Cf. *1 H 6,* IV. i. 192, "'Tis much when sceptres are in children's hands"; *Mer.V.,* III. v. 44.

190. *no fear*] no cause for fear.

For he will live, and laugh at this hereafter.

[*Clock strikes.*

Bru. Peace! count the clock.

Cas.   The clock hath stricken three.

Treb. 'Tis time to part.

Cas.   But it is doubtful yet
Whether Cæsar will come forth to-day or no;
For he is superstitious grown of late,   195
Quite from the main opinion he held once
Of fantasy, of dreams, and ceremonies.
It may be these apparent prodigies,
The unaccustom'd terror of this night,
And the persuasion of his augurers,   200
May hold him from the Capitol to-day.

Dec. Never fear that: if he be so resolv'd,
I can o'ersway him; for he loves to hear
That unicorns may be betray'd with trees,
And bears with glasses, elephants with holes,   205
Lions with toils, and men with flatterers;
But when I tell him he hates flatterers,
He says he does, being then most flattered.
Let me work;

191. S.D. Clock strikes] An anachronism, since mechanical clocks were not invented until the thirteenth century. In l. 192, "The clock hath stricken three", Shakespeare is thinking in terms of modern chronology; cf. ii. ii. 114; ii. iv. 23. We learn in l. 221 that the sun has not yet risen, and Roman hours were divisions of the natural day starting from dawn, and varying with the length of the day at different seasons of the year.

195–6. *superstitious . . . held once*] There is no warrant in Plutarch for Cæsar's superstition, nor that he earlier followed the Epicureans in disregarding omens and the like. *Main opinion* means "strong, confident opinion"; and *quite from* is "at variance with"—cf. i. iii. 64.

197. *fantasy*] figments of imagination. *Ceremonies* here means "portents, omens"; cf. ii. ii. 13.

198. *apparent*] that have been appearing.

204. *unicorns . . . trees*] Steevens draws attention to the passage in *The Faerie Queene* (ii. v. 10), which describes how a lion, charged by a unicorn, stands in front of a tree, and at the last moment steps aside, so that his enemy's horn becomes fixed in the tree, and he gains "a bounteous feast".

205. *bears with glasses*] presumably by blinding them with mirrors.

elephants with holes] Pliny (*H.N.*, viii. 8) describes how elephants are caught by means of specially prepared ditches. Cf. Somerville's *Chase*, iii. 261 ff, where also tigers and leopards are caught by means of mirrors.

206. *toils*] nets, snares.

men with flatterers] Even as wild beasts may be betrayed by simple wiles, so may men.

For I can give his humour the true bent,   210
And I will bring him to the Capitol.
Cas. Nay, we will all of us be there to fetch him.
Bru. By the eighth hour: is that the uttermost?
Cin. Be that the uttermost, and fail not then.
Met. Caius Ligarius doth bear Cæsar hard,   215
Who rated him for speaking well of Pompey;
I wonder none of you have thought of him.
Bru. Now, good Metellus, go along by him:
He loves me well, and I have given him reasons;
Send him but hither, and I'll fashion him.   220
Cas. The morning comes upon 's: we'll leave you, Brutus.
And, friends, disperse yourselves; but all remember
What you have said, and show yourselves true Romans.
Bru. Good gentlemen, look fresh and merrily.
Let not our looks put on our purposes,   225
But bear it as our Roman actors do,
With untir'd spirits and formal constancy.
And so good morrow to you every one.
                              [*Exeunt. Manet Brutus.*
Boy! Lucius! Fast asleep? It is no matter;
Enjoy the honey-heavy dew of slumber: 230

213. eighth] *F4;* eight *F1.*   221.] *As Rowe;* The . . . upon's: / . . . *Brutus,* / *F.*
230. honey-heavy dew] *Theobald;* hony-heauy-Dew *F.*

210. *give his humour the true bent*] turn
his disposition in the right direction.
  213. *uttermost*] latest.
  215. *bear Cæsar hard*] bears ill will to
Cæsar. Cf. i. ii. 310. In Plutarch
Ligarius had been acquitted by Cæsar
after an accusation of siding with
Pompey, but nevertheless hated him
for his tyranny. See Appendix, pp.
144–5.
  216. *rated*] chided, scolded.
  218. *by him*] by his dwelling.
  225. *Let not . . . purposes*] let us not
betray our design in our looks. Tilley
provides a good parallel from William
Rankins, *A Mirrour of Monsters* (1587),
"Beware of such pernitious Gnaton-
ists who taking vs friendlie by the one
hand, haue in the other a naked blade
to shed our bloud, and smiling in our

faces, seeke to betraie our soules."
Cf. iv. i. 50.
  226–7. *But bear it . . . constancy*] but,
like our Roman actors, carry it off
without looking strained and with
dignified composure. Actually Roman
actors wore masks; Shakespeare is
thinking of Elizabethan actors. The
most famous Roman actors were Q.
Roscius in comedy, and Æsopus
Claudius in tragedy. Both had en-
joyed the friendship of Cicero, but
both died some years before the murder of Cæsar. Roscius in particular
was held to have reached perfection in
his art, and in modern literature references to him as the type of the good
actor are frequent: e.g., *Ham.,* ii. ii.
419.
  230. *honey-heavy dew*] a superbly

Thou hast no figures nor no fantasies
Which busy care draws in the brains of men;
Therefore thou sleep'st so sound.

Enter PORTIA.

Por.   Brutus, my lord.
Bru. Portia, what mean you? Wherefore rise you now?
    It is not for your health thus to commit   235
    Your weak condition to the raw cold morning.
Por. Nor for yours neither. Y' have ungently, Brutus,
    Stole from my bed; and yesternight at supper
    You suddenly arose, and walk'd about,
    Musing, and sighing, with your arms across;   240
    And when I ask'd you what the matter was,
    You star'd upon me with ungentle looks.
    I urg'd you further; then you scratch'd your head,
    And too impatiently stamp'd with your foot;
    Yet I insisted, yet you answer'd not,   245
    But with an angry wafture of your hand
    Gave sign for me to leave you. So I did,
    Fearing to strengthen that impatience
    Which seem'd too much enkindled, and withal
    Hoping it was but an effect of humour,   250

237. Y'have] *F;* You've *Rowe et al.*   246. wafture] *Rowe;* wafter *F.*

compressed image, suggesting sound, sweet, and refreshing sleep. Cf. *R 3*, IV. i. 83, "the golden dew of sleep".

231. *figures . . . fantasies*] Both words suggest figments of the imagination. Cf. l. 197 above, and *Wiv.*, IV. ii. 234, "if it be but to scrape the figures out of your husband's brains".

240. *your arms across*] The attitude of one absorbed in melancholy thoughts. The phrase occurs several times in Shakespeare: cf. *Lucr.*, 1662, "With sad set eyes and wretched arms across"; and the attitude is illustrated on the engraved title-pages of Rowlands's *The Melancholie Knight* (1615), and Burton's *Anatomy of Melancholy*, 3rd edn. (1628).

246. *wafture*] gesture, waving. The verb *waft*, in the sense of *wave*, occurs elsewhere in Shakespeare, e.g., *Ham.*, I. iv. 61, "It wafts you to a more removed ground", and I. iv. 78, "It wafts me still", where the 1604 Quarto has *waves*. The form *wafture* here for the *wafter* of the Folio was suggested by Rowe, and is generally accepted. We may compare *roundure* for the *rounder* of the Folio in *John*, II. i. 259; *rondure*, meaning "circle", is found in *Sonn.*, XXI. 8. Not recorded before Rowe, *wafture* has since his time become fairly common in literary use. It is of course possible that *wafter* is a dialect word related to the obsolete verb *wafter* (=wave) which is once recorded by *O.E.D.*

250. *an effect of humour*] a sign of some passing mood.

Which sometime hath his hour with every man.
It will not let you eat, nor talk, nor sleep;
And could it work so much upon your shape
As it hath much prevail'd on your condition,
I should not know you Brutus. Dear my lord,   255
Make me acquainted with your cause of grief.

Bru. I am not well in health, and that is all.

Por. Brutus is wise, and, were he not in health,
He would embrace the means to come by it.

Bru. Why, so I do. Good Portia, go to bed.   260

Por. Is Brutus sick, and is it physical
To walk unbraced and suck up the humours
Of the dank morning? What, is Brutus sick?
And will he steal out of his wholesome bed
To dare the vile contagion of the night,   265
And tempt the rheumy and unpurged air
To add unto his sickness? No, my Brutus;
You have some sick offence within your mind,
Which, by the right and virtue of my place,
I ought to know of; and, upon my knees,   270
I charm you, by my once commended beauty,
By all your vows of love, and that great vow
Which did incorporate and make us one,
That you unfold to me, your self, your half,
Why you are heavy, and what men to-night   275

255. know you Brutus] *F1*; know you, Brutus *F4, Cambridge, Macmillan.*

251. *his*] its: cf. I. ii. 123.

254. *condition*] state of mind.

255. *know you Brutus*] know you for Brutus. Most editors unnecessarily follow the Fourth Folio in reading *know you, Brutus.*

259. *come by*] get. Cf. l. 169.

261. *physical*] healthy. Cf. *Cor.*, I. v. 19, "The blood I drop is rather physical / Than dangerous to me."

262. *unbraced*] See note on *doublet,* I. ii. 262, and cf. I. iii. 48.

humours] Here in its primary sense, "moistures, dampness".

266. *tempt*] risk. Cf. *Troil.*, v. iii. 34, "tempt not yet the brushes of the war".

rheumy and unpurged air] air that causes rheum, or catarrh, since it has not yet been purified of its dampness by the sun.

268. *sick offence*] harmful sickness— a transferred epithet. *Offence* occurs several times in Shakespeare in the sense of "harm, injury". Cf. IV. iii. 200, "Doing himself offence".

271. *charm*] entreat, adjure.

273. *incorporate*] make one body of us. Cf. the use of the word in I. iii. 135, and in the next line the words *your self, your half.* For *half* in the sense of "wife" cf. *Ado*, II. iii. 188, and Horace' "animae dimidium meae".

275. *heavy*] sorrowful, depressed.

Have had resort to you; for here have been
Some six or seven, who did hide their faces
Even from darkness.

Bru.   Kneel not, gentle Portia.

Por. I should not need, if you were gentle Brutus.
Within the bond of marriage, tell me, Brutus,   280
Is it excepted I should know no secrets
That appertain to you? Am I your self
But, as it were, in sort or limitation,
To keep with you at meals, comfort your bed,
And talk to you sometimes? Dwell I but in the suburbs
Of your good pleasure? If it be no more,   286
Portia is Brutus' harlot, not his wife.

Bru. You are my true and honourable wife,
As dear to me as are the ruddy drops
That visit my sad heart.   290

Por. If this were true, then should I know this secret.
I grant I am a woman; but withal
A woman that Lord Brutus took to wife;
I grant I am a woman; but withal
A woman well reputed, Cato's daughter.   295
Think you I am no stronger than my sex,
Being so father'd, and so husbanded?
Tell me your counsels, I will not disclose 'em.

---

279. gentle Brutus] *F;* gentle, Brutus *Staunton.*   295. reputed, Cato's]
reputed: *Cato's F;* reputed Cato's *Warburton et al.*

281–3. *excepted . . . sort or limitation*]
Dover Wilson points out that these are
"legal terms of land-tenure, suggested
by 'bond' (l. 280)", and in his Glossary
he refers to the legal phrase "exceptis
excipiendis" found in leases. Cf. *Tw.
N.,* 1. iii. 7, "Let her except before excepted." *Limitation* is "the period specified for the continuance of an estate"
(*O.E.D.*). L. 283 may be rendered,
"Only after a fashion, as it were, or for
a specified period".

285. *suburbs*] "Women of bad character lived in the suburbs of London"
(Onions). Cf. *harlot* (l. 287).

287. *Brutus' harlot*] From Plutarch.
See Appendix, p. 145.

295. *Cato's daughter*] Marcus Porcius
Cato, the orator and statesman, re-
sembled his great-grandfather, Cato
the Censor, in the rigid morality of his
life. In the Civil War he joined Pompey, and after the battle of Pharsalia
continued his resistance to Cæsar in
Africa, with Metellus Scipio. When all
Africa submitted to Cæsar, Cato,
rather than be taken, killed himself at
Utica, where he made a last stand;
hence his surname of Uticensis. He became the subject of much panegyric,
e.g. in Lucan's *Pharsalia.* Brutus was
his nephew as well as son-in-law, and
greatly admired him. See apparatus
criticus for readings in this line.

I have made strong proof of my constancy,
Giving myself a voluntary wound   300
Here, in the thigh: can I bear that with patience,
And not my husband's secrets?

Bru.   O ye gods,
Render me worthy of this noble wife!   *[Knock.*
Hark, hark! one knocks. Portia, go in awhile;
And by and by thy bosom shall partake   305
The secrets of my heart.
All my engagements I will construe to thee,
All the charactery of my sad brows.
Leave me with haste.   *[Exit Portia.*

Enter LUCIUS *and* [CAIUS] LIGARIUS.

               Lucius, who's that knocks?

Luc. Here is a sick man that would speak with you.   310

Bru. Caius Ligarius, that Metellus spake of.
     Boy, stand aside. Caius Ligarius, how?

Cai. Vouchsafe good morrow from a feeble tongue.

Bru. O, what a time have you chose out, brave Caius,
     To wear a kerchief! Would you were not sick!   315

Cai. I am not sick if Brutus have in hand
     Any exploit worthy the name of honour.

Bru. Such an exploit have I in hand, Ligarius,
     Had you a healthful ear to hear of it.

Cai. By all the gods that Romans bow before,   320
     I here discard my sickness. Soul of Rome!

299. *strong proof of my constancy*] severe trial of my resolution. *Proof* in this sense is frequent in Shakespeare; for *constancy* cf. l. 227 above. The incident is taken from Plutarch.

307. *construe*] explain, interpret.

308. *charactery of my sad brows*] what is written in my sad brows, i.e., what the furrows of sadness on my brows mean. For *charactery* cf. *Wiv.*, v. v. 77, "Fairies use flowers for their charactery." *Character* is used several times by Shakespeare for "writing".

311. *Ca us Ligarius*] Thus Plutarch. Actually Quintus Ligarius. In Plutarch Brutus visits Ligarius.

313. *Vouchsafe*] deign to accept. Cf. *Tim.*, I. i. 153, "Vouchsafe my labour"; *John*, III. i. 294. Normally it means "deign to grant".

315. *wear a kerchief*] be ill. Malone compares Fuller, *Worthies* (*Cheshire*, ed. 1662, p. 190), "if any here be sick, *They make him a posset, and tye a kerchieff on his head; and if that will not mend him, then God be mercifull to him.*" Cf. also Scot, *Discoverie of Witchcraft*, XII. xviii, ". . . a Gentleman that had beene vexed with sicknesse, named Elibert, hauing a kerchiefe on his head, according to the guise of sicke folke".

Brave son, deriv'd from honourable loins!
Thou, like an exorcist, hast conjur'd up
My mortified spirit. Now bid me run,
And I will strive with things impossible,   325
Yea, get the better of them. What's to do?
Bru. A piece of work that will make sick men whole.
Cai. But are not some whole that we must make sick?
Bru. That must we also. What it is, my Caius,
I shall unfold to thee, as we are going   330
To whom it must be done.
Cai.   Set on your foot,
And with a heart new-fir'd I follow you,
To do I know not what; but it sufficeth
That Brutus leads me on.   [*Thunder.*
Bru.   Follow me then.   [*Exeunt.*

[SCENE II.—*The Same. Cæsar's House.*]

Thunder and lightning. Enter JULIUS CÆSAR *in his
night-gown.*

Cæs. Nor heaven nor earth have been at peace to-night:
Thrice hath Calphurnia in her sleep cried out,
"Help, ho! they murther Cæsar!" Who's within?

Enter a Servant.

Serv. My lord?
Cæs. Go bid the priests do present sacrifice,   5
And bring me their opinions of success.

327.] *As Rowe;* A . . . worke, / . . . whole. / *F.*   330. going] *Capell;* going, F.

Scene II

1.] *As Rowe;* Nor . . . Earth / . . . to night: / *F.*

322. *Brave*] noble.   *Scene* II
324. *mortified*] deadened.
327. *whole*] sound, healthy. The   S.D. night-gown] dressing-gown.
slaying of Cæsar will cure those whom   Cf. *Mac.*, II. ii. 71, *Oth.*, IV. iii. 34.
his dictatorial tendencies make sick by
robbing them of freedom.   5. *present*] immediate. Cf. *presently*,
328. *make sick*] A euphemism for   IV. i. 45; IV. iii. 196.
"kill".
                                                      6. *success*] result, whether good or
331. *To whom*] to his house to whom.   bad. Cf. v. iii. 65; and *Ant.*, III. v. 6,
                                                      "what is the success?"

Serv. I will, my lord.   [*Exit.*

                    Enter CALPHURNIA.

Cal. What mean you, Cæsar? Think you to walk forth?
   You shall not stir out of your house to-day.
Cæs. Cæsar shall forth. The things that threaten'd me   10
   Ne'er look'd but on my back; when they shall see
   The face of Cæsar, they are vanished.
Cal. Cæsar, I never stood on ceremonies,
   Yet now they fright me. There is one within,
   Besides the things that we have heard and seen,   15
   Recounts most horrid sights seen by the watch.
   A lioness hath whelped in the streets,
   And graves have yawn'd and yielded up their dead;
   Fierce fiery warriors fight upon the clouds

19. fight] *F;* fought *Grant White;* did fight *Keightley.*

10. *shall forth*] Abbott, ¶41, gives several examples of the omission of verbs of motion before *forth, hence,* and *hither.*

13. *stood on ceremonies*] attached importance to omens, or portents. Plutarch says that "Calphurnia until that time was never given to any fear and superstition." For *stand on* in the sense of "make much of, attach importance to" cf. *Mac.,* III. iv. 119, "Stand not upon the order of your going." For *ceremonies* cf. II. i. 197.

16. *the watch*] There do not appear to have been night-watchmen in Rome at this period. Augustus instituted city guards, the *cohortes urbanae,* or *urbana militia,* and a body of night-watchers, the *cohortes vigilum,* whose main duty was to put out fires. Shakespeare no doubt had in mind the watchmen of Elizabethan London, like those of whom he gives us comic representatives in *Ado.*

16–24. *horrid sights . . . the streets*] For a similar account of the prodigies of this night cf. *Ham.,* I. i. 113 ff.

19. *fight*] I retain *fight* from the Folio, but many editors since Grant White (1861) change to *fought.* Cal-

phurnia is agitated, and the events she describes are very vivid in her mind; she might well drop into the graphic present. It is at least possible that there has been some revision in the speech, which may have stood elsewhere, in I. iii, for instance; in l. 23 the Folio has another discordant tense, *do neigh.*

19–22 *Fierce fiery . . . the air*] Cf. Milton, *Par. L.,* II. 533–8, "As when to warn proud Cities warr appears / Wag'd in the troubl'd Skie, and Armies rush / To Battel in the Clouds, before each Van / Pric forth the Aerie Knights, and couch thir spears / Till thickest Legions close; with feats of Arms / From either end of Heav'n the welkin burns." Milton's lines are based on Josephus's account of the prodigies that preceded the destruction of Jerusalem. This account was used and expanded by Dekker in *Canaans Calamitie* (entered *Stat. Reg.* 1598), and it is possible that Shakespeare had seen Dekker's version. Tacitus's description of the siege of Jerusalem (*Hist.,* v. xiii.) reports the prodigies in similar terms, and perhaps owes something to Josephus. Strange's company had a play (now

In ranks and squadrons and right form of war,   20
Which drizzled blood upon the Capitol;
The noise of battle hurtled in the air,
Horses did neigh, and dying men did groan,
And ghosts did shriek and squeal about the streets.
O Cæsar, these things are beyond all use,   25
And I do fear them.

Cæs.   What can be avoided
Whose end is purpos'd by the mighty gods?
Yet Cæsar shall go forth; for these predictions
Are to the world in general as to Cæsar.

Cal. When beggars die, there are no comets seen;   30
The heavens themselves blaze forth the death of princes.

23. did neigh] *F2;* do neigh *F1.*

lost) entitled *Jerusalem* in 1592 (Henslowe's *Diary*, ed. Greg, I. 13–14), and in 1584 and 1591 a play on this subject was acted at Coventry, 16 miles from Stratford (*N. & Q.*, 8 Aug. 1931). See E. Honigmann's note (Arden edition) on *John*, II. i. 378, "the mutines of Jerusalem". It is at least possible that Shakespeare partly drew on his memory of an old play for some of the present passage. The lost *Titus and Vespasian* (played in 1592) may also have helped. Sir Edmund Chambers calls this one of the best-known stories of ancient times current in Elizabethan England.

20. *right form of war*] regular order of war.

22. *hurtled*] clattered, clashed. Cf. *AYL.*, IV. iii. 133, "In which hurtling / From miserable slumber I awaked", where *hurtling* refers to the battle between Orlando and the lioness.

24. *shriek and squeal*] In the parallel account in *Ham.* mentioned above (see note on ll. 16–24), "the sheeted dead / Did squeak and gibber in the Roman streets."

25. *beyond all use*] beyond all experience, quite abnormal.

26-7. *What can . . . mighty gods?*] Cf. Pettie, *A Petite Pallace* (ed. Gollancz), II. 128, "No policy may prevent the

power of the heavens, no doings of men can undo the destinies."

28. *Yet Cæsar shall go forth*] Cf. l. 10 and l. 48. With these words and their context in the present passage cf. Marlowe, *The Massacre at Paris* (ed. H. S. Bennett), XVIII. 65–9, "*Third Murd.* . . . therefore, good my lord, go not forth. / *Guise.* Yet Cæsar shall go forth./ Let mean consaits and baser men fear death: / Tut, they are peasants; I am Duke of Guise; / And princes with their looks engender fear." This parallel was used by Robertson and Wells to support their arguments that *Julius Cæsar* was a revision, by Shakespeare and others, of a play by Marlowe. (See Introduction, p. xxii.) The Octavo of *The Massacre* has with some probability been dated 1594 by W. W. Greg (Mal. Soc. edn., p. vii), and the most likely explanation of the close parallel is that Marlowe and Shakespeare both based their lines on a passage in an earlier play about Cæsar. See note on *Et tu, Brute*, III. i. 77.

31. *blaze forth*] proclaim. Cf. *Ven.*, 219, "Red cheeks and fiery eyes blaze forth her wrong." But we must also read into the phrase its literal meaning of "flame forth". The notion that the deaths of mighty persons are attended with prodigies is not uncommon: cf.

Cæs. Cowards die many times before their deaths;
The valiant never taste of death but once.
Of all the wonders that I yet have heard,
It seems to me most strange that men should fear,   35
Seeing that death, a necessary end,
Will come when it will come.

Enter a Servant.

What say the augurers?
Serv. They would not have you to stir forth to-day.
Plucking the entrails of an offering forth,
They could not find a heart within the beast.   40
Cæs. The gods do this in shame of cowardice:
Cæsar should be a beast without a heart
If he should stay at home to-day for fear.
No, Cæsar shall not. Danger knows full well
That Cæsar is more dangerous than he.   45
We are two lions litter'd in one day,

44–8. No, . . . forth.] *F; in margin Pope, Hanmer.*   46. are] *Upton, Capell;* heare
Ff1, 2; hear *Ff3, 4;* were *Theobald.*

1 H 6, i. i. 1–5; Googe, *The Zodiake of
Life* (1576), p. 224, "The blasing
starres do oft appeare, that fall of
Prince doth showe." Plutarch relates
that a very bright comet appeared for
some nights after Cæsar's death.

32–3. *Cowards die . . . but once*] Plutarch (*Cæsar*, Sk., p. 92): "And when
some of his friends did counsel him to
have a guard for the safety of his person, and some also did offer themselves to serve him, he would never
consent to it, but said: 'It was better to
die once, than always to be afraid of
death.'" Cf. Marston and Barkstead,
The Insatiate Countess (ed. Wood), IV.
iii. 97, "A hundred times in life a
coward dies."

36–7. *Seeing that . . . will come*] Cf.
Ham., v. ii. 232–8. Hamlet faces death
with similar equanimity: "the readiness is all."

39–40. *Plucking . . . the beast*] In Plutarch it is Cæsar himself who carries out
this sacrifice and discovers the omen.

46. *we are*] The Folios read *we
hear(e)*. Theobald suggested *we were,*
and Capell *we are,* which modern editors accept. It is a simple change and
gives good sense. But the Folio *heare* is
difficult to explain. Wilson's suggestion, that it "looks like an 'intelligent'
correction with reference to ll. 15–17",
is far-fetched. Moreover, the word is
retained in the later Folios. It is just
possible that Shakespeare is using *hear*
in one of the senses of the Greek
ἀκούειν and the Latin *audire*: i.e.,
(*a*) "to be called or styled, to pass for";
and (*b*) with the adverbs εὖ and
κακῶς, *bene* and *male*, "to be reputed
in such and such a way". With (*a*) cf.
Milton, *Par. L.*, III. 7, "Or hear'st thou
rather pure ethereal stream"; with (*b*)
cf. Spenser, *F.Q.*, I. v. 23, "If old
Aveugles sonnes so evil hear", and
Milton, *Areop.* (ed. Hales), p. 24, "for
which England hears ill abroad".
Though this might to some readers
seem too bold a classical construction

And I the elder and more terrible,
And Cæsar shall go forth.

Cal.   Alas, my lord,
Your wisdom is consum'd in confidence.
Do not go forth to-day: call it my fear   50
That keeps you in the house, and not your own.
We'll send Mark Antony to the Senate House,
And he shall say you are not well to-day.
Let me upon my knee prevail in this.

Cæs. Mark Antony shall say I am not well,   55
And for thy humour I will stay at home.

Enter DECIUS.

Here's Decius Brutus; he shall tell them so.

Dec. Cæsar, all hail! Good morrow, worthy Cæsar.
I come to fetch you to the Senate House.

Cæs. And you are come in very happy time   60
To bear my greeting to the senators,
And tell them that I will not come to-day:
Cannot, is false; and that I dare not, falser;
I will not come to-day. Tell them so, Decius.

Cal. Say he is sick.

Cæs.   Shall Cæsar send a lie?   65
Have I in conquest stretch'd mine arm so far,
To be afeard to tell greybeards the truth?

for Shakespeare to use, its recognition as an English usage might explain the retention of *hear(e)* in the later Folios, even if it were a mistake in the First. On the supposition that the Folio *heare* may be a corruption, Dr Harold Brooks has suggested to me the possibility that it is due to an error of the copyist, who, having just written *he* at the end of the previous line, unconsciously began the new line with *He are* instead of *We are*. The corrector, perhaps preparing the MS. as copy, correctly supplied *We*, but failed to delete *He*. The compositor, altering the *H* to lower-case *h* because it did not begin the line, set up *We he are*; then either he or the proof-corrector closed up *he are*,

producing the Folio reading *We heare*.

49. *Your wisdom ... confidence*] A fair comment on Cæsar's thrasonical bragging in this scene.

56. *for thy humour*] to fall in with your mood, or caprice.

60. *happy time*] favourable time, time of good hap. Cf. *Oth.*, III.i. 32, "in a happy hour"; and *Ham.*, v. ii. 214.

65. *Shall Cæsar . . . lie?*] But note l. 55. It seems to be one thing to send a lie by a confidential friend like Antony, who in any case has not seen Cæsar this morning; another thing to do so by Decius, who, though Cæsar loves him (l. 74), is not on such intimate terms with him, and who can see that he is not sick.

    Decius, go tell them Cæsar will not come.

Dec. Most mighty Cæsar, let me know some cause,
    Lest I be laugh'd at when I tell them so.   70

Cæs. The cause is in my will: I will not come;
    That is enough to satisfy the Senate.
    But for your private satisfaction,
    Because I love you, I will let you know:
    Calphurnia here, my wife, stays me at home.   75
    She dreamt to-night she saw my statue,
    Which like a fountain with an hundred spouts
    Did run pure blood; and many lusty Romans
    Came smiling, and did bathe their hands in it.
    And these does she apply for warnings and portents   80
    And evils imminent; and on her knee
    Hath begg'd that I will stay at home to-day.

Dec. This dream is all amiss interpreted;
    It was a vision fair and fortunate:
    Your statue spouting blood in many pipes,   85
    In which so many smiling Romans bath'd,
    Signifies that from you great Rome shall suck
    Reviving blood, and that great men shall press
    For tinctures, stains, relics, and cognizance.

---

76. to-night] to night *F;* last night *Rowe.*   81. And] *F;* Of *Hanmer et al.*

---

71. *will . . . will*] The first *will* suggests rather "caprice" than any normal modern sense of the word. Cæsar, the mighty conqueror (l. 66), will not stoop to provide explanations for the *greybeards* of the Senate. The second *will* emphasizes his "wilful" determination: "I am not willing to come, and there's an end to the matter."

76 ff. *She dreamt to-night . . .*] According to Plutarch, Calphurnia "dreamed that Cæsar was slain" (Sk., p. 98). Shakespeare gives her a dream which deliberately anticipates the fact (reported later by Plutarch) that at Cæsar's death Pompey's statue ran blood; Antony refers to this "fact" in his oration (III.ii. 190–1). The dream also anticipates the episode in which the conspirators bathe their hands

in Cæsar's blood (III. i. 105–13).

76. *statue*] Here and in III.ii. 190 the word must be pronounced as a trisyllable to preserve the pentameter, though in l. 85 below it is disyllabic. Some editors respell it *statua*, which was a common Elizabethan variant.

80. *And these . . . portents*] One of the rare alexandrines in the play. *Portent*, as normally in Shakespeare, is accented on the second syllable. It is possible that the initial *And* was not intended by Shakespeare, and crept in because the compositor's eye caught the initial *And* in the following line. Without the *And* it would be possible to scan the line as a pentameter.

89. *For tinctures . . . cognizance*] Johnson explains thus: "There are two allusions: one to coats armorial, to which princes make additions, or give

This by Calphurnia's dream is signified.   90
Cæs. And this way have you well expounded it.
Dec. I have, when you have heard what I can say:
And know it now. The Senate have concluded
To give this day a crown to mighty Cæsar.
If you shall send them word you will not come,   95
Their minds may change. Besides, it were a mock
Apt to be render'd, for some one to say,
"Break up the Senate till another time,
When Cæsar's wife shall meet with better dreams."
If Cæsar hide himself, shall they not whisper,   100
"Lo, Cæsar is afraid"?
Pardon me, Cæsar; for my dear dear love
To your proceeding bids me tell you this,
And reason to my love is liable.
Cæs. How foolish do your fears seem now, Calphurnia!   105
I am ashamed I did yield to them.
Give me my robe, for I will go.

Enter BRUTUS, [CAIUS] LIGARIUS, METELLUS,
CASCA, TREBONIUS, CINNA, *and* PUBLIUS.

And look where Publius is come to fetch me.
Pub. Good morrow, Cæsar.

new *tinctures* and new marks of cognizance; the other to martyrs, whose reliques are preserved with veneration. The Romans, says Decius, all come to you, as to a saint, for reliques; as to a prince, for honours." We must suppose that the *relics* and *cognizances* envisaged by Decius would take some such form as handkerchiefs dipped in Cæsar's *reviving blood.* Cf. III. ii. 135. *Cognizance* is here used in something like its proper heraldic sense, "device or emblem worn by retainers". Cf. *I H 6*, II. iv. 108, where it is again associated with blood: "this pale and angry rose, / As cognizance of my blood-drinking hate, / Will I for ever and my faction wear." Taken in by Decius's flattering interpretation of the dream, Cæsar rejects Calphurnia's, seeing himself as a symbol of vitality and nourishment for the Romans.

96–7. *a mock . . . render'd*] a sarcastic retort likely to be made.

102–3. *my dear . . . proceeding*] my very deep interest in your advancement.

104. *And reason . . . liable*] and my reason is subordinate to my love: i.e., my love makes me say what my judgement tells me is out of place.

107. *Give me my robe*] Cf. *Ant.*, v. ii. 282, where, however, Cleopatra goes consciously and gladly to her death.

108. *Publius*] Shakespeare may have taken the name from "Publius Silicius who, as Plutarch relates, wept when Brutus was summoned to appear before the judges. He was proscribed by the Triumvirs, and put to death" (Macmillan). See note on III. i. 85.

Cæs.   Welcome, Publius.
What, Brutus, are you stirr'd so early too?   110
Good morrow, Casca. Caius Ligarius,
Cæsar was ne'er so much your enemy
As that same ague which hath made you lean.
What is't a clock?
Bru.   Cæsar, 'tis strucken eight.
Cæs. I thank you for your pains and courtesy.   115

Enter ANTONY.

See! Antony, that revels long a-nights,
Is notwithstanding up. Good morrow, Antony.
Ant. So to most noble Cæsar.
Cæs.   Bid them prepare within.
I am to blame to be thus waited for.
Now, Cinna; now, Metellus; what, Trebonius: 120
I have an hour's talk in store for you;
Remember that you call on me to-day:
Be near me, that I may remember you.
Treb. Cæsar, I will: [*Aside.*] and so near will I be,
That your best friends shall wish I had been further.   125
Cæs. Good friends, go in, and taste some wine with me;
And we, like friends, will straightway go together.
Bru. [*Aside.*] That every like is not the same, O Cæsar!
The heart of Brutus earns to think upon.   [*Exeunt.*

129. earns] earnes *F;* yearns *Capell.*

113. *lean*] Unconscious irony. We
recall what Cæsar said about lean men
at I. ii. 191–2.

118. *prepare within*] Presumably,
prepare the wine (l. 126).

120–3. *Now, Cinna ... remember you*]
A touch of the great Cæsar, who has an
affable and courteous word for each of
his visitors.

124–5. *and so near ... further*] Actually Trebonius does not stab Cæsar;

his task is to lure Antony away.

128–9. *That every like ... think upon*]
Brutus grieves to think that being *like
friends* is not the same as actually being friends.

129. *earns*] grieves. Cf. *H* 5, II. iii. 3,
6, "my manly heart doth earn ... for
Falstaff he is dead, / And we must earn
therefore"; Jonson, *Bartholomew Fair,*
IV. vi. 143, "Alas poore wretch! how it
earnes my heart for him!"

[SCENE III.—*A Street near the Capitol.*]

Enter ARTEMIDORUS [*reading a paper*].

Art. Cæsar, beware of Brutus; take heed of Cassius; come not near Casca; have an eye to Cinna; trust not Trebonius; mark well Metellus Cimber; Decius Brutus loves thee not; thou hast wrong'd Caius Ligarius. There is but one mind in all these men, and it is bent against Cæsar. If thou beest not immortal, look about you: security gives way to conspiracy. The mighty gods defend thee! Thy lover, 5

> *Artemidorus.*

Here will I stand till Cæsar pass along,
And as a suitor will I give him this. 10
My heart laments that virtue cannot live
Out of the teeth of emulation.
If thou read this, O Cæsar, thou may'st live;
If not, the Fates with traitors do contrive.   [*Exit.*

Scene III

13. may'st] *Rowe;* mayest *F.*

S.D. *Artemidorus*] For Plutarch's account of Artemidorus, "a doctor of rhetoric in the Greek tongue", see Appendix, pp. 146–7.

1–5. Cæsar, beware . . . against Cæsar] Dr Harold Brooks has drawn my attention to this passage as one of several which seem to show that Shakespeare made use of the account of Cæsar's death in *A Mirror for Magistrates*. Plutarch does not tell us what was in the memorial that Artemidorus presented to Cæsar. In *Caius Iulius Cæsar* (*Parts Added to The Mirror for Magistrates*, ed. L. B. Campbell, p. 301), ll. 361–3, we find: "There met mee by the way a *Romayne* good, / Presenting mee a scrole of euery

name: / And all their whole deuise that sought my bloud."

6. security . . . conspiracy] freedom from suspicion leaves the way open for conspiracy. In Elizabethan English *security* normally has meanings close to those of the Latin *securitas*, "freedom from care or suspicion, over-confidence, want of caution". Cf. *Mac.*, III. v. 32, "And you all know, security / Is mortals' chiefest enemy."

7. lover] devoted friend. Cf. III. ii. 13; and 46, "as I slew my best lover for the good of Rome".

12. *Out of . . . emulation*] beyond the reach of envious rivalry.

14. *contrive*] conspire, plot. Cf. II. i. 158, "a shrewd contriver".

[SCENE IV.—*Before the House of Brutus.*]

Enter PORTIA *and* LUCIUS.

Por. I prithee, boy, run to the Senate House.
   Stay not to answer me, but get thee gone.
   Why dost thou stay?
Luc.   To know my errand, madam.
Por. I would have had thee there and here again
   Ere I can tell thee what thou should'st do there.   5
   O constancy, be strong upon my side;
   Set a huge mountain 'tween my heart and tongue!
   I have a man's mind, but a woman's might.
   How hard it is for women to keep counsel!
   Art thou here yet?
Luc.   Madam, what should I do?   10
   Run to the Capitol, and nothing else?
   And so return to you, and nothing else?
Por. Yes, bring me word, boy, if thy lord look well,
   For he went sickly forth; and take good note
   What Cæsar doth, what suitors press to him.   15
   Hark, boy, what noise is that?
Luc. I hear none, madam.
Por.   Prithee, listen well.
   I heard a bustling rumour, like a fray,

Scene IV

2. *thee*] In Shakespeare the pronoun *thou* is used "(1) In addressing relatives or friends affectionately, (2) by masters when speaking good-humouredly or confidentially to servants, . . . (3) in contemptuous or angry speech to strangers, . . . and (4) in solemn style generally" (Onions). In this scene Portia is addressing inferiors, whom she addresses as *thou*, and is answered as *you*. Shakespeare is by no means consistent about these distinctions; but note that Brutus and Cassius use *you* in their quarrel (IV. iii), until Cassius, moving towards a reconciliation, drops into *thou* at l. 102.

6. *constancy*] firmness, self-control. Cf. II. i. 227, 299.

9. *How hard . . . counsel*] It is clear that Portia now knows the secret that Brutus promised to impart to her (II. i. 305-6). In fact he has had no opportunity of seeing her since he made the promise; but the inconsistency would not be noticed in the theatre.

18. *bustling rumour*] "noise of stir and tumult" (Wright). Cf. *John*, v. iv. 45, "the noise and rumour of the field". With this use of *bustling* to describe a sound cf. Sir Arthur Gorges, *The Olympian Catastrophe (Poems*, ed. H. E. Sandison, p. 141), l. 64, "sturdie archers bearinge bowes ybent, / With sheaves of steele-shodd-shaftes, girt to there shancks / Whose feathers made a bustlinge as they went".

And the wind brings it from the Capitol.
Luc. Sooth, madam, I hear nothing.   20

Enter the Soothsayer.

Por. Come hither, fellow. Which way hast thou been?
Sooth. At mine own house, good lady.
Por. What is 't a clock?
Sooth.   About the ninth hour, lady.
Por. Is Cæsar yet gone to the Capitol?
Sooth. Madam, not yet. I go to take my stand,   25
   To see him pass on to the Capitol.
Por. Thou hast some suit to Cæsar, hast thou not?
Sooth. That I have, lady, if it will please Cæsar
   To be so good to Cæsar as to hear me:
   I shall beseech him to befriend himself.   30
Por. Why, know'st thou any harm's intended towards him?
Sooth. None that I know will be, much that I fear may
      chance.
   Good morrow to you. Here the street is narrow.
   The throng that follows Cæsar at the heels,
   Of senators, of prætors, common suitors,   35
   Will crowd a feeble man almost to death:
   I'll get me to a place more void, and there
   Speak to great Cæsar as he comes along.   [*Exit.*
Por. I must go in. Ay me, how weak a thing
   The heart of woman is! O Brutus,   40
   The heavens speed thee in thine enterprise!
   [*Aside.*] Sure, the boy heard me. Brutus hath a suit

32.] *As Rowe;* None . . . be, / . . . chance: / *F.*   39.] *As Rowe;* I . . . in: /
. . . thing / *F.*

20. *I hear nothing*] Actually Cæsar
has not yet gone to the Capitol (l. 25).
In her overwrought state Portia
imagines ominous sounds.

23. *ninth hour*] Shakespeare again
thinking in terms of modern chronology. Cf. II. i. 192, II. ii. 114.

28. *That I have*] Yet in the next
scene he presents no suit; hence Tyr-
whitt wished to give these speeches to
Artemidorus, who is waiting in the

street expressly to present a suit to
Cæsar. But the change is unnecessary,
for the Soothsayer does at any rate
speak to Cæsar at the beginning of the
next scene.

32. *None . . . may chance*] In the Folio
this is printed as two half lines, but
modern editors run them together as
an alexandrine.

37. *more void*] more empty, less
crowded.

That Cæsar will not grant. [*Aside.*] O, I grow faint.
Run, Lucius, and commend me to my lord;
Say I am merry; come to me again,　　　　　45
And bring me word what he doth say to thee.

　　　　　　　　　　[*Exeunt* [*severally*].

45. *merry*] in good spirits.

ACT III

[SCENE I.—*Rome. Before the Capitol.*]

Flourish. Enter Cæsar, Brutus, Cassius, Casca, Decius, Metellus [Cimber], Trebonius, Cinna, Antony, Lepidus, Artemidorus, Publius, [Popilius,] *and the Soothsayer.*

Cæs. The ides of March are come.
Sooth. Ay, Cæsar, but not gone.
Art. Hail, Cæsar! Read this schedule.
Dec. Trebonius doth desire you to o'er-read,
    At your best leisure, this his humble suit.   5
Art. O Cæsar, read mine first; for mine's a suit

ACT III
Scene 1

S.D. [Popilius]] Not in the Folio S.D.; but he speaks in l. 13.

1–2. *The ides . . . not gone*] In Plutarch's version: "Cæsar going unto the Senate-house, and speaking merrily unto the soothsayer, told him, 'the Ides of March be come': 'so they be,' softly answered the soothsayer, 'but yet are they not past.'" In the *Caius Iulius Cæsar* of the *Mirror for Magistrates* (*op. cit.*, p. 301), ll. 374–5: "(Quod I) the Ides of Marche bee come, yet harme is none. / (Quod hee) the Ides of Marche be come, yet th'ar not gone." Shakespeare's change from Plutarch's *not past* to *not gone* is small, and natural enough as providing a more direct antithesis to *are come*, but in view of the parallels noted at II. iii. 1–5 and 6–10 below, it may be due to Shakespeare's knowledge of the *Mirror* passage, as Dr Brooks has suggested.

3. *schedule*] paper, document.

4–5. *Trebonius . . . suit*] This is the first and last that we hear of a suit from Trebonius, who has the important task of removing Antony (l. 25) before Cæsar is killed. Decius is, rightly, suspicious of Artemidorus, and he breaks in to distract Cæsar's mind from Artemidorus's schedule. Possibly we are intended to think that he has had the foresight to provide against such a potential danger as now threatens; but in any case an audience will forget Trebonius's "suit" in the rapid course of the events that follow.

6–10. *O Cæsar . . . fellow mad?*] Cf. *Mirror for Magistrates* (*op. cit.*, p. 301), ll. 365–7, where Cæsar says: "But I supposde that for some suit hee came, / I heedelesse bare this scrole in my left hand, / And others more, till leasure, left unscand." Plutarch (see Appendix, p. 147) represents Cæsar as attempting to read the schedule,

That touches Cæsar nearer. Read it, great Cæsar.
Cæs. What touches us ourself shall be last serv'd.
Art. Delay not, Cæsar. Read it instantly.
Cæs. What, is the fellow mad?
Pub.   Sirrah, give place.   10
Cas. What, urge you your petitions in the street?
Come to the Capitol.

[CÆSAR, *and the rest, enter the Senate.*]

Pop. I wish your enterprise to-day may thrive.
Cas. What enterprise, Popilius?
Pop.   Fare you well.
[*Leaves him and joins Cæsar.*]
Bru. What said Popilius Lena?   15
Cas. He wish'd to-day our enterprise might thrive.
I fear our purpose is discovered.
Bru. Look how he makes to Cæsar: mark him.
Cas. Casca, be sudden, for we fear prevention.
Brutus, what shall be done? If this be known,   20
Cassius or Cæsar never shall turn back,
For I will slay myself.
Bru.   Cassius, be constant: ⸺
Popilius Lena speaks not of our purposes;
For look, he smiles, and Cæsar doth not change.
Cas. Trebonius knows his time; for look you, Brutus,   25

12. S.D. *Cæsar . . . Senate.*] *Capell; not in F.*   14. S.D. *Leaves . . . Cæsar.*] *Capell; not in F.*   21. or] *F; on conj. Malone, Craik.*

Shakespeare as refusing to do so. Shakespeare may have taken a hint here from the *Mirror* account, and improved on it by adding the character-revealing touch of l. 8. Perhaps not entirely irrelevant in this connection is the fact that Shakespeare, like the *Mirror*, uses the word *suit* in the Artemidorus passage (cf. *suitor*, II. iii. 10), whereas North speaks of "supplications" and "this memorial", and does not use *suit* until he comes to tell of Metellus Cimber's suit.

8. *What touches . . . last serv'd*] what concerns myself must be last attended to. Another glimpse of the "royal" Cæsar; his sense of his own greatness is emphasized by the "royal we" in *us ourself*.

18. *makes to*] advances towards.

19. *sudden*] speedy, prompt.

fear prevention] fear that we shall be forestalled. Cf. II. i. 85.

22. *constant*] composed, resolute. Cf. II. i. 227; II. iv. 6.

25–6. *Trebonius . . . the way*] Thus in Plutarch's *Cæsar*; in the *Brutus* Decius draws Antony out of the way.

He draws Mark Antony out of the way.

> [*Exeunt Antony and Trebonius.*]

Dec. Where is Metellus Cimber? Let him go,
And presently prefer his suit to Cæsar.

Bru. He is address'd. Press near and second him.

Cin. Casca, you are the first that rears your hand.   30

Cæs. Are we all ready? What is now amiss
That Cæsar and his senate must redress?

Met. Most high, most mighty, and most puissant Cæsar,
Metellus Cimber throws before thy seat
An humble heart,—   [*Kneeling.*]

Cæs.   I must prevent thee, Cimber.   35
These couchings and these lowly courtesies
Might fire the blood of ordinary men,
And turn pre-ordinance and first decree
Into the law of children. Be not fond,
To think that Cæsar bears such rebel blood   40
That will be thaw'd from the true quality

26 S.D. *Exeunt ... Trebonius.*] *Malone; not in F.* 35. S.D. *Kneeling.*] *Not in F.* 39. law] *Johnson;* lane *F;* line *conj. Steevens;* play *conj. Mason;* lune *conj. Macmillan.*

28. *presently*] immediately.

prefer] offer, present.

29. *address'd*] prepared, ready.

32. *Cæsar and his senate*] Shakespeare again emphasizes Cæsar's arrogant assumption of the rights of royalty. His words recall those of Wolsey, *H 8*, III. ii. 315, "Ego et rex meus".

36. *These couchings ... courtesies*] this bowing and humble obeisance. *Curtsies* in l. 43 is a disyllabic variant of *courtesies*; in modern usage the words have become differentiated in sense according to their spelling.

38–9. *And turn pre-ordinance ... law of children*] and change what has been ordained and decreed from the first in the capricious manner of children. Johnson emended the Folio *lane* to *law*, of which sense may be made. Macmillan proposed *lune* (="caprice"), comparing *Wint.*, II. ii. 30, "these dangerous unsafe lunes i' the king"; but there the meaning is rather "frenzies" than "caprices". Nearer

"caprice" is *lines* in *Troil.*, II. iii. 140, "His pettish lines, his ebbs, his flows", and perhaps in *Wiv.*, IV. ii. 22, "your husband is in his old lines again" (="fits of temper, 'goings-on'"); in both these passages most modern editors change *lines* to *lunes*, but probably unnecessarily, since there is a Warwickshire phrase, *on a line*, which means "in a rage" (Onions). No satisfactory justification of *lane* has been offered, and though it was retained in the later Folios, this may have been from ignorance of what was intended. Johnson's *law* seems the best emendation yet suggested, and perhaps it gains support from the proximity of *pre-ordinance* and *decree*. Moreover, the misreading of *lawe* as *lane* supposes only a minim miscount.

39–40. *Be not fond, To think*] be not so foolish as to think.

40. *rebel blood*] unreliable disposition.

41. *the true quality*] i.e., the stable quality it ought to have.

With that which melteth fools—I mean sweet words,
Low-crooked curtsies, and base spaniel fawning.
Thy brother by decree is banished:
If thou dost bend and pray and fawn for him,   45
I spurn thee like a cur out of my way.
Know, Cæsar doth not wrong, nor without cause

42–3. *sweet words . . . spaniel fawning*] Cf. *Ham.*, III. ii. 65–7; and *H 8*, v. iii. 126, "You play the spaniel / And think with wagging of your tongue to win me." Cf. also v. i. 41–4. Imagery associating flatterers with fawning dogs (and with sweetness and melting) is frequent in Shakespeare. See Caroline Spurgeon, *Shakespeare's Imagery*, pp. 195–9.

47–8. *Know, Cæsar doth . . . be satisfied*] Round these words there has accumulated a vast deal of commentary which has its source in two passages in Ben Jonson. In *Timber: Or Discoveries Made Vpon Men And Matter*, after the famous words which express his love of Shakespeare and admiration of his talents, Jonson goes on: "Many times hee fell into those things, could not escape laughter: As when hee said in the person of Cæsar, one speaking to him; *Cæsar thou dost me wrong.* Hee replyed: *Cæsar did never wrong, but with just cause:* and such like; which were ridiculous." Then in the Induction to *The Staple of News* (1626), the Prologue says to Expectation: "*Cry you mercy*, you neuer did wrong, but with iust cause", where the difference in the type shows that a quotation is intended, and the context that the quotation is used satirically. Both passages were written some years after the first production of *Julius Cæsar*; but the play was extremely popular and was frequently revived by the acting company of which Jonson himself was a member, and it is unlikely that either deliberately or accidentally he misquoted, as has been suggested, especially since he was renowned for the accuracy of his verbal memory; and, too, the point of the quotation in *The Staple of News* largely

depended on its being recognized by the audience. It seems probable, therefore, that the Folio version represents an alteration made by Shakespeare or his company, perhaps in deference to a spoken criticism by Jonson, though if it were made in the prompt-book, we must assume that the players nevertheless continued to use the earlier version if it was recognized by the audience of *The Staple of News* in 1626; if not in the actual prompt-book, it must at any rate, presumably on the earlier authority of Shakespeare, have been made in the MS. used by the compositors of the First Folio. Accepting the hypothesis of some alteration, supported perhaps by the broken line in the Folio, we may suppose some such original version as follows: "*Cæs.* . . . . I spurn thee like a cur out of my way. / *Met.* Cæsar, thou dost me wrong. / *Cæs.* Know, Cæsar doth not wrong but with just cause, / Nor without cause will he be satisfied." From this the Folio version would be produced by deleting *but with just cause*, and filling out the line from that which follows. I add a parallel to the Jonsonian form of the speech, for which I am indebted to Mr John Crow: Nicholas Breton, *A Floorish upon Fancie* (1577) (ed. Grosart, p. 20), "done her wrong without just cause". The passage cannot be adequately dealt with in a footnote; for a full and balanced treatment see Dover Wilson in *Shakespeare Survey, 2*, pp. 38–42. Also illuminating is John Palmer in *Political Characters of Shakespeare*, pp. 44–6. A summary of the comments of earlier editors is to be found in Furness's Variorum *Julius Cæsar*, pp. 136–40.

Will he be satisfied.

Met. Is there no voice more worthy than my own,
To sound more sweetly in great Cæsar's ear   50
For the repealing of my banish'd brother?

Bru. I kiss thy hand, but not in flattery, Cæsar,
Desiring thee that Publius Cimber may
Have an immediate freedom of repeal.

Cæs. What, Brutus?

Cas.   Pardon, Cæsar; Cæsar, pardon: 55
As low as to thy foot doth Cassius fall,
To beg enfranchisement for Publius Cimber.

Cæs. I could be well mov'd, if I were as you;
If I could pray to move, prayers would move me;
But I am constant as the northern star,   60
Of whose true-fix'd and resting quality
There is no fellow in the firmament.
The skies are painted with unnumber'd sparks,
They are all fire, and every one doth shine;
But there's but one in all doth hold his place.   65
So in the world: 'tis furnish'd well with men,
And men are flesh and blood, and apprehensive;
Yet in the number I do know but one
That unassailable holds on his rank,
Unshak'd of motion; and that I am he,   70
Let me a little show it, even in this,

61. true-fix'd] true-fixt *Capell;* true fixt *F;* true, fixt *Rowe.*

51–4. *repealing . . . freedom of repeal*]
recalling from banishment . . . permission to return (be recalled) from banishment.

53. *Publius Cimber*] Shakespeare
seems to have provided Metellus's
brother with the name Publius. Plutarch does not name him.

55–7. *Pardon . . . Cimber*] A piece of
consummate hypocrisy on the part of
Cassius. From the dramatic point of
view the servility of Metellus and
Cassius is important in that it pro-
vokes Cæsar into such extravagant expressions of arrogance that all sympathy for him is alienated, and the
action of the assassins is for the mo-

ment almost accepted as justifiable.

59. *If I could pray to move*] if, like you,
I could pray others to change their
minds.

60. *constant as the northern star*] un-
changing as the pole star.

61. *true-fix'd and resting quality*] immovable and changeless quality.

63. *unnumber'd*] innumerable. Cf.
Lr., IV. vi. 22, "unnumber'd idle
pebbles".

67. *apprehensive*] possessed of reason.
Cf. *All's W.*, I. ii. 60, "apprehensive
senses".

69. *holds on his rank*] keeps his position—like the pole star. Cf. *Oth.*, II. i.
15, "the ever fixed pole".

That I was constant Cimber should be banish'd,
And constant do remain to keep him so.
Cin. O Cæsar—
Cæs.   Hence! Wilt thou lift up Olympus?
Dec. Great Cæsar—
Cæs.   Doth not Brutus bootless kneel?   75
Casca. Speak hands for me!   [*They stab Cæsar.*
Cæs. Et tu, Brute?–Then fall Cæsar!   [*Dies.*
Cin. Liberty! Freedom! Tyranny is dead!
    Run hence, proclaim, cry it about the streets.
Cas. Some to the common pulpits, and cry out,   80
    "Liberty, freedom, and enfranchisement!"
Bru. People and senators, be not affrighted.
    Fly not; stand still; ambition's debt is paid.
Casca. Go to the pulpit, Brutus.
Dec.   And Cassius too.
Bru. Where's Publius?   85

74. *lift up Olympus*] try the impossibe. The metaphor is in keeping with the side of Cæsar that Shakespeare is for the moment emphasizing; it implies that gods like Cæsar are not to be moved.

75. *bootless*] without avail.

77. Et tu, Brute?] The origin of this is probably Suetonius's account of the assassination (*Jul. Cæs.*, 82): "atque ita tribus et viginti plagis confossus est uno modo ad primum ictum gemitu sine voce edito, etsi tradiderunt quidam Marco Bruto irruenti dixisse: καὶ σύ, τέκνον;" ("And thou, my son?"). According to Suetonius, Cæsar had an intrigue with Brutus's mother, Servilia; and Plutarch, developing the theme, says that "because Brutus was born in that time when their love was hottest, he persuaded himself that he begat him." Shakespeare makes no use of this supposed relationship. The actual words, *Et tu, Brute*, are not found in any classical writer; they are first known in *The True Tragedie of Richard Duke of Yorke* (printed 1595), Praetorius Facs., xxi. 53, "Et tu, Brute, wilt thou stab *Cæsar* too?" This line occurs also in Nichol-

son's *Acolastus his Afterwitte* (1600). It is possible, as Malone suggested, that the Latin phrase was used in the lost *Epilogus Cæsaris Interfecti*, written by Richard Edes, and acted at Oxford in 1582. Ben Jonson uses it for comic effect in *Every Man Out of His Humour*, v. vi. 79. Indeed it seems to have become something of a stage commonplace. Cf. "What, Brutus too?" in *Cæsar's Revenge* (*c.* 1594). In the *Caius Iulius Cæsar* added to the tragic stories of *A Mirror for Magistrates* in 1587 (ed. L. B. Campbell), l. 385, we find again, "And Brutus thou my sonne (quoth I) whom erst I loued best?"

80. *pulpits*] platforms, or stages (Latin, *pulpitum*). North's phrase is "the pulpit for orations", meaning the rostra in the Forum.

83. *ambition's debt*] what was due to Cæsar's ambition. Brutus is reassuring the frightened assembly; no one else is to be touched.

85. 89. *Publius*] "Shakespeare picks out one Senator . . . and focuses our attention on him—thus in effect dramatizing the situation. Publius is an aged man, too feeble and panic-stricken to move when the rest flee.

Cin. Here, quite confounded with this mutiny.
Met. Stand fast together, lest some friend of Cæsar's
    Should chance—
Bru. Talk not of standing. Publius, good cheer;
    There is no harm intended to your person,   90
    Nor to no Roman else. So tell them, Publius.
Cas. And leave us, Publius, lest that the people,
    Rushing on us, should do your age some mischief.
Bru. Do so; and let no man abide this deed
    But we the doers.   95

Enter TREBONIUS.

Cas. Where is Antony?
Tre.   Fled to his house amaz'd.
    Men, wives, and children stare, cry out, and run,
    As it were doomsday.
Bru.   Fates, we will know your pleasures.
    That we shall die, we know; 'tis but the time
    And drawing days out, that men stand upon.   100
Casca. Why, he that cuts off twenty years of life
    Cuts off so many years of fearing death.

101. *Casca.*] *Cask. F; Cas. Pope et al.*

The humane Brutus remembers him and wishes to protect him. Then, finding him safe, he tries to utilize the aged senator's influence in quieting the panic. Cf. II. ii. 108" (Kittredge).

86. *mutiny*] uproar, tumult.

89. *Talk not of standing*] Brutus is confident that, when the deed is explained to the people, they will be satisfied. There is no need for the conspirators to stand fast together to defend themselves, as Metellus has suggested.

94. *abide*] pay the penalty for. Cf. III. ii. 116, and *MND.*, III. ii. 175, 335 (Q1 *aby* in both passages).

96. *amaz'd*] utterly confounded.

99-100. *That we . . . stand upon*] A common proverb in Elizabethan literature. Cf. Greene, *Never Too Late* (ed. Grosart, vol. VIII, p. 125), "Wee haue nothing more certaine than to

dye, nor nothing more uncertaine than the houre of death." Brutus's words are, in fact, a paraphrase of Cæsar's at II. ii. 35–7.

100. *drawing days out*] prolonging life.

stand upon] attach importance to. Cf. II. ii. 13.

101–2. *Why, he . . . fearing death*] Pope and many other editors give this speech to Cassius, feeling that it is more appropriate to him; Aldis Wright on the grounds that he is a Stoic. But note v. i. 77, where he says he is an Epicurean. Admittedly Casca is not a very consistent character, but these words resemble what he says at I. iii. 101–2, and I think they must remain his. He now disappears from the play, "perhaps because the actor taking the part was required to play Octavius" (Dover Wilson).

Bru. Grant that, and then is death a benefit:
So are we Cæsar's friends, that have abridg'd
His time of fearing death. Stoop, Romans, stoop,   105
And let us bathe our hands in Cæsar's blood
Up to the elbows, and besmear our swords:
Then walk we forth, even to the market-place,
And waving our red weapons o'er our heads,
Let's all cry, "Peace, freedom, and liberty!"   110
Cas. Stoop then, and wash. How many ages hence
Shall this our lofty scene be acted over,
In states unborn, and accents yet unknown!
Bru. How many times shall Cæsar bleed in sport,
That now on Pompey's basis lies along,   115
No worthier than the dust!
Cas.   So oft as that shall be,
So often shall the knot of us be call'd
The men that gave their country liberty.
Dec. What, shall we forth?
Cas.   Ay, every man away.
Brutus shall lead, and we will grace his heels   120

105–10. Stoop, . . . liberty!"] *F; Casc.* Stoop, . . . liberty!" *Pope, Warburton.*
113. states] *F2;* State *F1.*   114. *Bru.*] *F; Casc. Pope, Hanmer.*   115. lies] lyes
F2; lye *F1.*   116. *Cas.*] *F; Bru. Pope, Hanmer.*

105–10. *Stoop, Romans . . . liberty*] Of
these lines Pope says: "In all the editions this speech is ascribed to Brutus,
than which nothing is more inconsistent with his mild and philosophical
character." He therefore ascribes them
to Casca, in which Warburton follows
him. But Brutus is inviting his fellow-
conspirators to join him in taking full
responsibility for the assassination, and
by this symbolical act to confirm what
he has said in ll. 94–5. Thus too the
prophecy in Calphurnia's dream is
fulfilled. This little ceremony is of
Shakespeare's own devising. According to Plutarch, "the conspirators
thronging one upon another, because
every man was desirous to have a cut
at him, so many swords and daggers
lighting upon one body, one of
them hurt another, and among them
Brutus caught a blow on his hand, be-

cause he would make one in murthering of him, and all the rest also were
every man of them bloodied" (Sk.,
p. 119).

111–14. *How many . . . in sport*] Cf.
Ham., III. ii. 108, "*Pol:* I did enact
Julius Cæsar: I was kill'd i' the Capi-
tol; Brutus killed me."

115. *Pompey's basis*] "the base
whereupon Pompey's image stood"
(North).

lies along] lies stretched out. Cf.
AYL., II. i. 30, "as he lay along /
Under an oak". The First Folio
wrongly prints *lye along.*

117. *knot*] group of men bound together in a conspiracy. Cf. *Wiv.,* IV.
ii. 126; and *R 3,* III. i. 182, "ancient
knot of dangerous adversaries". During the Interregnum the inner council
of the Royalist party in England was
called the Sealed Knot.

With the most boldest and best hearts of Rome.

Enter a Servant.

Bru. Soft, who comes here? A friend of Antony's.
Serv. Thus, Brutus, did my master bid me kneel;
Thus did Mark Antony bid me fall down;
And, being prostrate, thus he bade me say: 125
Brutus is noble, wise, valiant, and honest;
Cæsar was mighty, bold, royal, and loving:
Say I love Brutus, and I honour him;
Say I fear'd Cæsar, honour'd him, and lov'd him.
If Brutus will vouchsafe that Antony   130
May safely come to him, and be resolv'd
How Cæsar hath deserv'd to lie in death,
Mark Antony shall not love Cæsar dead
So well as Brutus living; but will follow
The fortunes and affairs of noble Brutus   135
Thorough the hazards of this untrod state,
With all true faith. So says my master Antony.
Bru. Thy master is a wise and valiant Roman;
I never thought him worse.
Tell him, so please him come unto this place,   140
He shall be satisfied; and, by my honour,
Depart untouch'd.
Serv.   I'll fetch him presently. [*Exit Servant.*
Bru. I know that we shall have him well to friend.
Cas. I wish we may: but yet have I a mind
That fears him much; and my misgiving still   145
Falls shrewdly to the purpose.

Enter ANTONY.

Bru. But here comes Antony. Welcome, Mark Antony.

122-3. A . . . Antony's. / *Serv.* Thus] *F; Serv.* A . . . Antony's. / Thus *Pope,*
Hanmer.   147.] *As Pope;* But . . . *Antony:* / Welcome . . . *Antony.* / *F.*

126. *honest*] honourable.
136. *this untrod state*] this unknown
state of affairs.
145-6. *my misgiving . . . purpose*] my

misgivings always turn out to be un-
pleasantly close to the truth. As usual
in the period, *still* means "always,
continually".

Ant. O mighty Cæsar! dost thou lie so low?
　　　Are all thy conquests, glories, triumphs, spoils,
　　　Shrunk to this little measure? Fare thee well.　　　150
　　　I know not, gentlemen, what you intend,
　　　Who else must be let blood, who else is rank:
　　　If I myself, there is no hour so fit
　　　As Cæsar's death's hour; nor no instrument
　　　Of half that worth as those your swords, made rich　　155
　　　With the most noble blood of all this world.
　　　I do beseech ye, if you bear me hard,
　　　Now, whilst your purpled hands do reek and smoke,
　　　Fulfil your pleasure. Live a thousand years,
　　　I shall not find myself so apt to die;　　　160
　　　No place will please me so, no mean of death,
　　　As here by Cæsar, and by you cut off,
　　　The choice and master spirits of this age.
Bru. O Antony, beg not your death of us.
　　　Though now we must appear bloody and cruel,　　　165
　　　As by our hands and this our present act
　　　You see we do, yet see you but our hands
　　　And this the bleeding business they have done.
　　　Our hearts you see not; they are pitiful;
　　　And pity to the general wrong of Rome—　　　170

154. death's hour] deaths houre *F;* death hour *Collier, Dover Wilson.*　　170. Rome—] Rome, *F.*

148–50. Contrast Antony's natural reaction at seeing Cæsar's body with his rhetorical message in ll. 123–37.

O mighty . . . measure] Cf. *A Mirror for Magistrates* (ed. L. B. Campbell, p. 378), *Shore's Wife*, ll. 155–8, "Duke haniball in all his *conquest* greate. / Or Cæsar yet, whose *tryumphes* did excede, / Of all their *spoyles* which made them toyle and sweat, / Were not so glad to haue so ryche a meade." (The italics are mine.) Shakespeare's lines are perhaps a reminiscence of this passage.

149–50. *Are all . . . little measure*] Cf. *Cym.*, III. i. 49, "Cæsar's ambition /

Which swelled so much, that it did almost stretch / The sides of the world"; *Ham.*, v. i. 235, "Imperious Cæsar, dead and turn'd to clay, / Might stop a hole to keep the wind away."

152. *be let blood*] A grim euphemism for "be put to death".

rank] swollen with disease, and hence to be cured by blood-letting.

158. *purpled*] crimsoned with blood.

159. *Fulfil your pleasure*] Ironical. Notice how skilfully Antony in this scene plays on Brutus.

160. *apt*] inclined, ready.

161. *mean of death*] means of death, way of dying.

As fire drives out fire, so pity pity—
Hath done this deed on Cæsar. For your part,
To you our swords have leaden points, Mark Antony:
Our arms in strength of malice, and our hearts
Of brothers' temper, do receive you in   175
With all kind love, good thoughts, and reverence.
Cas. Your voice shall be as strong as any man's
In the disposing of new dignities.
Bru. Only be patient till we have appeas'd
The multitude, beside themselves with fear,   180
And then we will deliver you the cause
Why I, that did love Cæsar when I struck him,
Have thus proceeded.
Ant.   I doubt not of your wisdom.
Let each man render me his bloody hand.
First, Marcus Brutus, will I shake with you;   185
Next, Caius Cassius, do I take your hand;
Now, Decius Brutus, yours; now yours, Metellus;

171–2. so pity pity— / Hath] so pitty, pitty / Hath *F.*   174. in strength of malice] *F;* exempt from malice *Pope;* no strength of malice *Capell;* in strength of amity *Singer, Hudson, Dover Wilson (N.C.S. Notes);* in strength of welcome *Collier MS., Craik;* forspent of malice *Anon. ap. Cambridge; and other conj.*

171. *As fire drives out fire*] A proverb several times used by Shakespeare. Cf. *Cor.,* IV. vii. 54, "One fire drives out one fire; one nail, one nail; / Rights by rights founder, strengths by strengths do fail." Also Chapman, *Monsieur D'Olive,* v. i. 8, "For one heat, all know, doth drive out another, / One passion doth expel another still."

so pity pity] Pity for the general wrong of Rome has driven out pity for Cæsar.

174. *Our arms . . . malice*] See apparatus criticus for emendations that have been proposed. Capell gave *no strength of malice* followed by a semicolon, with a comma after *Antony.* But this destroys the parallelism of phrase and antithesis of thought, both surely intended, of *our arms in strength of malice* and *our hearts of brothers' temper,* a parallelism made clear by the Folio punctuation, which I retain. Singer

(*N. & Q.,* Jan. 1857) proposed *in strength of amity.* I think that the Folio reading may be justified and should be retained. It may be paraphrased: "Both our arms, strong in enmity (*malice*) as they must seem to you, and our hearts, which cherish a true brotherly regard for you, are ready to receive you." Their arms are still bloody to the elbow, and must look very ominous to Cæsar's dearest friend. As Kittredge points out, there is the same antithesis between the bloodiness and apparent cruelty of their *hands* and the true kindness of their *hearts* in the earlier part of the speech.

177. *voice*] vote, authority. Cassius thinks an appeal to Antony's ambition more likely to sway him than Brutus's professions of brotherly kindness. Cassius is a "great observer" (I. ii. 199).

Yours, Cinna; and, my valiant Casca, yours;
Though last, not least in love, yours, good Trebonius.
Gentlemen all—alas, what shall I say?   190
My credit now stands on such slippery ground,
That one of two bad ways you must conceit me,
Either a coward, or a flatterer.
That I did love thee, Cæsar, O, 'tis true!
If then thy spirit look upon us now,   195
Shall it not grieve thee dearer than thy death,
To see thy Antony making his peace,
Shaking the bloody fingers of thy foes,
Most noble, in the presence of thy corse?
Had I as many eyes as thou hast wounds,   200
Weeping as fast as they stream forth thy blood,
It would become me better than to close
In terms of friendship with thine enemies.
Pardon me, Julius! Here wast thou bay'd, brave
        hart;
Here didst thou fall; and here thy hunters stand,   205
Sign'd in thy spoil, and crimson'd in thy lethe.

206. lethe] *F* (Lethee); death *Pope*.

188. *my valiant Casca*] More of
Antony's irony.

191. *My credit . . . slippery ground*] my
reputation (as Cæsar's intimate) has
put me in so equivocal a position. Perhaps too we can read into these words
a side-reference to Cæsar's blood on
the ground.

192. *conceit*] conceive, judge. Cf. I.
iii. 162.

199. *Most noble*] Do these words
apply ironically to *foes* in the previous
line, or reverently to Cæsar whose
body lies before him, or disgustedly to
himself for coming to terms with
Cæsar's enemies? From the tenor of
the rest of the speech, it seems most
natural to apply them to Cæsar.

202. *to close*] to come to an agreement.

204. *bay'd*] brought to bay, like a
hunted animal.

hart] For the rest of the speech

Antony plays on the words *hart* and
heart, a common pun in Elizabethan
literature.

206. *Sign'd in thy spoil*] "bearing the
bloody tokens of thy slaughter"
(Onions). *Sign'd* means literally
"marked". *Spoil* means "(in hunting)
capture of the quarry and division of
rewards to the hounds, (hence)
slaughter, massacre" (Onions). Cf.
Cor., II. ii. 125, "where he did / Run
reeking o'er the lives of men, as if /
'Twere a perpetual spoil."

lethe] The First Folio spelling *Lethee*
marks the word as a disyllable, as elsewhere in Shakespeare. Lethe was a
river in Hades, and the drinking of its
waters caused forgetfulness of the past;
hence its name is normally used as a
synonym for "oblivion". Here, however, the word suggests more specifically "the stream of death", and, by
transference of meaning, "life-blood".

O world, thou wast the forest to this hart;
And this indeed, O world, the heart of thee.
How like a deer, strucken by many princes,
Dost thou here lie!   210

Cas. Mark Antony—

Ant.   Pardon me, Caius Cassius:
The enemies of Cæsar shall say this;
Then, in a friend, it is cold modesty.

Cas. I blame you not for praising Cæsar so;
But what compact mean you to have with us?   215
Will you be prick'd in number of our friends,
Or shall we on, and not depend on you?

Ant. Therefore I took your hands, but was indeed
Sway'd from the point by looking down on Cæsar.
Friends am I with you all, and love you all,   220
Upon this hope, that you shall give me reasons
Why, and wherein, Cæsar was dangerous.

Bru. Or else were this a savage spectacle.
Our reasons are so full of good regard,
That were you, Antony, the son of Cæsar,   225
You should be satisfied.

Ant.   That's all I seek;
And am moreover suitor that I may
Produce his body to the market-place,
And in the pulpit, as becomes a friend,
Speak in the order of his funeral.   230

207–10. O world . . . lie!] *F; in margin Pope, Hanmer.*   208. heart] *Theobald;*
Hart *F.*   209. strucken] *Q 1691, Steevens;* stroken *F1;* stricken *F2.*

207–8. *O world . . . heart of thee*]
Coleridge doubts the genuineness of
these two lines, "first, on account of
the rhythm, which is not Shakespearean, but just the very tune of
some old play, from which the actor
might have interpolated them; and
secondly, because they interrupt not
only the sense and connection, but
likewise the flow both of the passion
and (what is with me still more decisive) of the Shakespearean link of association." Coleridge's doubt does not
seem to me to be justified on either
ground.

209. *strucken*] This seems the nearest
equivalent to the Folio form *stroken*,
and is supported by II. ii. 114.

213. *modesty*] moderation. Cf. *modestly* in I. ii. 68.

216. *prick'd*] marked down by a
prick, or tick. Cf. IV. i. 1, 3, 16.

224. *good regard*] sound considerations.

225. *son of Cæsar*] Perhaps some of
the audience would recall Suetonius's
"καὶ σύ, τέκνον;". See note on l. 77.

230. *order of his funeral*] ceremonial
arrangements made for his funeral. Cf.
note on I. ii. 25, "order of the course".

Bru. You shall, Mark Antony.
Cas.   Brutus, a word with you.
     [*Aside.*] You know not what you do. Do not consent
     That Antony speak in his funeral.
     Know you how much the people may be mov'd
     By that which he will utter?
Bru.   By your pardon: 235
     I will myself into the pulpit first,
     And show the reason of our Cæsar's death.
     What Antony shall speak, I will protest
     He speaks by leave and by permission:
     And that we are contented Cæsar shall   240
     Have all true rites and lawful ceremonies,
     It shall advantage more than do us wrong.
Cas. I know not what may fall; I like it not.
Bru. Mark Antony, here, take you Cæsar's body.
     You shall not in your funeral speech blame us,   245
     But speak all good you can devise of Cæsar,
     And say you do 't by our permission;
     Else shall you not have any hand at all
     About his funeral. And you shall speak
     In the same pulpit whereto I am going,   250
     After my speech is ended.
Ant.   Be it so;
     I do desire no more.
Bru. Prepare the body, then, and follow us.
                              [*Exeunt. Manet Antony.*

232. S.D. *Aside.*] *Rowe; not in F.*

231. *You shall, Mark Antony*] Plutarch comments on the two great mis-
takes that Brutus made after Cæsar's
death, his refusal to let Antony be
slain, and his consent to Antony's
requests about the funeral ceremonies.
See Appendix, pp. 151-2.
   236-7. *I will ... death*] "The infatuation is almost incredible, and it
springs not only from generosity to
Antony and Cæsar, but from the false
assumption of the justice of his cause,
and the Quixotic exaltation the assumption brings with it" (MacCal-

lum). Antony has played his hand
with consummate skill; the grim game
is entirely beyond Brutus's compre-
hension. *Our Cæsar's death:* as Kittredge says, the phrase "suggests, in
an indescribable way, the feeling
with which Brutus regards his dead
friend. In his opinion, all the conspirators in striking at Cæsar did so
regretfully, and purely for public
reasons."
   238. *protest*] proclaim. Cf. *Oth.*, IV.
ii. 205, "what I protest intendment of
doing".

Ant. O, pardon me, thou bleeding piece of earth,
That I am meek and gentle with these butchers.   255
Thou art the ruins of the noblest man
That ever lived in the tide of times.
Woe to the hand that shed this costly blood!
Over thy wounds now do I prophesy
(Which like dumb mouths do ope their ruby lips,   260
To beg the voice and utterance of my tongue),
A curse shall light upon the limbs of men;
Domestic fury and fierce civil strife
Shall cumber all the parts of Italy;
Blood and destruction shall be so in use,   265
And dreadful objects so familiar,
That mothers shall but smile when they behold
Their infants quartered with the hands of war,
All pity chok'd with custom of fell deeds;
And Cæsar's spirit, ranging for revenge,   270
With Ate by his side come hot from hell,
Shall in these confines with a monarch's voice
Cry havoc and let slip the dogs of war,

258. hand] *F;* hands *Grant White, Hudson, Dover Wilson.*   262. limbs] *F;* line *Warburton;* loins *Collier MS., Craik;* lives *conj. Johnson;* times *Walker;* minds *Dyce; and other conj.*

257. *the tide of times*] the course of ages.

260. *dumb mouths*] Cf. III. ii. 227, "Sweet Cæsar's wounds, poor poor dumb mouths". Shakespeare uses the image two or three times elsewhere.

262. *A curse … limbs of men*] Various emendations have been proposed for the Folio *limbes*. But Aldis Wright compares Timon's curse upon Athens, *Tim.*, IV. i. 21–5, and points out that Lear's curses were levelled at his daughters' limbs: e.g., *Lr.*, II. iv. 158–60. The curse visualized by Lear is some kind of plague; by Antony, the *blood and destruction* he goes on to describe.

264. *cumber*] burden, harass.

268. *quartered*] cut to pieces.

269. *custom of fell deeds*] the becoming accustomed to cruelty.

270. *ranging*] roving in search of prey.

271. *Ate*] Represented by Homer as a daughter of Zeus (*Il.*, XIX. 90 ff), and by Hesiod as the daughter of Strife, Ate was to the Greeks a personification of moral blindness or infatuation. In Shakespeare she personifies mischief and discord. Cf. *John*, II. i. 63, "An Ate stirring him to blood and strife"; *LLL.*, v. ii. 692; *Ado*, II. i. 263.

273. *Cry havoc*] To give the signal for "no quarter", for slaughter and pillage; this was the prerogative of monarchs. Cf. *John*, II. i. 357, "Cry havoc, kings!"

the dogs of war] Steele (*Tatler* 137) couples with this line a passage from the Prol. of *H 5* (ll. 5–8) which serves very well as a gloss: "Then should the warlike Harry, like himself, / Assume the port of Mars, and at his heels / (Leash'd in, like hounds) should

That this foul deed shall smell above the earth
With carrion men, groaning for burial.   275

Enter Octavius' Servant.

You serve Octavius Cæsar, do you not?
Serv. I do, Mark Antony.
Ant. Cæsar did write for him to come to Rome.
Serv. He did receive his letters, and is coming,
And bid me say to you by word of mouth—   280
O Cæsar!
Ant. Thy heart is big; get thee apart and weep.
Passion, I see, is catching, for mine eyes,
Seeing those beads of sorrow stand in thine,
Began to water. Is thy master coming?   285
Serv. He lies to-night within seven leagues of Rome.
Ant. Post back with speed, and tell him what hath chanc'd.
Here is a mourning Rome, a dangerous Rome,
No Rome of safety for Octavius yet.
Hie hence and tell him so. Yet stay awhile;   290
Thou shalt not back till I have borne this corse
Into the market-place; there shall I try,
In my oration, how the people take
The cruel issue of these bloody men;
According to the which thou shalt discourse   295
To young Octavius of the state of things.
Lend me your hand.   [*Exeunt.*

---

275. S.D. *Octavius'*] *Octavius's | Rowe; Octauio's F.*   283. catching, for] *F2;*
catching from *F1.*   285. Began] *F;* Begin *Hanmer et al.*   287.] *As Rowe;*
Post . . . speede, / . . . chanc'd: / *F.*

famine, sword, and fire / Crouch for   her son"; *LLL.*, v. ii. 118.
employment."   289. *No Rome of safety*] Again the
    282. *big*] swelling with grief.   pun on *Rome* and *room.* Cf. I. ii. 154.
    283. *Passion*] sorrow. Cf. *Tit.*, I. i.   294. *The cruel issue*] the outcome of
106, "A mother's tears in passion for   the cruelty.

[SCENE II.—*The Forum.*]

Enter BRUTUS *and goes into the pulpit, and* CASSIUS, *with the Plebeians.*

Plebeians. We will be satisfied: let us be satisfied.
Bru. Then follow me, and give me audience, friends.
       Cassius, go you into the other street,
       And part the numbers.
       Those that will hear me speak, let 'em stay here;   5
       Those that will follow Cassius, go with him;
       And public reasons shall be rendered
       Of Cæsar's death.
1. Pleb.   I will hear Brutus speak.
2. Pleb. I will hear Cassius, and compare their reasons,
       When severally we hear them rendered.   10
           [*Exit Cassius, with some of the Plebeians.*]
3. Pleb. The noble Brutus is ascended: silence!
Bru. Be patient till the last.
       Romans, countrymen, and lovers, hear me for my
       cause, and be silent, that you may hear. Believe me
       for mine honour, and have respect to mine honour,   15
       that you may believe. Censure me in your wisdom,
       and awake your senses, that you may the better
       judge. If there be any in this assembly, any dear

Scene II

10. S.D. *Exit Cassius . . . Plebeians.*] *Not in* F.

S.D. goes into the pulpit] Clearly he does not do this until Cassius's departure at l. 10.

10. *severally*] separately.

13–35. *Romans, countrymen,* ff] For Plutarch's account of this oration see Appendix, pp. 150–1. Plutarch tells us elsewhere (Sk., p. 107) that Brutus in some of his Greek letters "counterfeited that brief compendious manner of speech of the Lacedaemonians. As, when the war was begun, he wrote unto the Pergamenians in this sort: 'I understand you have given Dolabella money: if you have done it willingly, you confess you have offended me; if against your wills, shew it then by giving me willingly.'" Macmillan, drawing attention to the repetition of the word "offended" and the use of the conditional clauses, suggests that Shakespeare had this letter in mind when he composed Brutus's oration. Brutus's calm reasonableness is in very marked contrast to Antony's eloquence later.

15. *have respect to mine honour*] bear in mind that I am honourable.

16. *Censure*] judge.

17. *your senses*] your reason, understanding—as when we talk of people being "in their senses". Brutus appeals to the reason of the crowd, Antony to their passions.

friend of Cæsar's, to him I say that Brutus' love to
Cæsar was no less than his. If then that friend   20
demand why Brutus rose against Cæsar, this is my
answer: Not that I loved Cæsar less, but that I loved
Rome more. Had you rather Cæsar were living, and
die all slaves, than that Cæsar were dead, to live all
free men? As Cæsar loved me, I weep for him; as he   25
was fortunate, I rejoice at it; as he was valiant, I
honour him; but, as he was ambitious, I slew him.
There is tears, for his love; joy, for his fortune;
honour, for his valour; and death, for his ambition.
Who is here so base, that would be a bondman? If   30
any, speak; for him have I offended. Who is here so
rude, that would not be a Roman? If any, speak; for
him have I offended. Who is here so vile, that will not
love his country? If any, speak; for him have I
offended. I pause for a reply.   35

All. None, Brutus, none.

Bru. Then none have I offended. I have done no more to
Cæsar than you shall do to Brutus. The question of
his death is enroll'd in the Capitol; his glory not
extenuated, wherein he was worthy; nor his offences   40
enforc'd, for which he suffered death.

Enter MARK ANTONY [*and others*], *with Cæsar's body.*

Here comes his body, mourned by Mark Antony,
who, though he had no hand in his death, shall receive the benefit of his dying, a place in the common-

---

41. S.D. *and others*] *Malone; not in F.*

32. *rude*] ignorant, barbarous.

38–9. *The question . . . Capitol*] the
considerations that made his death
necessary are recorded in the archives
of the Capitol. As Macmillan points
out, there can hardly have been time
for a debate in the Senate. Perhaps
Shakespeare, though he does not use it
in his play, has in mind another speech
that Plutarch says (Sk., p. 120) Brutus
made in the Capitol when he and
the other conspirators took refuge

there immediately after the assassination.

39–41. *his glory . . . offences enforc'd*]
his glory not being depreciated . . . nor
his offences unduly stressed.

44–5. *place in the commonwealth*] "In
a letter extant in Cicero's correspondence, Brutus and Cassius wrote to
Antony, 'Nos in hac sententia sumus
ut te cupiamus in libera re publica
magnum et honestum esse'" (Macmillan). In the words that follow ("as

wealth, as which of you shall not? With this I depart,   45
that, as I slew my best lover for the good of Rome, I
have the same dagger for myself, when it shall please
my country to need my death.

All. Live, Brutus! live! live!

1. Pleb. Bring him with triumph home unto his house.   50

2. Pleb. Give him a statue with his ancestors.

3. Pleb. Let him be Cæsar.

4. Pleb.   Cæsar's better parts
Shall be crown'd in Brutus.

1. Pleb. We'll bring him to his house with shouts and
clamours.

Bru. My countrymen—

2. Pleb.   Peace! Silence! Brutus speaks.   55

1. Pleb. Peace, ho!

Bru. Good countrymen, let me depart alone,
And, for my sake, stay here with Antony.
Do grace to Cæsar's corpse, and grace his speech
Tending to Cæsar's glories, which Mark Antony,   60
By our permission, is allow'd to make.
I do entreat you, not a man depart,
Save I alone, till Antony have spoke.   [*Exit.*

1. Pleb. Stay, ho! and let us hear Mark Antony.

3. Pleb. Let him go up into the public chair.   65
We'll hear him. Noble Antony, go up.

Ant. For Brutus' sake, I am beholding to you.

4. Pleb. What does he say of Brutus?

3. Pleb.   He says, for Brutus' sake
He finds himself beholding to us all.

4. Pleb. 'Twere best he speak no harm of Brutus here!   70

54.] *As Capell;* Wee'l . . . House, / . . . Clamors. / *F.*

which of you shall not?") the implication is perhaps that there was no place
for any one in a free commonwealth
while Cæsar lived.

51. *ancestors*] See note on Lucius
Junius Brutus, I. ii. 157.

52. *Let him be Cæsar*] This is intended
to seem bitterly ironical to the audience. Brutus had slain his friend to prevent him from becoming "Cæsar" and
destroying the Republic.

59. *Do grace . . . his speech*] pay respect to Cæsar's body, and give a re-
spectful hearing to Antony's speech.

65. *chair*] Shakespeare found the
word in North: "the chair or pulpit for
orations".

67. *beholding*] obliged, indebted.
The form is a fairly common corruption of the earlier *beholden*, which is
used here in the Fourth Folio and in
several later editions.

1. Pleb. This Cæsar was a tyrant.
3. Pleb.   Nay, that's certain.
    We are blest that Rome is rid of him.
2. Pleb. Peace! let us hear what Antony can say.
Ant. You gentle Romans,—
All.   Peace, ho! let us hear him.
Ant. Friends, Romans, countrymen, lend me your ears;   75
    I come to bury Cæsar, not to praise him.
    The evil that men do lives after them,
    The good is oft interred with their bones;
    So let it be with Cæsar. The noble Brutus
    Hath told you Cæsar was ambitious.   80
    If it were so, it was a grievous fault,
    And grievously hath Cæsar answer'd it.
    Here, under leave of Brutus and the rest,
    (For Brutus is an honourable man,
    So are they all, all honourable men)   85
    Come I to speak in Cæsar's funeral.
    He was my friend, faithful and just to me;
    But Brutus says he was ambitious,
    And Brutus is an honourable man.
    He hath brought many captives home to Rome,   90
    Whose ransoms did the general coffers fill:
    Did this in Cæsar seem ambitious?
    When that the poor have cried, Cæsar hath wept;
    Ambition should be made of sterner stuff:
    Yet Brutus says he was ambitious,   95
    And Brutus is an honourable man.
    You all did see that on the Lupercal
    I thrice presented him a kingly crown,
    Which he did thrice refuse. Was this ambition?
    Yet Brutus says he was ambitious,   100
    And sure he is an honourable man.
    I speak not to disprove what Brutus spoke,

---

72. blest] *F;* most blest *Capell.*

77–8. *The evil . . . their bones*] Cf. Whetstone, *1 Promos and Cassandra*, III. iv, "The Prouerbe saies, that tenne good turnes lye dead, / And one yll deede, tenne tymes beyonde pretence,/ By enuious tongues, report abrode doth spread."
  82. *answer'd it*] atoned for it.
  97. *on the Lupercal*] on the day of the Lupercalia. Cf. I. i. 67.

But here I am to speak what I do know.
You all did love him once, not without cause;
What cause withholds you then to mourn for him?　105
O judgment, thou art fled to brutish beasts,
And men have lost their reason. Bear with me.
My heart is in the coffin there with Cæsar,
And I must pause till it come back to me.

1. Pleb. Methinks there is much reason in his sayings.　110

2. Pleb. If thou consider rightly of the matter,
　Cæsar has had great wrong.

3. Pleb.　　　　　　　　　　　　Has he, masters?
　I fear there will a worse come in his place.

4. Pleb. Mark'd ye his words? He would not take the crown;
　Therefore 'tis certain he was not ambitious.　115

1. Pleb. If it be found so, some will dear abide it.

2. Pleb. Poor soul! His eyes are red as fire with weeping.

3. Pleb. There's not a nobler man in Rome than Antony.

4. Pleb. Now mark him; he begins again to speak.

Ant. But yesterday the word of Cæsar might　120
　Have stood against the world; now lies he there,
　And none so poor to do him reverence.
　O masters! if I were dispos'd to stir
　Your hearts and minds to mutiny and rage,
　I should do Brutus wrong, and Cassius wrong,　125
　Who, you all know, are honourable men.
　I will not do them wrong; I rather choose

---

106. thou art] *F2;* thou are *F1.*　　112. Has he, masters?] *F4;* Has' hee
Masters? *F1;* Has he, my masters? *Capell;* Has he not, masters? *Craik, Kittredge;*
That he has, masters. *conj. H. Morley, Hunter;* That has he, masters. *conj.
Macmillan.*　　112–13. Has . . . place.] *As Capell;* one line *F.*

106–7. *O judgment . . . their reason*] It
is possible that Jonson is mocking this
passage, or its sentiment, when in
*Every Man Out of His Humour,*III. iv. 33,
"Reason long since is fled to animals"
is quoted as an illustration of "fustian
philosophy". See Dover Wilson, "Ben
Jonson and *Julius Cæsar*", in *Shakespeare Survey, 2.*

110. *much reason in his sayings*] But is
there? Rather, Antony has been play-
ing with emotions.

113. *I fear . . . his place*] Proverbial.

Tilley quotes parallels: e.g., Pettie.
A Petite Pallace (ed. Gollancz, II. 32),
"The common saying is, the change is
seldom made for the better"; *R 3,* II.
iii. 4, "Ill news, by'r lady; seldom
comes the better."

116. *dear abide it*] pay dearly for it.
Cf. III. i. 94.

122. *And none . . . reverence*] "that is,
the meanest man is now too high to do
reverence to Cæsar" (Johnson).

124. *mutiny*] disorder, riot. Cf. l. 213
below.

To wrong the dead, to wrong myself and you,
Than I will wrong such honourable men.
But here's a parchment with the seal of Cæsar;   130
I found it in his closet; 'tis his will.
Let but the commons hear this testament,
Which, pardon me, I do not mean to read,
And they would go and kiss dead Cæsar's wounds,
And dip their napkins in his sacred blood,   135
Yea, beg a hair of him for memory,
And, dying, mention it within their wills,
Bequeathing it as a rich legacy
Unto their issue.

4. Pleb. We'll hear the will. Read it, Mark Antony.   140
All. The will, the will! We will hear Cæsar's will!
Ant. Have patience, gentle friends; I must not read it.
It is not meet you know how Cæsar lov'd you.
You are not wood, you are not stones, but men;
And being men, hearing the will of Cæsar,   145
It will inflame you, it will make you mad.
'Tis good you know not that you are his heirs;
For if you should, O, what would come of it?
4. Pleb. Read the will! We'll hear it, Antony!
You shall read us the will, Cæsar's will!   150
Ant. Will you be patient? Will you stay awhile?
I have o'ershot myself to tell you of it.
I fear I wrong the honourable men
Whose daggers have stabb'd Cæsar; I do fear it.
4. Pleb. They were traitors. Honourable men!   155
All. The will!—The testament!
2. Pleb. They were villains, murderers! The will! Read
the will!
Ant. You will compel me then to read the will?
Then make a ring about the corpse of Cæsar,   160

---

133. Which, pardon me,] *Rowe;* Which (pardon me) *Q 1691;* (Which pardon
me) *F.*   159. will?] *Pope;* Will: *F.*

131. *his will*] According to Plutarch
(Sk., p. 121), the will was read in the
Senate before Antony's speech.

135. *napkins*] handkerchiefs. The
line refers to the practice of preserving

cloths dipped in the blood of martyrs
as sacred relics; and the next line to another kind of relic. See note on II. ii. 89.

152. *o'ershot myself*] gone further
than I meant.

And let me show you him that made the will.
Shall I descend? and will you give me leave?
All. Come down.
2. Pleb. Descend.   [*Antony comes down.*]
3. Pleb. You shall have leave.   165
4. Pleb. A ring! Stand round.
1. Pleb. Stand from the hearse! stand from the body!
2. Pleb. Room for Antony, most noble Antony!
Ant. Nay, press not so upon me; stand far off.
All. Stand back! Room! Bear back!   170
Ant. If you have tears, prepare to shed them now.
    You all do know this mantle. I remember
    The first time ever Cæsar put it on;
    'Twas on a summer's evening in his tent,
    That day he overcame the Nervii.   175
    Look, in this place ran Cassius' dagger through:
    See what a rent the envious Casca made:
    Through this the well-beloved Brutus stabb'd;
    And as he pluck'd his cursed steel away,
    Mark how the blood of Cæsar follow'd it,   180
    As rushing out of doors, to be resolv'd
    If Brutus so unkindly knock'd or no;
    For Brutus, as you know, was Cæsar's angel.
    Judge, O you gods, how dearly Cæsar lov'd him.

164. S.D. *Antony comes down.*] Rowe (*He comes down from the Pulpit*); not in F.

169. *far off*] Probably the comparative, "further off". Cf. v. iii. 11, and
Wint., IV. iv. 442, "Far than Deucalion
off". In all three examples the Folio
spelling is *farre*.

175. *overcame the Nervii*] This was
one of Cæsar's most hardly-won and
most decisive victories in the Gallic
Wars (57 B.C.). In North's *Plutarch*
(*Julius Cæsar*, Sk., p. 61) there is a side-
note: "Nervii the stoutest warriors of
all the Belgae". Cæsar himself fought
with conspicuous bravery, and set an
inspiring example to his men; and the
victory was celebrated in Rome with
feasts and solemn processions on a
thitherto unparalleled scale. Actually
Antony was not present at the battle,
since he did not join Cæsar in Gaul

until three years later; but the mention of this victory in his speech is a
telling stroke.

177. *envious*] malicious, spiteful—
the normal Shakespearian sense. Cf.
II. i. 178, and contrast III. i. 188, "my
valiant Casca", spoken ironically.

181. *to be resolv'd*] to learn for certain. Cf. III. i. 131.

182. *unkindly*] Perhaps a play on the
two meanings, "unnaturally" and
"cruelly". Cf. *Lr.*, III. iv. 70, "his un-
kind daughters".

183. *Cæsar's angel*] Probably no
more than "Cæsar's darling", a sense
in which *angel* is several times used in
Sidney's *Arcadia*. But some editors have
regarded it as almost synonymous with
genius at II. i. 66.

This was the most unkindest cut of all;   185
For when the noble Cæsar saw him stab,
Ingratitude, more strong than traitors' arms,
Quite vanquish'd him: then burst his mighty heart;
And in his mantle muffling up his face,
Even at the base of Pompey's statue   190
(Which all the while ran blood) great Cæsar fell.
O, what a fall was there, my countrymen!
Then I, and you, and all of us fell down,
Whilst bloody treason flourish'd over us.
O, now you weep, and I perceive you feel   195
The dint of pity. These are gracious drops.
Kind souls, what weep you when you but behold
Our Cæsar's vesture wounded? Look you here!
Here is himself, marr'd, as you see, with traitors.
1. Pleb. O piteous spectacle!   200
2. Pleb. O noble Cæsar!
3. Pleb. O woeful day!
4. Pleb. O traitors! villains!
1. Pleb. O most bloody sight!
2. Pleb. We will be revenged.   205
All. Revenge!—About!—Seek!—Burn!—Fire!—Kill!—
    Slay!—Let not a traitor live.
Ant. Stay, countrymen.
1. Pleb. Peace there! Hear the noble Antony.

205–7. *2. Pleb.* . . . revenged. / *All.* Revenge!—. . . live. /] *As Grant White*;
2. . . . reueng'd: Reuenge / . . . slay, / . . . liue. / F.

185. *most unkindest*] This could mean
"most cruel", or "most unnatural".
Perhaps both meanings should be read
into it. Cf. l. 182 above.
    191. *ran blood*] The implication is
that even Pompey, Cæsar's former
enemy, could not forbear to show
sympathy. However, Plutarch took
the blood as a token "that the image
took just revenge of Pompey's enemy,
being thrown down on the ground at
his feet, and yielding up his ghost
there". An Elizabethan audience
would also, no doubt, see in this passage an allusion to a current superstition that the corpse of a murdered man

bled in the presence of the murderer.
Cf. *R 3*, I. ii. 55–9, and *Arden of Fever-*
sham (Mal. Soc.), ll. 2474–6.
    194. *flourish'd*] Perhaps, as Dover
Wilson suggests, a double meaning is
implied, "brandish a sword in
triumph", and "swagger".
    196. *dint*] stroke, or impression.
    199. *Here is himself*] The uncovering
of Cæsar's body is mentioned by Plutarch in the life of Cæsar; in the lives of
Brutus and Antonius, Antony shows
only the rent and bloody garments.
Shakespeare provides a powerful and
moving climax with the uncovering of
the body.

2. *Pleb.* We'll hear him, we'll follow him, we'll die with   210
him.
Ant. Good friends, sweet friends, let me not stir you up
To such a sudden flood of mutiny.
They that have done this deed are honourable.
What private griefs they have, alas, I know not,   215
That made them do it. They are wise and honourable,
And will, no doubt, with reasons answer you.
I come not, friends, to steal away your hearts.
I am no orator, as Brutus is,
But (as you know me all) a plain blunt man,   220
That love my friend; and that they know full well
That gave me public leave to speak of him.
For I have neither wit, nor words, nor worth,
Action, nor utterance, nor the power of speech
To stir men's blood; I only speak right on.   225
I tell you that which you yourselves do know,
Show you sweet Cæsar's wounds, poor poor dumb
mouths,
And bid them speak for me. But were I Brutus,
And Brutus Antony, there were an Antony

223. wit] *F2;* writ *F1, Johnson, Malone, Collier.*

214-32. *They that have done . . . rise*
and mutiny] Antony skilfully discredits
the motives of the conspirators by re-
ducing them to "private griefs", and
by disclaiming powers of oratory in
himself subtly implies that he lacks the
"glib and oily art" of Brutus to work
on the feelings of his audience. We recall, as Antony's hearers do not, the
entirely unglib nature of Brutus's
oratory.
215. *griefs*] grievances. Cf. I. iii. 118.
217. *reasons*] Brutus has, of course,
already given these reasons, but the
crowd are by now in no condition to
remember them. Antony himself was
not present when Brutus made his
speech.
220-1. In these two lines of mono-
syllables the orator gives a practical
demonstration of his powers as *a plain*
blunt man.

222. *public leave to speak*] leave to
speak in public—another transferred
epithet.
223-5. *neither wit . . . men's blood*] "A
complete list of the qualities of a good
orator: (1) intellectual cleverness
(*wit*); (2) fluency (*words*); (3) *auctori-*
tas, the weight that comes from character or standing (*worth*); (4) gesture
and bearing (*action*); (5) skilful elocu-
tion, good delivery (*utterance*)—and
finally (6) *the power of speech to stir men's*
blood, without which all other accom-
plishments avail but little" (Kittredge).
223. *wit*] The First Folio has *writ*,
which Johnson and Malone wished to
retain, Johnson explaining it as a
"penned or premeditated oration".
Surely both context and euphony
demand *wit*. The Second Folio makes
the change to *wit*.

Would ruffle up your spirits, and put a tongue   230
In every wound of Cæsar that should move
The stones of Rome to rise and mutiny.
All. We'll mutiny.
1. Pleb.   We'll burn the house of Brutus.
3. Pleb. Away then! Come, seek the conspirators.
Ant. Yet hear me, countrymen. Yet hear me speak.   235
All. Peace, ho!—Hear Antony, most noble Antony.
Ant. Why, friends, you go to do you know not what.
Wherein hath Cæsar thus deserv'd your loves?
Alas! you know not: I must tell you then.
You have forgot the will I told you of.   240
All. Most true.—The will!—Let's stay and hear the will.
Ant. Here is the will, and under Cæsar's seal.
To every Roman citizen he gives,
To every several man, seventy-five drachmas.
2. Pleb. Most noble Cæsar! We'll revenge his death.   245
3. Pleb. O royal Cæsar!
Ant. Hear me with patience.
All. Peace, ho!
Ant. Moreover, he hath left you all his walks,
His private arbours, and new-planted orchards,   250
On this side Tiber; he hath left them you,
And to your heirs for ever: common pleasures,
To walk abroad and recreate yourselves.
Here was a Cæsar! when comes such another?
1. Pleb. Never, never! Come, away, away!   255
We'll burn his body in the holy place,
And with the brands fire the traitors' houses.
Take up the body.
2. Pleb. Go fetch fire.

251. this side] *F;* that side *Theobald.*

230. *ruffle up*] stir up to rage.
231–2.*move The stones*] Cf. *Luke,* xix. 40, "If these should hold their peace, the stones would immediately cry out."
246. *O royal Cæsar!*] Contrast l. 71, "This Cæsar was a tyrant", and l. 52, "Let him be Cæsar".
250–1. *orchards, On this side Tiber*]

Cæsar's gardens (*orchards:* cf. II. i, S.D.) actually lay on the other side of the river (Plut., πέραν τοῦ ποταμοῦ). Amyot mistranslated, "deçà la rivière du Tibre", and was followed by North, and hence by Shakespeare.
252. *common pleasures*] public pleasure-grounds.

3. Pleb. Pluck down benches.   260
4. Pleb. Pluck down forms, windows, any thing.
                              [*Exeunt Plebeians* [*with the body*].
Ant. Now let it work. Mischief, thou art afoot,
    Take thou what course thou wilt! How now, fellow?

Enter Servant.

Serv. Sir, Octavius is already come to Rome.
Ant. Where is he?   265
Serv. He and Lepidus are at Cæsar's house.
Ant. And thither will I straight to visit him.
    He comes upon a wish. Fortune is merry,
    And in this mood will give us any thing.
Serv. I heard him say Brutus and Cassius   270
    Are rid like madmen through the gates of Rome.
Ant. Belike they had some notice of the people,
    How I had mov'd them. Bring me to Octavius.   [*Exeunt.*

[SCENE III.—*The Same. A Street.*]

Enter CINNA *the Poet, and after him the Plebeians.*

Cin. I dreamt to-night that I did feast with Cæsar,

261. S.D. *Exeunt . . . body.*] *Rowe; Exit Plebeians. F.*   263.] *As Pope;* Take
. . . wilt. / . . . Fellow? / *F.*

261. *windows*] shutters. See K. Tillotson, in G. Tillotson's *Essays in Criticism and Research* (1942), pp. 204–7.
Mrs Tillotson notes several examples
of *window* in this or kindred senses.

264. *Octavius . . . come to Rome*]
Actually it was about six weeks before
Octavius came to Rome, from Apol-
lonia.

268. *upon a wish*] exactly according
to my wishes. From Plutarch we learn
that Antony was far from desiring the
return of Octavius, since he was man-
aging affairs entirely to his own satis-
faction and regarded him as a dangerous rival. Indeed it was not until
the autumn of the following year, after
battles between the soldiers of Octavius and those of Antony and Lepidus,

that the two settled their differences
and formed the Triumvirate with
Lepidus. Marcus Aemilius Lepidus, a
supporter of Cæsar, and consul with
him in 46, was in the neighbourhood
of Rome at the time of the assassination, and on the next night entered
the city with his troops. Shakespeare
telescopes these events for dramatic
effect.

272–3. *some notice . . . mov'd them*]
some notice of how I had moved the
people.

Scene III

S.D. Enter Cinna the Poet] Hel-
vetius Cinna was a poet of some renown, a friend of Catullus.

1. *to-night*] last night. Cf. II. ii. 76.

　　And things unluckily charge my fantasy.
　　I have no will to wander forth of doors,
　　Yet something leads me forth.
1. Pleb. What is your name?　　　　　　　　　　　　　5
2. Pleb. Whither are you going?
3. Pleb. Where do you dwell?
4. Pleb. Are you a married man or a bachelor?
2. Pleb. Answer every man directly.
1. Pleb. Ay, and briefly.　　　　　　　　　　　　　　10
4. Pleb. Ay, and wisely.
3. Pleb. Ay, and truly, you were best.
Cin. What is my name? Whither am I going? Where do
　　I dwell? Am I a married man or a bachelor? Then,
　　to answer every man directly and briefly, wisely and　15
　　truly: wisely I say, I am a bachelor.
2. Pleb. That's as much as to say they are fools that
　　marry. You'll bear me a bang for that, I fear. Pro-
　　ceed, directly.
Cin. Directly, I am going to Cæsar's funeral.　　　　20
1. Pleb. As a friend or an enemy?
Cin. As a friend.
2. Pleb. The matter is answered directly.
4. Pleb. For your dwelling, briefly.
Cin. Briefly, I dwell by the Capitol.　　　　　　　25
3. Pleb. Your name, sir, truly.
Cin. Truly, my name is Cinna.
1. Pleb. Tear him to pieces! He's a conspirator.
Cin. I am Cinna the poet, I am Cinna the poet.
4. Pleb. Tear him for his bad verses, tear him for his bad　30
　　verses.
Cin. I am not Cinna the conspirator.
1. Pleb. It is no matter, his name's Cinna; pluck but his

---

2. unluckily] *F;* unlucky *Warburton;* unlikely *Collier MS., Craik.*

2. *things . . . fantasy*] the things that
have happened weigh ominously on
my imagination. Shylock had a pre-
sentiment of evil when he dreamed of
money-bags (*Mer.V.,*II. v. 16–18), and
Romeo had happy dreams the night
before his death (*Rom.,* v. i. 1–5).
Kittredge quotes, from Adlington's
Apuleius (Tudor Transl., p. 97), and
from Lyly's *Mother Bombie* (ed. Bond,
III. 203), passages which speak of the
danger of dreaming of good cheer.

9. *directly*] straightforwardly, to the
point. Cf. I. i. 12.

18. *You'll bear . . . for that*] you'll get
a bang for that.

name out of his heart, and turn him going.

3. Pleb. Tear him, tear him! Come, brands, ho! fire-   35
    brands! To Brutus', to Cassius'; burn all! Some to
    Decius' house, and some to Casca's; some to Lig-
    arius'. Away! go!

        [*Exeunt all the Plebeians* [,*dragging off Cinna*].

38. S.D. *dragging off Cinna*] *Not in F.*

ACT IV

[SCENE I.—*Rome. A Room in Antony's House.*]

Enter ANTONY, OCTAVIUS, *and* LEPIDUS.

Ant. These many then shall die; their names are prick'd.
Oct. Your brother too must die; consent you, Lepidus?
Lep. I do consent—
Oct.   Prick him down, Antony.
Lep. Upon condition Publius shall not live,
  Who is your sister's son, Mark Antony.   5
Ant. He shall not live. Look, with a spot I damn him.
  But, Lepidus, go you to Cæsar's house;
  Fetch the will hither, and we shall determine
  How to cut off some charge in legacies.
Lep. What, shall I find you here?   10

ACT IV
Scene 1

1. *prick'd*] ticked, marked by a
"prick" on the list. Cf. the use of the
word in III. i. 216.

2. *Your brother . . . die*] Lepidus's
brother, Lucius Aemilius Paullus, had
held the highest offices, including the
consulate in 50 B.C. On the assassination of Cæsar he joined the republican
party, and was one of those who, in
June, 43 B.C., declared Lepidus a public enemy for having joined Antony.
When the Triumvirate was formed a
few months later his name was put at
the head of the proscription list by
Lepidus; he escaped, probably with
Lepidus's connivance, and joined
Brutus. Although pardoned after the
Battle of Philippi, he refused to return
to Rome, and died abroad.

4. *Publius*] Antony had no nephew
Publius, but his uncle, Lucius Cæsar,
as Plutarch mentions, was among

those who were proscribed by the
Triumvirs. Whether by mistake or
design, Shakespeare brings a nephew
into the story, and, by showing Antony's readiness to *damn* him as a pre-
cautionary measure to further the
suppression of the conspiracy, brings
about a contrast with Brutus's refusal
to take the precaution of killing Antony himself, which was essential for
the success of the conspiracy. Or perhaps he wants to show Antony as a just
and unsentimental man. (See Introduction, p. li.)

6. *with a spot I damn him*] with a prick
I condemn him.

9. *cut off some charge*] lessen some ex-
penditure. Cæsar's legacies had served
a useful purpose in Antony's oration;
now the Triumvirs will not scruple
to use some of the money in other
ways.

91

Oct. Or here or at the Capitol.   *[Exit Lepidus.*

Ant. This is a slight unmeritable man,
    Meet to be sent on errands. Is it fit,
    The three-fold world divided, he should stand
    One of the three to share it?

Oct.   So you thought him,   15
    And took his voice who should be prick'd to die
    In our black sentence and proscription.

Ant. Octavius, I have seen more days than you;
    And though we lay these honours on this man,
    To ease ourselves of divers sland'rous loads,   20
    He shall but bear them as the ass bears gold,
    To groan and sweat under the business,
    Either led or driven, as we point the way;
    And having brought our treasure where we will,
    Then take we down his load, and turn him off,   25
    Like to the empty ass, to shake his ears,
    And graze in commons.

12. *slight unmeritable*] insignificant and undeserving of consideration. Cf. IV. iii. 37, "Away, slight man!" where, however, *slight* has the rather stronger meaning of "worthless". In *Ant.*, II. vii, Shakespeare presents a Lepidus to whom these epithets might very suitably be applied.

14. *The three-fold world divided*] the world being divided into three. When in the autumn of 43 B.C. Octavius, Antony, and Lepidus established themselves as *Triumviri Reipublicae Constituendae*, the first two having been reconciled by the mediation of Lepidus, they agreed to share the government of the state. Antony was to have Gaul as his province, Lepidus Spain, and Octavius Africa, Sardinia, and Sicily. In using the term *three-fold*, Shakespeare is perhaps thinking of the three areas of the Roman world, Europe, Africa, and Asia. Cf. *Ant.*, IV. vi. 6, "the three-nook'd world"; and *Ant.*, I. i. 12, "The triple pillar of the world".

16. *voice*] opinion, vote. Cf. III. i. 177.

17. *black sentence*] sentence of death.

20. *To ease . . . sland'rous loads*] to lighten for ourselves some of the burden of reproach or disgrace that we may encounter: i.e., by causing Lepidus to share, or laying on him, the blame of some of their unpopular acts. For the construction of *sland'rous loads*, cf. I. ii. 9, "sterile curse".

21. *as the ass bears gold*] Proverbial. Cf. *Meas.*, III. i. 25–8, "If thou art rich, thou'rt poor; / For, like an ass whose back with ingots bows, / Thou bear'st thy heavy riches but a journey, / And death unloads thee"; T. Heywood, *1 Iron Age*, IV, "An Asse fit for service and good for burthens, to carry gold, and to feede on thistles".

26. *to shake his ears*] Also proverbial. Cf. *Tw.N.*, II. iii. 134, "Go shake your ears"; Gabriel Harvey, *Letter Book* (ed. Scott, p. 42), "And as for M. Gawber, his Mastership may go shake his eares elsewhere, and appoint his diet at sum other table."

27. *in commons*] i.e., on the public pasture-lands, or commons, with which most villages were provided, and on to which the villagers could turn their beasts to graze.

Oct.   You may do your will;
      But he's a tried and valiant soldier.
Ant. So is my horse, Octavius, and for that
      I do appoint him store of provender.   30
      It is a creature that I teach to fight,
      To wind, to stop, to run directly on,
      His corporal motion govern'd by my spirit.
      And, in some taste, is Lepidus but so:
      He must be taught, and train'd, and bid go forth: 35
      A barren-spirited fellow; one that feeds
      On objects, arts, and imitations,
      Which, out of use and stal'd by other men,
      Begin his fashion. Do not talk of him
      But as a property. And now, Octavius,   40
      Listen great things. Brutus and Cassius
      Are levying powers; we must straight make head.
      Therefore let our alliance be combin'd,

37. objects, arts] *F;* abject orts *Theobald;* abjects, orts *conj. Staunton;* abject arts *conj. Grant White.*

32. *To wind*] to turn, or wheel.

33. *His corporal . . . my spirit*] his physical movements controlled by my mind.

34. *in some taste*] in some measure.

36. *barren-spirited*] having no ideas of his own, no originality.

36–9. *one that feeds . . . his fashion*] one that feeds his understanding with curiosities, artifices, and imitations—things which become part of his mental stock only when they have been worn out and made cheap by other men. Antony amplifies the epithet "barren-spirited" by saying that Lepidus's ideas are all second-hand and out of date. In *Ant.*, II. vii, Shakespeare illustrates this side of Lepidus, and his credulity.

37. *objects, arts, and imitations*] I take *objects* to mean "wonders, curiosities". *O.E.D.* gives under *object*, "a sight, spectacle, gazing-stock", and with other illustrations quotes *Tim.*, IV. iii. 122, "Swear against objects, / Put armour on thine ears and on thine eyes." Perhaps it is relevant to quote also *LLL.*, IV. ii. 70, "a foolish, extravagant spirit, full of forms, figures, shapes, objects, ideas, apprehensions, motions, and revolutions". Two further passages show the word in contexts that give it the same meaning: *Gent.*, I. i. 13, "when thou haply seest / Some rare noteworthy object in thy travel", and *Ham.*, III. i. 180, "Haply the seas and countries different / With variable objects shall expel / This something-settled matter in his heart." The words *arts, and imitations* suggest things and ideas that are artificial and secondhand. Theobald, followed by most 18th-c. editors, read *abject orts*, i.e., "rejected scraps". Staunton and some others read *abjects, orts*. But emendation is unnecessary.

38. *stal'd*] made common or cheap. Cf. I. ii. 72.

40. *a property*] a mere tool.

42. *make head*] raise a force—as several times in Shakespeare.

Our best friends made, our means stretch'd;
And let us presently go sit in council,   45
How covert matters may be best disclos'd,
And open perils surest answered.
Oct. Let us do so: for we are at the stake,
And bay'd about with many enemies;
And some that smile have in their hearts, I fear,   50
Millions of mischiefs.   [*Exeunt.*

[SCENE II.—*Camp near Sardis. Before Brutus's Tent.*]

Drum. Enter BRUTUS, LUCILIUS, [LUCIUS,] *and the Army.*
TITINIUS *and* PINDARUS *meet them.*

Bru. Stand ho!
Lucil. Give the word, ho! and stand.

44. our means stretch'd] our meanes stretcht *F1;* and our best meanes stretcht
out *F2;* our best means stretcht *Johnson;* our means stretch'd to the utmost
Malone; our means, our plans stretch'd out *Bulloch; and other conj.*

44. *Our best friends made, our means
stretch'd*] Most editors give the line as it
is in the later Folios (see app. crit.).
But there are plenty of defective lines
in Shakespeare's plays, and the later
Folios have no textual authority. I
therefore think it best to leave the
reading of the First Folio.

stretch'd] made to go as far as possible.

45. *presently*] at once, forthwith. Cf.
II. ii. 5, and III. i. 28.

46–7. *How covert . . . surest answered*]
how hidden threats may best be
brought to light, and open dangers
most safely met.

48–9. *at the stake . . . many enemies*] A
metaphor from bear-baiting: "tied to
the stake, with many dogs barking
about us, eager to get their teeth into
us". There is perhaps also a suggestion
that they are "at bay", cornered like
hunted animals that must turn on their
pursuers and make a fight of it. Cf. III.
i. 204, "Here wast thou bay'd, brave
hart." For the whole picture cf. *Mac.*,
v. vii. 1, "They have tied me to a
stake; I cannot fly, / But bear-like I

must fight the course." It is not very
long since Cæsar was the bear, and the
conspirators the dogs.

51. *mischiefs*] injuries. Cf. *2 H 6*, IV.
viii. 59, "The name of Henry the
Fifth hales them to an hundred mischiefs."

Scene II

S.D. Drum. Enter Brutus . . . meet
them] This stage-direction is mis-
leading. It is clear from the end of the
scene that the various encounters take
place before Brutus's tent, from which
he presumably enters on hearing the
drum, perhaps attended by Lucius, for
it is probably Lucius, and not Lucilius,
whom he addresses in the last speech of
the scene. Lucilius, returning from an
official visit to Cassius, comes in at the
head of Brutus's troops, and *with* him,
not meeting him, comes Pindarus.
Dover Wilson is perhaps right in suggesting that Titinius should not enter
until l. 30, since, as an officer of
Cassius, he could not have been ignored so long by Brutus.

2. *Give . . . stand*] Lucilius passes

Bru. What now, Lucilius, is Cassius near?
Lucil. He is at hand, and Pindarus is come
    To do you salutation from his master.   5
Bru. He greets me well. Your master, Pindarus,
    In his own change, or by ill officers,
    Hath given me some worthy cause to wish
    Things done undone; but if he be at hand,
    I shall be satisfied.
Pin.   I do not doubt   10
    But that my noble master will appear
    Such as he is, full of regard and honour.
Bru. He is not doubted. A word, Lucilius;
    How he receiv'd you, let me be resolv'd.
Lucil. With courtesy and with respect enough,   15
    But not with such familiar instances,
    Nor with such free and friendly conference,
    As he hath us'd of old.
Bru.   Thou hast describ'd
    A hot friend cooling. Ever note, Lucilius,
    When love begins to sicken and decay   20
    It useth an enforced ceremony.
    There are no tricks in plain and simple faith;
    But hollow men, like horses hot at hand,

13–14. Lucilius; ... you,] *Malone; Lucillius ... you: F.*

Brutus's command on to his subordinate officers.

6. *He greets me well*] he sends his greeting by a good man.

7. *In his own ... ill officers*] whether from a change in his feelings for me (cf. *a hot friend cooling*, l. 19), or through the actions of bad subordinates (e.g., Lucius Pella, iii. 2, below).

8. *worthy*] considerable.

8–9. *to wish Things done undone*] Proverbial. Cf. *Mac.*, v. i. 75, "What's done cannot be undone."

10. *satisfied*] receive a satisfactory explanation.

12. *full of regard and honour*] worthy of all respect and honour.

16. *familiar instances*] marks of friendship. *O.E.D.*, under *instance* (III. 7), gives "a proof. evidence; a sign,

token, mark". For the construction cf. iv. i. 20, "sland'rous loads", and i. ii. 9, "sterile curse".

17. *conference*] conversation.

20–1. *When love . . . enforced ceremony*] Cf. *Tim.*, i. ii. 15–18, "Nay, my lords, ceremony was but devis'd at first / To set a gloss on faint deeds, hollow welcomes, / Recanting goodness, sorry ere 'tis shown; / But where there is true friendship, there needs none."

21. *enforced*] strained, forced.

22. *tricks*] artifices.

23. *hollow*] insincere.

hot at hand] lively at the start. *O.E.D.*, under *hand* (II. 25c), shows that *at hand*, meaning "at the immediate moment, at the start", is a not uncommon phrase.

Make gallant show and promise of their mettle;
                                [*Low march within.*
But when they should endure the bloody spur,   25
They fall their crests, and like deceitful jades
Sink in the trial. Comes his army on?
Lucil. They mean this night in Sardis to be quarter'd;
        The greater part, the horse in general,
        Are come with Cassius.

                Enter CASSIUS *and his Powers.*

Bru.   Hark! he is arriv'd.   30
        March gently on to meet him.
Cas. Stand ho!
Bru. Stand ho! Speak the word along.
[*First Sold.*] Stand!
[*Second Sold.*] Stand!   35
[*Third Sold.*] Stand!
Cas. Most noble brother, you have done me wrong.
Bru. Judge me, you gods; wrong I mine enemies?
        And if not so, how should I wrong a brother?
Cas. Brutus, this sober form of yours hides wrongs;   40
        And when you do them—
Bru.   Cassius, be content.
        Speak your griefs softly; I do know you well.
        Before the eyes of both our armies here,
        Which should perceive nothing but love from us,

34, 35, 36. *First Sold., Second Sold., Third Sold.*] *Cambridge; not in* F.

24. *mettle*] spirit, courage.
26. *fall*] let fall: transitive, as often in Shakespeare.
  crests] the ridge of a horse's neck. Cf. *Ven.*, 272, and 297, where a "high crest" is given among the attributes of a spirited horse.
27. *Sink in the trial*] fail when put to the test.
30. S.D. Enter . . . Powers] Most editors put this after l. 31. I think we can justify its place in l. 30, as in the Folio. As the *low march* ceases, Brutus begins, "Hark . . . meet him," and at that moment Cassius and his powers

appear at an entrance to the stage at some distance from him. By the time he has finished speaking, Cassius is within speaking distance at the front of the stage, and halts and gives his command, "Stand ho!"
40. *this sober form*] this calm, grave demeanour.
41. *be content*] keep calm. Cf. I. iii. 142, where the sense of the phrase is much the same.
42. *griefs*] grievances, as in l. 46, where *enlarge your griefs* means, "freely express your grievances". Cf. I. iii. 118, III. ii. 215.

Let us not wrangle. Bid them move away;   45
Then in my tent, Cassius, enlarge your griefs,
And I will give you audience.

Cas.   Pindarus,
Bid our commanders lead their charges off
A little from this ground.

Bru. Lucius, do you the like; and let no man   50
Come to our tent till we have done our conference.
Lucilius and Titinius guard our door.   [*Exeunt.*
          Manent Brutus and Cassius.

[Scene iii.—*Within the tent of Brutus.*]

Cas. That you have wrong'd me doth appear in this:
You have condemn'd and noted Lucius Pella
For taking bribes here of the Sardians;
Wherein my letters, praying on his side,
Because I knew the man, was slighted off.   5

---

50. Lucius] *Craik; Lucillius* F.   52. Lucilius] *Craik;* Let *Lucius* F.   S.D.
Manent] *F2; Manet F1.*

4–5. letters, praying . . . man, was] *Dover Wilson;* Letters, praying . . . man was
F1; Letter, praying . . . man, was *F2, Rowe, Capell;* letter (praying . . . man) was
Pope, Theobald, Hanmer, Warburton, Johnson; letters, praying . . . man, were
Malone and most mod. edd.

48. *their charges*] their troops.

50, 52. *Lucius . . . Lucilius*] The Folio reads *Lucillius* in l. 50, and *Let Lucius* in l. 52. Craik's transposition of the names is surely justified. Craik points out the absurdity of associating Titinius and Lucius in the guarding of the door, "an officer of rank and a servant boy. . . The function of Lucius was to carry messages. As Cassius sends *his* servant Pindarus with a message to his division of the force, Brutus sends his servant Lucius with a similar message to his division. Nothing can be clearer than that Lucilius in the first line is a misprint for Lucius, and Lucius in the third a misprint for Lucilius. . . At the close of the conference we have Brutus in iii. 138 again addressing himself to Lucilius and Titinius, who had evidently kept together all the time it lasted." To this might be added that at

iii. 126 it is Lucilius, obviously on guard at the door, who tries to prevent the poet from entering. Craik further suggests that the *Let* of l. 52 was added by the compositor for the sake of the metre. The mistake might easily have arisen through the use of abbreviated forms of *Lucius* and *Lucilius* in the MS. copy for the Folio.

Scene-heading] See Introduction, p. lxx.

2. *noted*] stigmatized, branded with disgrace. Cf. North (Sk., p. 135): "Brutus . . . did condemn and note Lucius Pella for a defamed person."

5. *slighted off*] slightingly disregarded. I depart from the punctuation of the Folio in supplying a comma after *man*. There is no need to change *was* to *were*, as did Malone and many later

Bru. You wrong'd yourself to write in such a case.
Cas. In such a time as this it is not meet
            That every nice offence should bear his comment.
Bru. Let me tell you, Cassius, you yourself
            Are much condemn'd to have an itching palm,   10
            To sell and mart your offices for gold
            To undeservers.
Cas.   I an itching palm!
            You know that you are Brutus that speaks this,
            Or, by the gods, this speech were else your last.
Bru. The name of Cassius honours this corruption,   15
            And chastisement doth therefore hide his head.
Cas. Chastisement!
Bru. Remember March, the ides of March remember.
            Did not great Julius bleed for justice' sake?
            What villain touch'd his body, that did stab,   20
            And not for justice? What, shall one of us,
            That struck the foremost man of all this world
            But for supporting robbers, shall we now

13. speaks] *F;* speak *Pope et al.*

editors. A singular verb with a plural
subject is common enough in Shakespeare when, as here, an intervening
noun in the singular attracts the verb
into the singular.

8. *That every . . . comment*] that every
trifling offence should come in for
criticism. *His = its:* see note on I. ii.
123.

10. *condemn'd to have*] accused of
having.

itching palm] mercenary streak, itch
for money. Dover Wilson quotes Jonson, *Cynthia's Revels,* III. iv. 39, "Itchie
palmes".

11. *mart*] traffic in.

15–16. *The name . . . his head*] That
the name of Cassius should be associated with this corrupt practice gives
it a spurious credit, and so lesser men
enjoy the same immunity from pun-
ishment as he does by virtue of his high
authority.

19. *for justice' sake*] This is the first
time that justice has figured among

Brutus's motives for the assassination;
in his soliloquy at II. i. 10 ff, he reasons
that, though he knows nothing to
Cæsar's discredit, he must die because
he might, if crowned, be led by his
ambition into courses dangerous to the
state. Shakespeare's immediate purpose requires the change of ground;
nor is it necessarily inconsistent, as is
sometimes suggested, if we may suppose that Brutus's interpretation of his
motives has changed since Cæsar's
death.

20–21. *What villain . . . justice?*] Who
that touched his body was such a villain as to stab with any other motive
than a desire for justice?

23. *supporting robbers*] There has
been no earlier suggestion that Cæsar
supported robbers. This further motive for killing Cæsar crops up because
Shakespeare is following Plutarch very
closely at this point. See Appendix,
p. 157, and cf. footnote on p. xxxvi of
the Introduction.

Contaminate our fingers with base bribes,
And sell the mighty space of our large honours   25
For so much trash as may be grasped thus?
I had rather be a dog, and bay the moon,
Than such a Roman.
Cas.   Brutus, bait not me;
I'll not endure it. You forget yourself,
To hedge me in. I am a soldier, I,   30
Older in practice, abler than yourself
To make conditions.
Bru.   Go to! you are not, Cassius.
Cas. I am.
Bru. I say you are not.
Cas. Urge me no more, I shall forget myself;   35
Have mind upon your health; tempt me no farther.
Bru. Away, slight man!
Cas. Is 't possible?

27. bay] *F1;* baite *F2;* bait *Rowe.*   28. bait] *F;* bay *Theobald, Warburton,*
Capell, et al.

25. *the mighty space . . . honours*] i.e., the high offices of honour that it was in their power to confer.

26. *trash*] For the basic meaning of the word, and its common sense of "dross, rubbish", see note on I. iii. 108. It was also used as a contemptuous term for money, as here and at l. 74, *vile trash.* Cf. Florio, *A Worlde of Wordes,* "Pelfe, trash, *id est* mony"; and Greene, *James the Fourth* (Mal. Soc.), l. 1210, "and therefore must I bid him prouide trash, for my Maister is no friend without mony."

grasped thus] Presumably he makes a grasping gesture.

27. *bay the moon*] Proverbial, especially of wolves barking against the moon. Cf. *AYL.,* v. ii. 118, "Pray you, no more of this; 'tis like the howling of Irish wolves against the moon"; Marston, *Antonio's Revenge,* III. i. 184, "Now barks the wolf against the full-cheek'd moon."

28. *bait*] harass, worry. This is the reading of the Folio. Theobald, followed by many modern editors, in-

cluding Dover Wilson, reads *bay;* "but *bait* yields the better sense and accords with *urge, tempt,* and *move* (ll. 35, 36, 58), all in the same general meaning" (Kittredge). Even if it is possible for *bay* to have the sense of "dam in", according with *hedge in* (l. 30), as Dover Wilson says, with support for this meaning from *O.E.D.,* it would surely be understood in the same sense as it bears in l. 27 if Cassius merely echoed it. His stronger word, *bait,* suggests his feeling that he is being worried by Brutus as a bear tied to a stake is worried by the dogs.

30. *hedge me in*] limit my freedom of action.

32. *To make conditions*] to manage affairs; or perhaps to make decisions about the place of subordinates in their affairs, with reference to Lucius Pella.

35. *Urge*] drive, harry (Latin, *urgere*).

36. *health*] welfare. In the same line, *tempt* means "provoke".

37. *slight man*] worthless fellow, trifler. Cf. note on IV. i. 12.

Bru.   Hear me, for I will speak.
　　　Must I give way and room to your rash choler?
　　　Shall I be frighted when a madman stares?   40
Cas. O ye gods, ye gods! Must I endure all this?
Bru. All this? ay, more: fret till your proud heart break;
　　　Go show your slaves how choleric you are,
　　　And make your bondmen tremble. Must I budge?
　　　Must I observe you? Must I stand and crouch   45
　　　Under your testy humour? By the gods,
　　　You shall digest the venom of your spleen,
　　　Though it do split you; for, from this day forth,
　　　I'll use you for my mirth, yea, for my laughter,
　　　When you are waspish.
Cas.   Is it come to this?   50
Bru. You say you are a better soldier:
　　　Let it appear so; make your vaunting true,
　　　And it shall please me well. For mine own part,
　　　I shall be glad to learn of noble men.
Cas. You wrong me every way; you wrong me, Brutus.   55
　　　I said, an elder soldier, not a better:
　　　Did I say better?
Bru.   If you did, I care not.
Cas. When Cæsar liv'd, he durst not thus have mov'd me.
Bru. Peace, peace! you durst not so have tempted him.
Cas. I durst not?   60
Bru. No.
Cas. What? durst not tempt him?

55.] *As Rowe;* You . . . way: / . . . *Brutus: F.*

39. *Must I give . . . rash choler?*] must
I give "free course and scope to your
quick temper?" (Kittredge).

40. *stares*] glares.

44. *budge*] flinch. Cf. *Cor.*, I. vi. 44.
"The mouse ne'er shunn'd the cat as
they did budge / From rascals worse
than they."

45. *observe*] pay court to, be obsequious to. Cf. *2 H 4*, IV. iv. 30, "For he
is gracious, if he be observed"; *Ham.*,
III. i. 163, "The observed of all obser-
vers".

46. *testy humour*] irritability, iras-
cibility.

47. *You shall digest . . . spleen*] you
shall swallow the poison of your fiery
temper. The spleen was thought to be
the seat of sudden passions.

49. *mirth . . . laughter*] object of mirth
and ridicule. Cf. l. 113 below, and note
on I. ii. 71.

54. *learn of*] take lessons from. Cf.
AYL., III. ii. 68, "Learn of the wise".
Forgetting his habitual fair-minded-
ness, Brutus implies that Cassius is not
noble. But contrast l. 231, "Noble,
noble Cassius".

58. *mov'd*] exasperated.

59. *tempted*] tried, provoked. Cf. l. 36.

Bru.   For your life you durst not.

Cas. Do not presume too much upon my love.
     I may do that I shall be sorry for.

Bru. You have done that you should be sorry for.   65
     There is no terror, Cassius, in your threats;
     For I am arm'd so strong in honesty
     That they pass by me as the idle wind,
     Which I respect not. I did send to you
     For certain sums of gold, which you denied me;   70
     For I can raise no money by vile means:
     By heaven, I had rather coin my heart,
     And drop my blood for drachmas, than to wring
     From the hard hands of peasants their vile trash
     By any indirection. I did send   75
     To you for gold to pay my legions,
     Which you denied me: was that done like Cassius?
     Should I have answer'd Caius Cassius so?
     When Marcus Brutus grows so covetous,
     To lock such rascal counters from his friends,   80
     Be ready, gods, with all your thunderbolts,
     Dash him to pieces!

Cas.   I denied you not.

Bru. You did.

Cas.   I did not. He was but a fool
     That brought my answer back. Brutus hath riv'd my
          heart.
     A friend should bear his friend's infirmities;   85
     But Brutus makes mine greater than they are.

Bru. I do not, till you practise them on me.

Cas. You love me not.

Bru.   I do not like your faults.

Cas. A friendly eye could never see such faults.

Bru. A flatterer's would not, though they do appear   90
     As huge as high Olympus.

Cas. Come, Antony, and young Octavius, come,

---

67. *honesty*] uprightness, integrity.
Cf. II.i. 127.
  75. *indirection*] irregular and unjust
means. Cf. *John.*, III. i. 276, "Yet indirection thereby grows direct."

80. *rascal counters*] rubbishy coins.
Cf. *vile trash* in l. 74. Brutus uses
counter as a derogatory word for
"coin".
  84. *riv'd*] cleft, broken.

Revenge yourselves alone on Cassius,
For Cassius is aweary of the world:
Hated by one he loves; brav'd by his brother;   95
Check'd like a bondman; all his faults observ'd,
Set in a note-book, learn'd, and conn'd by rote,
To cast into my teeth. O, I could weep
My spirit from mine eyes! There is my dagger,
And here my naked breast; within, a heart   100
Dearer than Pluto's mine, richer than gold:
If that thou be'st a Roman, take it forth.
I, that denied thee gold, will give my heart:
Strike, as thou didst at Cæsar; for I know,   104
When thou didst hate him worst, thou lov'dst him better
Than ever thou lov'dst Cassius.

Bru.   Sheathe your dagger.
Be angry when you will, it shall have scope;
Do what you will, dishonour shall be humour.
O Cassius, you are yoked with a lamb
That carries anger as the flint bears fire,   110
Who, much enforced, shows a hasty spark,

101. Pluto's] *F;* Plutus' *Pope et al.*   108. humour] *F;* honour *conj. Craik.*
109. lamb] *F;* man *Pope;* temper *Anon. ap. Cambridge;* heart *Herr.*

96. *Check'd*] reproved, rebuked.

98. *To cast into my teeth*] A proverbial expression. Cf. *Err.*, II. ii. 22, "Yea, dost thou jeer and flout me in the teeth?"; Lyly, *Euphues, the Anatomy of Wyt* (ed. Bond, vol. II, p. 262), "The trecheries of his parents . . . wil be cast in his teeth."

101. *Dearer*] more precious.

Pluto's mine] Pope and many later editors read *Plutus' mine*, but the change is unnecessary. Plutus, the god of wealth (the personification of wealth), and Pluto, the god of the nether world (the giver of wealth, i.e., of corn) were already confused in classical times: Liddell and Scott cite Aristophanes, *Plutus*, l. 727, and Sophocles, *Fr.*, l. 259. Elizabethan writers often identify the two gods with each other. Several editors quote *Troil.*, III. iii. 197, "every grain of Pluto's gold", and Webster *Duchess of*

Malfi, III. ii. 283, "Pluto, the god of riches"; and Kittredge illustrates further from *The Rare Triumphs of Love and Fortune* (1589), Dekker, *If this be not a Good Play*, and Thynne, *Embleames and Epigrames* (1600).

103. *I, that denied thee gold*] In l. 82 Cassius had said, "I denied you not." The contradiction is only apparent. One who is ready to give his heart is not likely to have denied mere gold to his friend. The words imply, "I that (if you will have it so) denied . . ."

107. *it shall have scope*] your anger shall have free play.

108. *dishonour shall be humour*] I shall take any insult from you as mere caprice.

111–12. *Who, much enforced . . . cold again*] A proverbial expression. The antecedent of *who* is *flint*; *enforced* means "struck forcibly". Cf. *Lucr.*, 181, "As from this cold flint I enforc'd this fire, /

And straight is cold again.
Cas.   Hath Cassius liv'd
To be but mirth and laughter to his Brutus,
When grief and blood ill-temper'd vexeth him?
Bru. When I spoke that, I was ill-temper'd too.   115
Cas. Do you confess so much? Give me your hand.
Bru. And my heart too.
Cas.   O Brutus!
Bru.   What's the matter?
Cas. Have not you love enough to bear with me,
When that rash humour which my mother gave me
Makes me forgetful?
Bru.   Yes, Cassius; and from henceforth
When you are over-earnest with your Brutus,   121
He'll think your mother chides, and leave you so.

Enter a Poet [, *followed by* LUCILIUS, TITINIUS, *and* LUCIUS].

Poet. Let me go in to see the generals.
There is some grudge between 'em; 'tis not meet

122. S.D. *followed . . . Lucius*] *Cambridge; not in* F.   123–8. Let me . . . matter?]
F; *in margin* Pope, Hanmer.

So Lucrece must I force to my desire";
Troil., III. iii. 257, "It [wit] lies as
coldly in him as fire in a flint, which
will not show without knocking."
    114. *blood ill-temper'd*] a badly-
balanced disposition, presumably containing too much of *that rash humour*
which Cassius admits to having in
l. 119. Aldis Wright quotes from
Davies of Hereford's *Microcosmos*:
"Well-tempred, is an equal counter-
poise / Of th' Elements' forementioned
qualities. / . . . Ill-tempred's that where
some one Element / Hath more dominion then it ought to haue." In l. 115
ill-temper'd suggests as well something
closer to its modern sense.
    117. *What's the matter?*] "Spoken in
a tone of conscious sympathy, for
Cassius's 'O Brutus!' expresses almost
uncontrollable agitation"(Kittredge).
    119. *rash humour*] irascible tempera-
ment. There is no warrant in Plutarch

for Cassius's having inherited this from
his mother. But it is a vivid touch, and
is effectively taken up in Brutus's
reply.
    121. *over-earnest*] A few moments
earlier it was Cassius's *rash choler*, and
the *venom* of his *spleen*.
    122. *and leave you so*] and leave it at
that.
    122. S.D. Enter a Poet . . .] Marked
rather early in the Folio, whether by
the prompter, so that it should catch
his eye in good time, or because we
must suppose that the entry was from
a far corner of the stage, and it took
some moments for the new arrivals to
be within speaking distance of Cassius.
    123. Poet] In Plutarch he is one
Marcus Phaonius, who "took upon
him to counterfeit a [Cynic] Philosopher, not with wisdom and discretion, but with a certain bedlam and
frantic motion".

They be alone.   125
Lucil. You shall not come to them.
Poet. Nothing but death shall stay me.
Cas. How now? What's the matter?
Poet. For shame, you generals! What do you mean?
　　Love, and be friends, as two such men should be;   130
　　For I have seen more years, I'm sure, than ye.
Cas. Ha, ha! how vildly doth this cynic rhyme!
Bru. Get you hence, sirrah! Saucy fellow, hence!
Cas. Bear with him, Brutus; 'tis his fashion.
Bru. I'll know his humour, when he knows his time.   135
　　What should the wars do with these jigging fools?
　　Companion, hence!
Cas.　　　　　　　　Away, away, be gone!   [*Exit Poet.*
Bru. Lucilius and Titinius, bid the commanders
　　Prepare to lodge their companies to-night.
Cas. And come yourselves, and bring Messala with you   140
　　Immediately to us.   [*Exeunt Lucilius and Titinius.*]
Bru.　　　　　　Lucius, a bowl of wine. [*Exit Lucius.*]
Cas. I did not think you could have been so angry.
Bru. O Cassius, I am sick of many griefs.
Cas. Of your philosophy you make no use,
　　If you give place to accidental evils.   145
Bru. No man bears sorrow better. Portia is dead.
Cas. Ha? Portia?
Bru. She is dead.
Cas. How 'scap'd I killing, when I cross'd you so?

141. S.D. *Exeunt . . . Titinius.*] *Rowe; not in* F.   S.D. *Exit Lucius.*] *Not in* F.

130–1. *Love, and be friends . . . than ye*]
From North (Sk., p. 135): "This
Phaonius . . . with a certain scoffing
and mocking gesture . . . rehearsed the
verses which old Nestor said in Homer:
My lords, I pray you hearken both to
me, / For I have seen mo years than
suchie three." In Plutarch he actually
quotes Homer's line from the *Iliad*
(i. 259): ἀλλὰ πίθεσθ'· ἄμφω δὲ
νεωτέρω ἐστὸν ἐμεῖο ("But listen to
me. You are both younger than I.")
Disregarding the reference to Homer,
and improving very slightly on North's
version, Shakespeare attributes the
verse to Phaonius himself; and probably it is on the strength of this that
he transforms him from a pseudo-
philosopher into a poet.

135. *I'll know . . . his time*] I'll accept
his eccentricity when he knows the
right time for it.

137. *Companion*] fellow—contemptuously used, as elsewhere in Shakespeare.

144–5. *Of your philosophy . . . accidental evils*] As a Stoic Brutus should
not have allowed himself to give way
to *accidental evils*, i.e., the evils brought
about by chance.

   O insupportable and touching loss!   150
   Upon what sickness?
Bru.   Impatient of my absence,
   And grief that young Octavius with Mark Antony
   Have made themselves so strong; for with her death
   That tidings came. With this she fell distract,
   And, her attendants absent, swallow'd fire.   155
Cas. And died so?
Bru.   Even so.
Cas.   O ye immortal gods!

Enter Boy [LUCIUS] *with wine and tapers.*

Bru. Speak no more of her. Give me a bowl of wine.
   In this I bury all unkindness, Cassius.   [*Drinks.*
Cas. My heart is thirsty for that noble pledge.
   Fill, Lucius, till the wine o'erswell the cup.   160
   I cannot drink too much of Brutus' love.   [*Exit Lucius.*]

Enter TITINIUS *and* MESSALA.

Bru. Come in, Titinius. Welcome, good Messala.
   Now sit we close about this taper here,
   And call in question our necessities.
Cas. Portia, art thou gone?
Bru.   No more, I pray you.   165
   Messala, I have here received letters,
   That young Octavius and Mark Antony
   Come down upon us with a mighty power,
   Bending their expedition toward Philippi.
Mes. Myself have letters of the self-same tenor.   170

---

161. S.D. *Exit Lucius.*] *Not in* F.   162.] *As Rowe;* Come . . . *Titinius:* |
. . . *Messala:* | F.   170. tenor] *Theobald* (tenour); Tenure F.

150. *touching*] grievous.

151–2. *Impatient . . . grief*] The construction changes, but the meaning is plain. "*Impatience* and 'absence' concurring wounded the poet's ear; he put up with 'impatient' and hopes his reader will do so" (Capell).

153–4. *for with . . . came*] for together with the news of her death came tid-

ings of that (i.e., of the strength of Antony and Octavius).

155. *swallow'd fire*] For Plutarch on this incident, see Appendix, p. 157.

157–8. *Give me . . . unkindness*] Cf. *Wiv.*, I. i. 103, "I hope we shall drink down all unkindness."

170. *tenor*] purport. The Folio has the variant spelling *tenure*.

Bru. With what addition?

Mes. That by proscription and bills of outlawry
    Octavius, Antony, and Lepidus
    Have put to death an hundred senators.

Bru. Therein our letters do not well agree.   175
    Mine speak of seventy senators that died
    By their proscriptions, Cicero being one.

Cas. Cicero one?

Mes.   Cicero is dead,
    And by that order of proscription.
    [Had you your letters from your wife, my lord?   180

178–9. Cicero is dead, / And . . . proscription. /] *As Capell; Cicero* is dead, and . . . proscription / *F.*

172. *proscription*] condemnation to outlawry or death; here, as the context shows, to death.

180–94. *Had you . . . bear it so*] This passage contradicts what Brutus has told Cassius of Portia's death (ll. 146–56). Resch (*Archiv für das Studium der Neueren Sprachen*, 1882) suggested that the inconsistency could be explained only by the supposition that the copy from which the Folio was printed contained two versions of the account of Portia's death, of which one was a revision, and that both were printed by mistake. Macmillan reached this conclusion independently: "It is very possible that when Shakespeare first wrote the play his intention was to give an impressive illustration of Brutus's stoicism and subordination of private feelings to public necessities. . . Afterwards he may have seen that such a representation of Brutus would be inconsistent with the gentleness previously ascribed to him, and added the lines in which he reveals his loss to Cassius." With most recent editors, I accept these views, and take the present passage to be the original version of the announcement of Portia's death, not clearly cancelled in the MS. when the revelation to Cassius was added. I therefore enclose it in square brackets. If this hypothesis is correct, I take the "revised version" which Shakespeare

added to replace this passage to be ll. 142–57 and l. 165. In the "original version" of the scene without these lines, Brutus would presumably have carried on from l. 141 to what is now l. 158:

Bru.   Lucius, a bowl of wine.
    In this I bury all unkindness,
        Cassius.

Lucius would not then have left the tent to fetch the wine—but it is natural to suppose that Brutus would keep his wine in his own tent; and there would have been time during the pledges for Lucilius and Titinius to go out at l. 141 (as they obviously do, though the Folio neglects to give the necessary S.D.) to pass on Brutus's orders to the commanders, and for Titinius to return with Messala at l. 161. We must also presume that, having decided to make the revision, Shakespeare sent Lucius out of the tent while Brutus told Cassius of Portia's death, as the re-entry S.D. after l. 156 indicates; but he neglected to add the *Exit* S.D. which modern editions supply at l. 141. All this assumes that no other deletions or alterations were made to fit in the new lines; other changes may of course have been necessary. What appear to be similar uncancelled duplications are found in other Shakespearian texts: e.g., *LLL.*, IV. iii, where in Berowne's great speech

Bru. No, Messala.
Mes. Nor nothing in your letters writ of her?
Bru. Nothing, Messala.
Mes.　　　　　　　　That, methinks, is strange.
Bru. Why ask you? Hear you aught of her in yours?
Mes. No, my lord.　　　　　　　　　　　　　　185
Bru. Now as you are a Roman, tell me true.
Mes. Then like a Roman bear the truth I tell;
　　　For certain she is dead, and by strange manner.
Bru. Why, farewell, Portia. We must die, Messala.
　　　With meditating that she must die once,　　　190
　　　I have the patience to endure it now.
Mes. Even so great men great losses should endure.
Cas. I have as much of this in art as you,
　　　But yet my nature could not bear it so.]
Bru. Well, to our work alive. What do you think　195
　　　Of marching to Philippi presently?
Cas. I do not think it good.
Bru.　　　　　　　　　Your reason?
Cas.　　　　　　　　　　　This it is:
　　　'Tis better that the enemy seek us;
　　　So shall he waste his means, weary his soldiers,
　　　Doing himself offence, whilst we, lying still,　200
　　　Are full of rest, defence, and nimbleness.
Bru. Good reasons must of force give place to better.

184.] *As Rowe;* Why . . . you? / . . . yours? / *F.*

ll. 293–314 have been reworked in the
remaining fifty-odd lines of the speech,
and v. ii, where ll. 807–12 appear in a
revised form in ll. 831–44. (See
Richard David's notes on these passages in his Arden *LLL.*, and his Introduction, pp. xx–xxi.) For arguments
that Shakespeare intended both passages announcing Portia's death to
stand, see Warren D. Smith, 'The
Duplicate Revelation of Portia's
Death' (*Shak. Quarterly*, IV, no. 2, pt I,
Apr. 1935, pp. 153–61).

190. *once*] at some time. Cf. *Mac.*,
v. I. v-7, "She should have (i.e., must
have) died hereafter", where, however, Macbeth's state of mind is very

different from that of Brutus.

193. *I have . . . in art as you*] theo-
retically I have as much of this philosophic fortitude as you.

195. *to our work alive*] to the work
that is our present concern, perhaps
with some implication that work
which concerns the living is of more
immediate importance than grief for
the dead. Thus, subordinating "private feelings to public necessities,"
according to the "original version" of
the scene he dismisses Portia's death,
according to the "revised version"
Cicero's.

200. *offence*] harm. Cf. II. i. 268.
202. *of force*] of necessity, perforce

The people 'twixt Philippi and this ground
Do stand but in a forc'd affection;
For they have grudg'd us contribution.   205
The enemy, marching along by them,
By them shall make a fuller number up,
Come on refresh'd, new-added, and encourag'd;
From which advantage shall we cut him off
If at Philippi we do face him there,   210
These people at our back.

Cas.   Hear me, good brother.

Bru. Under your pardon. You must note beside
That we have tried the utmost of our friends,
Our legions are brim-full, our cause is ripe.
The enemy increaseth every day;   215
We, at the height, are ready to decline.
There is a tide in the affairs of men,
Which, taken at the flood, leads on to fortune;
Omitted, all the voyage of their life
Is bound in shallows and in miseries.   220
On such a full sea are we now afloat,
And we must take the current when it serves,
Or lose our ventures.

Cas.   Then, with your will, go on;

208. *new-added*] *Capell;* new added *F;* new aided *Singer;* new-hearted *Collier.*
223-4.] *As Capell;* Then ... along / ... *Philippi.* / *F.*

208. *new-added*] reinforced.

212 ff. *Under your pardon...*] We may
compare the speech at III. i. 235 beginning, "By your pardon", in which,
against the better judgement of
Cassius, Brutus insists that Antony be
allowed to speak at Cæsar's funeral.
As there, and as earlier at II. i. 162 ff,
Cassius lets himself be overruled, with
serious consequences for the conspira-
torial party. At v. i. 74-6 he disclaims
responsibility for the present decision.

217-20. *There is a tide ... in miseries*]
Editors cite many passages that express
the same thought: e.g., Chaucer,
Troilus and Criseyde, II. 281-7; Chapman, *Bussy D'Ambois,* I. i. 114-18;
Beaumont and Fletcher, *The Custom of*
the Country, II. iii. 63-8; and *The Bloody*
Brother, II. i. 2-6, etc. Kittredge suggests that the sentiment may be traced
back to "a philosophical commonplace that Shakespeare had read in
one of his earliest schoolbooks—*Cato's*
Distichs, II. 26: Rem tibi quam noris
aptam dimittere noli: / Fronte capil-
lata, post est occasio calva." He adds
parallels from *All's W.* and *Oth.*

219. *Omitted*] missed, neglected.

220. *bound in*] limited to, confined
to.

shallows . . . miseries] The metaphorical *shallows* is emphasized and
explained by *miseries.*

223. *ventures*] merchandise risked in
trade. Cf. *Mer.V.,*I. i. 15, etc.

with your will] as you desire it.

We'll along ourselves, and meet them at Philippi.

Bru. The deep of night is crept upon our talk,   225
And nature must obey necessity,
Which we will niggard with a little rest.
There is no more to say?

Cas.   No more. Good night.
Early to-morrow will we rise, and hence.

Bru. Lucius!

Enter LUCIUS.

My gown.   [*Exit Lucius.*]
                Farewell, good Messala.   230
Good night, Titinius. Noble, noble Cassius,
Good night, and good repose.

Cas.   O my dear brother,
This was an ill beginning of the night.
Never come such division 'tween our souls!
Let it not, Brutus.

Enter LUCIUS, *with the gown.*

Bru.   Every thing is well.   235

Cas. Good night, my lord.

Bru.   Good night, good brother.

Tit., Mes. Good night, Lord Brutus.

Bru.   Farewell, every one.
                Exeunt [*Cassius, Titinius, and Messala*].
Give me the gown. Where is thy instrument?

Luc. Here in the tent.

Bru.   What, thou speak'st drowsily?

228. to say?] *Capell;* to say. *F.*   230. S.D. *Enter Lucius.*] *After* hence (*l. 229*) *F.*
S.D. *Exit Lucius.*] *Not in F.*   236. *Cas.* Good night, . . . brother.] *F; omitted*
Pope, Theobald, Hanmer, Warburton, Johnson.   237. S.D. *Cassius . . . Messala*]
Not in F.

227. *niggard*] "stint or put off with
short allowance" (Aldis Wright).
230. S.D. Enter Lucius] In the
Folio this appears before l. 230, which
is printed as an unbroken line,
"*Lucius* my Gowne: farewell good
Messala". It is most unlikely that
Lucius would break into a council of
war without being summoned, and I
have therefore broken the line to let
Brutus call him, and have supplied the
exit stage-direction which is rendered
necessary by the Folio re-entry direction in l. 235.
gown] See note on night-gown, II. ii.
S.D.

Poor knave, I blame thee not; thou art o'er-watch'd. 240
Call Claudius and some other of my men;
I'll have them sleep on cushions in my tent.
Luc. Varro and Claudius!

Enter VARRO *and* CLAUDIUS.

Var. Calls my lord?
Bru. I pray you, sirs, lie in my tent and sleep.   245
It may be I shall raise you by and by
On business to my brother Cassius.
Var. So please you, we will stand and watch your pleasure.
Bru. I will not have it so; lie down, good sirs;
It may be I shall otherwise bethink me.   250
                    [*Varro and Claudius lie down.*]
Look, Lucius, here's the book I sought for so;
I put it in the pocket of my gown.
Luc. I was sure your lordship did not give it me.
Bru. Bear with me, good boy, I am much forgetful.
Canst thou hold up thy heavy eyes awhile,   255
And touch thy instrument a strain or two?
Luc. Ay, my lord, an't please you.
Bru.   It does, my boy.
I trouble thee too much, but thou art willing.
Luc. It is my duty, sir.
Bru. I should not urge thy duty past thy might;   260

241. Claudius] *Rowe; Claudio F. (So for rest of scene.)*   243. Varro] *Rowe;
Varrus F. (So for rest of scene.)*   248.] *As Rowe;* So . . . stand, / . . . pleasure. / F.
250. S.D. *Varro . . . down.*] *Not in F.*

240. *Poor knave*] poor lad. Cf. German *Knabe*, meaning "boy".
  I blame thee not] The Second Folio
misprints *not* as *art*, presumably a compositor's anticipation of the *art* which
follows. The Third Folio, printed from
the Second, omits the word as mean-
ingless, and its reading is followed in
the Fourth Folio.
  241, 243. *Varro and Claudius*] Here
and for the rest of the scene these two
names appear in the Folio as Varrus
and Claudio.
  246. *raise*] rouse.

248. *watch your pleasure*] be on the
watch for anything you wish us to do.
But there is something of the basic
meaning of *watch* as well, i.e., "remain
awake": cf. *o'erwatch'd* in l. 240, meaning "tired out by lack of sleep". Dover
Wilson suggests, "keep awake and
wait for".
  250. *otherwise bethink me*] change my
mind.
  251. *the book*] Plutarch more than
once mentions Brutus's fondness for
reading far into the night. See, e.g.,
Appendix, pp. 134, 158.

I know young bloods look for a time of rest.
Luc. I have slept, my lord, already.
Bru. It was well done, and thou shalt sleep again;
I will not hold thee long. If I do live,
I will be good to thee.   [*Music, and a Song.* 265
This is a sleepy tune: O murd'rous slumber!
Layest thou thy leaden mace upon my boy,
That plays thee music? Gentle knave, good night;
I will not do thee so much wrong to wake thee.
If thou dost nod, thou break'st thy instrument;   270
I'll take it from thee; and, good boy, good night.
Let me see, let me see; is not the leaf turn'd down
Where I left reading? Here it is, I think.

Enter the Ghost of CÆSAR.

How ill this taper burns! Ha! who comes here?
I think it is the weakness of mine eyes   275
That shapes this monstrous apparition.
It comes upon me. Art thou any thing?
Art thou some god, some angel, or some devil,
That mak'st my blood cold, and my hair to stare?

266. *murd'rous slumber*] "Because it is the 'death of each day's life' (*Mac.*, II. iii. 81)" (Macmillan).

267. *leaden mace*] The sergeant, or sheriff's officer, carried a mace with which he touched the shoulder of the person whom he arrested. Cf. Spenser, *F.Q.*, I. iv. 44, "But whenas *Morpheus* had with leaden mace / Arrested all that courtly company".

272. *leaf turn'd down*] An anachronism, since Brutus would be reading from a scroll.

274. *How ill this taper burns*] ". . . looking towards the light of the lamp that waxed very dim, he saw a horrible vision of a man, of a wonderful greatness, and dreadful look, which at the first made him marvellously afraid" (North). It was a common superstition that lights burned dim, or blue, in the presence of a ghost or evil spirit. Cf. *The Merry Devil of Edmonton*, Induction, 12, "The lights burne dim,

affrighted with thy presence." Kittredge cites *R 3*, v. iii. 181; Lyly's *Gallathea*, II. iii; and Melton's *Astrologaster* (1620).

276. *apparition*] Plutarch does not specifically say it is Cæsar's ghost. Shakespeare says so in the stage-direction, and Brutus at v. v. 18. But it would be obvious enough to the audience.

277. *Art thou any thing?*] In Plutarch Cassius says in reference to the ghost that, according to the Epicureans, the senses when idle "are induced to imagine they see and conjecture that which in truth they do not". With the next line we may compare *Ham.*, I. iv and II. ii, where, in spite of the unmistakable resemblance, Hamlet and the others cannot be sure that the Ghost is that of the dead king.

279. *stare*] stand on end. Cf. *Tp.*, I. ii. 213, "With hair upstaring".

Speak to me what thou art.   280
Ghost. Thy evil spirit, Brutus.
Bru.   Why com'st thou?
Ghost. To tell thee thou shalt see me at Philippi.
Bru. Well; then I shall see thee again?
Ghost. Ay, at Philippi.
Bru. Why, I will see thee at Philippi then. [*Exit Ghost.*] 285
  Now I have taken heart thou vanishest.
  Ill spirit, I would hold more talk with thee.
  Boy! Lucius! Varro! Claudius! Sirs, awake!
  Claudius!
Luc. The strings, my lord, are false.   290
Bru. He thinks he still is at his instrument.
  Lucius, awake!
Luc. My lord?
Bru. Didst thou dream, Lucius, that thou so criedst out?
Luc. My lord, I do not know that I did cry.   295
Bru. Yes, that thou didst. Didst see anything?
Luc. Nothing, my lord.
Bru. Sleep again, Lucius. Sirrah Claudius!
  Fellow thou, awake!
Var.   My lord?
Clau.   My lord?
Bru. Why did you so cry out, sirs, in your sleep?   300
Both. Did we, my lord?
Bru.   Ay. Saw you any thing?
Var. No, my lord, I saw nothing.
Clau.   Nor I, my lord.
Bru. Go and commend me to my brother Cassius.
  Bid him set on his powers betimes before,
  And we will follow.
Both.   It shall be done, my lord.   [*Exeunt.* 305

---

285. S.D. *Exit Ghost.*] *Rowe; not in F.*   298–9.] *As Capell;* Sleepe . . . Fellow, /
. . . Awake. / *F.*

286. *Now I . . . vanishest*] ". . . Does   is imaginary. . . The very next verse
not indicate that the vision is only sub-   shows that he believes he has seen a
jective and therefore overcome by an   spirit" (Kittredge).
exertion of Brutus's will, but merely   290. *false*] out of tune.
that he tries to persuade himself that it   304. *betimes*] early in the morning.

ACT V

[SCENE I.—*The Plains of Philippi.*]

Enter OCTAVIUS, ANTONY, *and their Army.*

Oct. Now, Antony, our hopes are answered.
　　You said the enemy would not come down,
　　But keep the hills and upper regions.
　　It proves not so; their battles are at hand;
　　They mean to warn us at Philippi here,　　　　　　　5
　　Answering before we do demand of them.
Ant. Tut, I am in their bosoms, and I know
　　Wherefore they do it. They could be content
　　To visit other places, and come down
　　With fearful bravery, thinking by this face　　　　10
　　To fasten in our thoughts that they have courage;
　　But 'tis not so.

Enter a Messenger.

ACT V
Scene I

4. *battles*] armies. Cf. *Mac.*, v. vi. 4, "Lead our first battle."

5. *warn*] summon, challenge. Cf. *John*, II. i. 201, "Who is it that hath warn'd us to the walls?"

at Philippi here] Historically the meeting at Sardis took place early in 42 B.C., and the Battle of Philippi in the following autumn.

6. *Answering . . . of them*] accepting our challenge before we have called them to battle.

7. *in their bosoms*] Cf. II. i. 305, "thy bosom shall partake / The secrets of my heart."

8–9. *could be content . . . other places*] would gladly be elsewhere.

10. *fearful bravery*] Either, with a frightening show of splendour, or, with a show of splendour that covers their fear. The context supports rather the latter interpretation. In Shakespeare *fearful* may have either the objective sense, "inspiring fear", or the subjective, "full of fear". *Bravery* means "splendour, finery", and may also imply "bravado", as here; it never means merely "courage". Cf. *gallant show* (l. 13). North tells us, "For bravery and rich furniture, Brutus' army far excelled Cæsar's. For the most part of their armours were silver and gilt."

face] outward show.

113

Mess.   Prepare you, generals.
    The enemy comes on in gallant show;
    Their bloody sign of battle is hung out,
    And something to be done immediately.   15
Ant. Octavius, lead your battle softly on
    Upon the left hand of the even field.
Oct. Upon the right hand I. Keep thou the left.
Ant. Why do you cross me in this exigent?
Oct. I do not cross you; but I will do so.   [*March.*   20

        Drum. Enter BRUTUS, CASSIUS, *and their Army;*
        [LUCILIUS, TITINIUS, MESSALA, *and others.*]

Bru. They stand, and would have parley.
Cas. Stand fast, Titinius; we must out and talk.
Oct. Mark Antony, shall we give sign of battle?
Ant. No, Cæsar, we will answer on their charge.
    Make forth; the generals would have some words.   25
Oct. Stir not until the signal.
Bru. Words before blows: is it so, countrymen?
Oct. Not that we love words better, as you do.
Bru. Good words are better than bad strokes, Octavius.
Ant. In your bad strokes, Brutus, you give good words;   30
    Witness the hole you made in Cæsar's heart,
    Crying, "Long live! hail, Cæsar!"
Cas.   Antony,
    The posture of your blows are yet unknown;

20. S.D. *Lucilius . . . others.*] *Rowe; not in F.*

    14. *bloody sign of battle*] "The signal
of battle was set out in Brutus' and
Cassius' camp, which was an arming
scarlet coat" (North). A red flag was
the Roman signal for battle.

    16. *softly*] slowly.

    18. *Upon the right hand I*] In Plu-
tarch Brutus insists on commanding
the right wing, in spite of the greater
experience of Cassius. Whether by a
slip of memory, or to bring out the
character of Octavius, Shakespeare
transfers the incident to the opposite
camp.

    19. *exigent*] exigency, crisis.

    20. *I do not cross . . . do so*] I am not
merely perversely thwarting you; but
I will do as I said.

    24. *answer on their charge*] meet them
when they attack.

    25. *Make forth*] go forward.

    27 ff.] Kittredge gives many paral-
lels from Shakespeare and other Elizabethan dramatists to this "flyting" of
the leaders before a battle. It does not
occur in Plutarch.

    33. *The posture of your blows*] what
kind of blows you can strike. The verb
are is attracted into the plural by *blows*
immediately before it.

But for your words, they rob the Hybla bees,
And leave them honeyless.

Ant.   Not stingless too.   35

Bru. O yes, and soundless too;
For you have stol'n their buzzing, Antony,
And very wisely threat before you sting.

Ant. Villains! you did not so when your vile daggers
Hack'd one another in the sides of Cæsar: 40
You show'd your teeth like apes, and fawn'd like hounds,
And bow'd like bondmen, kissing Cæsar's feet;
Whilst damned Casca, like a cur, behind
Struck Cæsar on the neck. O you flatterers!

Cas. Flatterers? Now, Brutus, thank yourself.   45
This tongue had not offended so to-day,
If Cassius might have rul'd.

Oct. Come, come, the cause. If arguing make us sweat,
The proof of it will turn to redder drops.
Look,   50
I draw a sword against conspirators.
When think you that the sword goes up again?
Never, till Cæsar's three and thirty wounds
Be well aveng'd; or till another Cæsar
Have added slaughter to the sword of traitors.   55

Bru. Cæsar, thou canst not die by traitors' hands,
Unless thou bring'st them with thee.

Oct.   So I hope.

36–8. O yes . . . sting.] *F;* You threat before you sting. *Pope, Hanmer, with original
in margin.*   41.] *As Rowe;* You . . . Apes, / . . . Hounds, / *F.*   teeth] *F3;*
teethes *F1.*   50–1.] *As Steevens;* Looke, I *F.*   53. thirty] *F;* twenty *Theobald
and other 18th-c. edd.*

34. *Hybla*] A mountain, and a town,
of Sicily, proverbially famous for
honey. Cf. *1 H 4,* I. ii. 47. Cassius recalls the honeyed words with which
Antony declared his friendship for the
conspirators after the assassination of
Cæsar.

41. *show'd your teeth*] grinned. For
fawn'd like hounds, cf. III. i. 45–6.

47. *If Cassius might have rul'd*] If
Cassius had had his way when he
advised that Antony too should be
slain (II. i. 155–61).

48. *the cause*] the business in hand,
the case being argued.

49. *The proof*] the practical test.

52. *goes up again*] goes back into its
sheath.

53. *three and thirty wounds*] Plutarch
and Suetonius say "three and twenty",
and Theobald emended according-
ly.

54–5. *or till . . . sword of traitors*] or
till another Cæsar (viz., himself) shall
have been slaughtered by the swords
of traitors.

I was not born to die on Brutus' sword.

Bru. O, if thou wert the noblest of thy strain,
Young man, thou could'st not die more honourable.   60

Cas. A peevish school-boy, worthless of such honour,
Join'd with a masker and a reveller.

Ant. Old Cassius still!

Oct.   Come, Antony; away!
Defiance, traitors, hurl we in your teeth.
If you dare fight to-day, come to the field;   65
If not, when you have stomachs.

                    [*Exeunt Octavius, Antony, and Army.*

Cas. Why now, blow wind, swell billow, and swim bark!
The storm is up, and all is on the hazard.

Bru. Ho, Lucilius, hark, a word with you.

Lucil. [*Standing forth.*] My lord?   70

                    [*Brutus and Lucilius talk apart.*]

Cas. Messala.

Mes. [*Standing forth*]. What says my general?

Cas.   Messala,
This is my birth-day; as this very day
Was Cassius born. Give me thy hand, Messala:
Be thou my witness that against my will
(As Pompey was) am I compell'd to set   75
Upon one battle all our liberties.
You know that I held Epicurus strong,
And his opinion; now I change my mind,

67.] *As Rowe;* Why . . . Billow, / . . . Barke: / *F.*   70, 71. S.D. *Standing forth.*]
This edn.; Lucillius and Messala stand forth. F (*after* you, *l.* 69).   70. S.D.
Brutus . . . apart.] *Not in* F.   71–2. Messala, / This] *As Pope; Messala,* this F.

---

61. *A peevish school-boy*] Peevish here
has the sense of "silly, childish". Cf.
AYL., III. v. 110, "'Tis but a peevish
boy." Octavius was actually twenty-
one at this time. In the same line
worthless means "unworthy".

62. *a masker and a reveller*] Cf. I. ii.
200–1, and II. ii. 116.

66. *stomachs*] appetite, inclination.
Cf. *H 5*, IV. iii. 35, "he which hath no
stomach to this fight".

67–8. *blow wind . . . on the hazard*] Cf.
Mac., V. v. 51, "Blow wind, come
wrack, / At least we'll die with har-

ness on our back."

68. *on the hazard*] at stake.

75. *As Pompey was*] At Pharsalia
Pompey was persuaded to give battle
against his better judgement. For the
wording here, close to that of North,
see Appendix, p. 160.

set] stake. North's word is *jeopard*.

77. *held Epicurus strong*] was a firm
follower of Epicurus. The Epicureans
did not believe in omens, for they
thought that the gods were not interested in human affairs. Cf. Horace,
Odes, I. xxxiv.

And partly credit things that do presage.
Coming from Sardis, on our former ensign   80
Two mighty eagles fell, and there they perch'd,
Gorging and feeding from our soldiers' hands,
Who to Philippi here consorted us.
This morning are they fled away and gone,
And in their steads do ravens, crows, and kites   85
Fly o'er our heads, and downward look on us,
As we were sickly prey; their shadows seem
A canopy most fatal, under which
Our army lies, ready to give up the ghost.

Mes. Believe not so.
Cas.   I but believe it partly,   90
For I am fresh of spirit, and resolv'd
To meet all perils very constantly.

Bru. Even so, Lucilius.
Cas.   Now, most noble Brutus,
The gods to-day stand friendly, that we may,
Lovers in peace, lead on our days to age!   95
But since the affairs of men rests still incertain,
Let's reason with the worst that may befall.
If we do lose this battle, then is this
The very last time we shall speak together:
What are you then determined to do?   100

Bru. Even by the rule of that philosophy

---

95. Lovers in peace,] *F*; Lovers, in peace *conj. Furness.*   96. rests] *F*; rest
Rowe and most edd.

---

80. *former ensign*] "Two eagles . . .
lighted upon two of the foremost
ensigns" (North).

85. *ravens, crows, and kites*] Birds of
ill omen which proverbially anticipate
the death of their prey.

88. *fatal*] presaging death.

90. *I but . . . partly*] I only partly
believe it.

92. *constantly*] firmly, resolutely. Cf.
II. i. 227.

93. *Even so, Lucilius*] Presumably
Brutus has been giving instructions to
Lucilius while Cassius speaks to
Messala.

94. *stand*] Subjunctive: "may the

gods stand friendly."

95. *Lovers*] dear friends. Cf.III.ii. 13.

96. *rests*] The third person plural
ending in –*s* is common in Shakespeare. Abbott, ¶333, gives many
examples.

still] always.

97. *Let's reason . . . befall*] let us consider what is to be done if the worst
happens. A proverbial expression. Cf.
Troil., III. ii. 78, "To fear the worst oft
cures the worse"; Udall, *Roister
Doister* (Mal. Soc.), l. 645, "It is good
to cast the wurst."

101. *that philosophy*] The Stoics regarded suicide as *cowardly and vile.*

By which I did blame Cato for the death
Which he did give himself, I know not how,
But I do find it cowardly and vile,
For fear of what might fall, so to prevent   105
The time of life, arming myself with patience
To stay the providence of some high powers
That govern us below.

Cas.   Then, if we lose this battle,
You are contented to be led in triumph
Thorough the streets of Rome?   110

Bru. No, Cassius, no: think not, thou noble Roman,
That ever Brutus will go bound to Rome;
He bears too great a mind. But this same day
Must end that work the ides of March begun;
And whether we shall meet again I know not.   115
Therefore our everlasting farewell take.
For ever, and for ever, farewell, Cassius.
If we do meet again, why, we shall smile;
If not, why then this parting was well made.

Cas. For ever, and for ever, farewell, Brutus.   120
If we do meet again, we'll smile indeed;
If not, 'tis true this parting was well made.

Bru. Why then, lead on. O, that a man might know
The end of this day's business ere it come!

---

106. time] *F*; term *Capell*.   107. some] *F*; those *Collier MS.*, *Craik*.   110. Rome?] *Theobald*; Rome. *F*.   111.] *As Rowe*; No ... no: / ... Romane, / *F*.

Some critics have drawn attention to the apparent inconsistency between Brutus's sentiments here, and those of his next speech—and his suicide later. It is only a partial inconsistency. The views of Brutus the philosopher conflict with those of Brutus the Roman soldier facing the possibility of capture and degradation: "in the midst of the danger I am of a contrary mind" (North).

102. *Cato*] Cato the younger. See note on II. i. 295.

105–6. *to prevent . . . of life*] to anticipate the term of life, the natural end of life. For *prevent*, cf. II. i. 28.

107–8. *To stay . . . us below*] to wait for the fate ordained by higher powers that govern the lives of mortal men. The word *some* suggests that the Stoic Brutus does not believe in the conventional gods of the Roman mythology.

109. *led in triumph*] Perhaps there was little danger of this. The granting and the procedure of triumphs were governed by strict laws. They could be granted only for victories won against external enemies, not in civil wars. As Plutarch makes clear (see Appendix, p. 138) Caesar gave great offence by celebrating a triumph over Pompey's sons.

But it sufficeth that the day will end,   125
And then the end is known. Come, ho! away!   [*Exeunt.*

[SCENE II.—*The Same. The Field of Battle.*]

Alarum. Enter BRUTUS *and* MESSALA.

Bru. Ride, ride, Messala, ride, and give these bills
     Unto the legions on the other side.   [*Loud alarum.*
     Let them set on at once, for I perceive
     But cold demeanour in Octavius' wing,
     And sudden push gives them the overthrow.   5
     Ride, ride, Messala; let them all come down.   [*Exeunt.*

[SCENE III.—*Another Part of the Field.*]

Alarums. Enter CASSIUS *and* TITINIUS.

Cas. O, look, Titinius, look, the villains fly.
     Myself have to mine own turn'd enemy:
     This ensign here of mine was turning back;
     I slew the coward, and did take it from him.
Tit. O Cassius, Brutus gave the word too early,   5

Scene II

4. Octavius'] *Pope; Octauio's F.*

Scene II

S.D. Alarum. Enter Brutus and
Messala] In the Folio this S.D. follows, after a space, the S.D. *Exeunt* at
the end of Brutus's previous speech.
There is of course no other indication
of change of scene. The same thing
happens at the beginning of Scene iv
below, where *Exeunt* at the end of a
speech by Brutus is followed by a new
S.D., *Alarum. Enter* BRUTUS, MESSALA
. . . FLAVIUS. I can recall no other
place in Shakespeare where a S.D. indicating the clearing of the stage is
followed by one indicating the imme-

diate re-entry of persons who have
just left the stage.
     1. *bills*] written orders. ". . . little
bills . . . in the which he wrote the
word of the battle" (North).
     2. *the other side*] the other wing, com-
manded by Cassius.
     4. *cold demeanour*] lack of ardour in
fighting.

Scene III

     1. *the villains*] his own men, of
course.
     3. *ensign*] standard-bearer. In l. 4 it
is the standard itself.

Who, having some advantage on Octavius,
Took it too eagerly; his soldiers fell to spoil,
Whilst we by Antony are all enclos'd.

Enter PINDARUS.

Pin. Fly further off, my lord, fly further off!
Mark Antony is in your tents, my lord.   10
Fly, therefore, noble Cassius, fly far off!
Cas. This hill is far enough. Look, look, Titinius!
Are those my tents where I perceive the fire?
Tit. They are, my lord.
Cas.   Titinius, if thou lov'st me,
Mount thou my horse, and hide thy spurs in him,   15
Till he have brought thee up to yonder troops
And here again, that I may rest assur'd
Whether yond troops are friend or enemy.
Tit. I will be here again, even with a thought.   [*Exit.*
Cas. Go, Pindarus, get higher on that hill;   20
My sight was ever thick. Regard Titinius,
And tell me what thou not'st about the field.
                                    [*Exit Pindarus.*]
This day I breathed first. Time is come round,
And where I did begin, there shall I end.
My life is run his compass. Sirrah, what news?   25
Pin. [*Above.*] O my lord!
Cas. What news?
Pin. Titinius is enclosed round about
With horsemen, that make to him on the spur,
Yet he spurs on. Now they are almost on him.   30
Now, Titinius! now some light. O, he lights too!
He's ta'en!   [*Shout.*
                And, hark! they shout for joy.
Cas. Come down; behold no more.
O, coward that I am, to live so long,

22. S.D. *Exit Pindarus.*] *Hanmer; not in* F.

11. *far*] Probably comparative, the
same as *further off* in l. 9. Cf. III. ii. 169.
19. *with a thought*] as quick as
thought—as often in Shakespeare.

21. *thick*] dim. *Regard* means "observe".
25. *his compass*] its full circuit.
31. *light*] alight.

To see my best friend ta'en before my face!   35

Enter PINDARUS [*from above*].

Come hither, sirrah.
In Parthia did I take thee prisoner;
And then I swore thee, saving of thy life,
That whatsoever I did bid thee do,
Thou shouldst attempt it. Come now, keep thine
    oath.   40
Now be a freeman; and with this good sword,
That ran through Cæsar's bowels, search this
    bosom.
Stand not to answer. Here, take thou the hilts,
And when my face is cover'd, as 'tis now,
Guide thou the sword.—Cæsar, thou art reveng'd,   45
Even with the sword that kill'd thee.   [*Dies.*]
Pin. So, I am free; yet would not so have been,
Durst I have done my will. O Cassius!
Far from this country Pindarus shall run,
Where never Roman shall take note of him.   [*Exit.*]

Enter TITINIUS *and* MESSALA.

Mes. It is but change, Titinius; for Octavius   51
Is overthrown by noble Brutus' power,
As Cassius' legions are by Antony.
Tit. These tidings will well comfort Cassius.
Mes. Where did you leave him?
Tit.   All disconsolate,   55
With Pindarus his bondman, on this hill.
Mes. Is not that he that lies upon the ground?
Tit. He lies not like the living. O my heart!
Mes. Is not that he?

36–7. Come . . . sirrah. / In . . . prisoner; /] *As Pope;* Come . . . sirrah: In . . .
Prisoner, / F.   46. S.D. *Dies.*] *Capell; not in* F.   47.] *As Rowe;* So, . . . free, /
. . . beene / F.   50. S.D. *Exit.*] *Not in* F.

38. *swore thee*] made thee swear—as
in "the jury were sworn."
42. *search*] probe, penetrate. Cf.
LLL., 1. i. 85, "glorious sun, / That will
not be deep search'd with saucy looks".

46. *the sword that kill'd thee*] "He . . .
slew himself with the same sword,
with the which he strake Cæsar"
(North).
51. *change*] exchange of fortune.

Tit.   No, this was he, Messala,
But Cassius is no more. O setting sun,   60
As in thy red rays thou dost sink to night,
So in his red blood Cassius' day is set.
The sun of Rome is set. Our day is gone;
Clouds, dews, and dangers come; our deeds are
    done.
Mistrust of my success hath done this deed.   65
Mes. Mistrust of good success hath done this deed.
O hateful Error, Melancholy's child,
Why dost thou show to the apt thoughts of men
The things that are not? O Error, soon conceiv'd,
Thou never com'st unto a happy birth,   70
But kill'st the mother that engender'd thee.
Tit. What, Pindarus! Where art thou, Pindarus?
Mes. Seek him, Titinius, whilst I go to meet
The noble Brutus, thrusting this report
Into his ears. I may say thrusting it;   75
For piercing steel and darts envenomed
Shall be as welcome to the ears of Brutus
As tidings of this sight.
Tit.   Hie you, Messala,
And I will seek for Pindarus the while.   [*Exit Messala.*]
Why didst thou send me forth, brave Cassius?   80
Did I not meet thy friends, and did not they
Put on my brows this wreath of victory,
And bid me give it thee? Didst thou not hear their
    shouts?
Alas, thou hast misconstrued every thing.
But hold thee, take this garland on thy brow;   85
Thy Brutus bid me give it thee, and I
Will do his bidding. Brutus, come apace,
And see how I regarded Caius Cassius.

79. S.D. *Exit Messala.*] *Not in F.*

60. *O setting sun*] But note l. 109,
"'Tis three a clock."

65. *Mistrust . . . success*] fear of the
outcome of my mission. Cf. II. ii. 6.

67. *Melancholy's child*] Melancholy
people imagine non-existent evils.

68. *apt*] willing (to be deceived).

71. *the mother*] i.e., Melancholy, and
by transference the melancholy person
who conceived the error, here Cassius.

80. *brave*] noble. Cf. l. 96.

88. *regarded*] honoured.

By your leave, gods. This is a Roman's part:
Come, Cassius' sword, and find Titinius' heart.   [*Dies.*

Alarum. Enter BRUTUS, MESSALA, YOUNG CATO,
STRATO, VOLUMNIUS, *and* LUCILIUS.

Bru. Where, where, Messala, doth his body lie?   91
Mes. Lo, yonder, and Titinius mourning it.
Bru. Titinius' face is upward.
Cato.   He is slain.
Bru. O Julius Cæsar, thou art mighty yet!
   Thy spirit walks abroad, and turns our swords   95
   In our own proper entrails.   [*Low alarums.*
Cato.   Brave Titinius!
   Look where he have not crown'd dead Cassius.
Bru. Are yet two Romans living such as these?
   The last of all the Romans, fare thee well!
   It is impossible that ever Rome   100
   Should breed thy fellow. Friends, I owe moe tears
   To this dead man than you shall see me pay.
   I shall find time, Cassius, I shall find time.
   Come therefore, and to Thasos send his body.
   His funerals shall not be in our camp,   105
   Lest it discomfort us. Lucilius, come;
   And come, young Cato; let us to the field.
   Labeo and Flavius, set our battles on.

97. where] *F;* whe'r *Capell;* whether *Variorum 1773;* if *Pope.*   99. The last] *F;*
Thou last *Rowe.*   101. moe] mo *F;* more *Rowe.*   104. Thasos] *Cambridge;*
Thassos *Theobald; Tharsus F.*   108. Labeo] *Hanmer; Labio F.*   Flavius] *F2;*
Flauio F1.

89. *By your leave, gods*] Because he is
ending his life before the time appointed by the gods.

94–5. *O Julius Cæsar . . . walks
abroad*] Cf. II. i. 167–70, and III. i.
270 ff.

96. *proper*] own (Latin, *proprius*).
Own proper is an emphatic repetition.

97. *where*] whether. Cf. I. i. 61, and
v. iv. 30.

99–101. *The last . . . thy fellow*]
"After he had lamented the death of
Cassius, calling him the last of all the
Romans, being impossible that Rome
should ever breed again so noble and
valiant a man as he, he caused his body
to be buried, and sent it unto the city
of Thasos" (North).

104. *Thasos*] An island off the coast
of Thrace near Philippi. The *Tharsus*
of the Folio is an alternative spelling of
Tarsus, whether the chief city of
Cilicia or the town in Bithynia.

106. *discomfort us*] dishearten our
troops.

'Tis three a clock; and, Romans, yet ere night
We shall try fortune in a second fight.   [*Exeunt.*   110

[SCENE IV.—*Another Part of the Field.*]

Alarum. Enter BRUTUS, MESSALA, [YOUNG] CATO,
LUCILIUS, *and* FLAVIUS.

Bru. Yet, countrymen, O, yet hold up your heads!   [*Exit.*]
Cato. What bastard doth not? Who will go with me?
I will proclaim my name about the field.
I am the son of Marcus Cato, ho!
A foe to tyrants, and my country's friend.   5
I am the son of Marcus Cato, ho!

Enter Soldiers, and fight.

Lucil. And I am Brutus, Marcus Brutus, I!

Scene IV

1. S.D. *Exit.*] *This edn.; not in F.*   6. S.D. *Enter . . . fight.*] *F; before l. 1 most edd.*
7. *Lucil.* And] *Macmillan, Dover Wilson; And F; Bru. And Rowe and most other edd.*

110. *second fight*] Historically the
second fight took place twenty days
later.

Scene IV

S.D. Enter Brutus . . . Flavius] See
note on S.D. at the beginning of v. ii.
   2. *What bastard doth not?*] who is of
such base blood that he does not?
   4. *son of Marcus Cato*] Son of Cato of
Utica, and hence Brutus's brother-in-
law.
   7–8. *And I am Brutus . . . know me for
Brutus*] There is no speech-heading at
l. 7 in the Folio, which has *Luc.* before l. 9. Rowe supplied *Bru.* at l. 7, and
Pope [*Exit*] after l. 8; in this they were
followed by subsequent editors until
Macmillan made the change which is
shown in the present text, and which
Dover Wilson supports, though both
have transferred to the beginning of
the scene the Folio stage-direction
after l. 6 which was perhaps the cause

of the compositor's mistake. I restore
the stage-direction to its original
place, allowing the first two speeches
of the scene to be spoken in a place
from which the fighting has for the
moment withdrawn. Macmillan's reasons for the change in speech-heading
seem convincing: ". . . Brutus was so
well known that it is strange that he
should tell his name with such emphasis, and it is still more strange that
he should follow the lead of such a
young man as Cato. The iteration of
the name Brutus sounds like the language of a man who was pretending to
be what he was not. The ascription of
these two lines to Lucilius would make
the motive and action of Lucilius much
plainer to the audience, who would
have some difficulty in taking in the
situation with only the words 'Kill
Brutus' in l. 14, to enlighten them.
It seems probable that the printers of
the Folio by mistake put the heading

Brutus, my country's friend; know me for Brutus!
O young and noble Cato, art thou down?
Why, now thou diest as bravely as Titinius,   10
And mayst be honour'd, being Cato's son.
1. Sold. Yield, or thou diest.
Lucil.   Only I yield to die:
There is so much that thou wilt kill me straight:
Kill Brutus, and be honour'd in his death.
1. Sold. We must not. A noble prisoner!   15

Enter ANTONY.

2. Sold. Room, ho! Tell Antony, Brutus is ta'en.
1. Sold. I'll tell the news. Here comes the general.
Brutus is ta'en, Brutus is ta'en, my lord.
Ant. Where is he?
Lucil. Safe, Antony; Brutus is safe enough.   20
I dare assure thee that no enemy
Shall ever take alive the noble Brutus.

8. Brutus!] *Brutus. F; Brutus. Exit. | Pope and most edd.*   9. O] *Macmillan,*
Dover Wilson; Luc. O F, *Rowe and most edd.*   13.] *As F;* S.D. *Giving him money.*
added Hanmer and most edd.   17. the news] *Pope;* thee news *F.*

'*Luc.*' two lines too low down." The
source (see Appendix, p. 163) makes it
quite clear too that Lucilius is here intended to impersonate Brutus. It must
be assumed, I think, that after his
rallying words in l. 1, Brutus hurries
away to encourage or lead others of his
soldiers, and I have indicated this by
inserting the stage-direction [*Exit*]
after l. 1.

13–14. *There is so much . . . honour'd in
his death*] After l. 13 Hanmer added the
stage-direction [*Giving him money*], and
in this he was followed by later editors
until Macmillan, while retaining it,
cast doubts on its rightness in his
notes: "Possibly Lucilius, speaking in
the character of Brutus, means that so
much can be laid to his charge that the
soldier is sure to kill him immediately."
Although I do not accept this interpretation, I agree that the stage-
direction is unnecessary. I paraphrase
as follows: "Here is a great induce-

ment for you to kill me at once: that
in doing so you will be killing Brutus
and winning great honour." We can
scarcely imagine Brutus behaving in
this way (cf. ll. 21–5); obviously Lucilius hopes to distract the enemy by his
stratagem. We may compare with
this episode that in *1 H 4,* v. III in
which Blunt is killed while imperson-
ating the King in the Battle of
Shrewsbury.

15. S.D. Enter Antony] This Folio
stage-direction occurs rather early,
whether because it was marked so by
the prompter so that it should catch
his eye in good time, or because
we must assume that he enters at
some distance from the soldiers, and
it is a few moments before he is
noticed by them and within speaking
distance.

20–9. *Safe, Antony . . . than enemies*]
Very close to North. See Appendix,
p. 164.

The gods defend him from so great a shame!
When you do find him, or alive or dead,
He will be found like Brutus, like himself.   25
Ant. This is not Brutus, friend; but, I assure you,
A prize no less in worth. Keep this man safe;
Give him all kindness. I had rather have
Such men my friends than enemies. Go on,
And see where Brutus be alive or dead;   30
And bring us word unto Octavius' tent
How every thing is chanc'd.   [*Exeunt.*

[SCENE V.—*Another Part of the Field.*]

Enter BRUTUS, DARDANIUS, CLITUS, STRATO, *and*
VOLUMNIUS.

Bru. Come, poor remains of friends, rest on this rock.
Cli. Statilius show'd the torch-light; but, my lord,
He came not back; he is or ta'en or slain.
Bru. Sit thee down, Clitus. Slaying is the word;
It is a deed in fashion. Hark thee, Clitus.   [*Whispers.*]
Cli. What, I, my lord? No, not for all the world.   6
Bru. Peace then. No words.
Cli.   I'll rather kill myself.
Bru. Hark thee, Dardanius.   [*Whispers.*]
Dar.   Shall I do such a deed?
Cli. O Dardanius!

30. where] *F;* whe'r *Capell;* whether *Variorum 1773;* if *Pope.*

Scene v

5, 8. S.D. *Whispers.*] *Not in F; Whispering. Rowe.*

30. *where*] whether, as at v. iii. 97,
and earlier in the play.

Scene v

2. *show'd the torch-light*] Statilius had
volunteered to make his way to the
camp through the body of the enemy,
and to hold up a torch if he found all
well there. The context would make it
clear enough to the audience that

Statilius was a scout who had not
returned. Dover Wilson points out
that "the reference to 'torchlight'
shows the time as already night."

5. *a deed in fashion*] He refers to the
suicide of Cassius and Titinius in
v. iii. See the note on *that philosophy* at
v. i. 101.

8. *Dardanius*] North rightly calls
him Dardanus.

Dar. O Clitus!   10
Cli. What ill request did Brutus make to thee?
Dar. To kill him, Clitus. Look, he meditates.
Cli. Now is that noble vessel full of grief,
  That it runs over even at his eyes.
Bru. Come hither, good Volumnius: list a word.   15
Vol. What says my lord?
Bru.   Why, this, Volumnius:
  The ghost of Cæsar hath appear'd to me
  Two several times by night: at Sardis once,
  And this last night, here in Philippi fields.
  I know my hour is come.
Vol.   Not so, my lord.   20
Bru. Nay, I am sure it is, Volumnius.
  Thou seest the world, Volumnius, how it goes:
  Our enemies have beat us to the pit.   [*Low alarums.*
  It is more worthy to leap in ourselves
  Than tarry till they push us. Good Volumnius,   25
  Thou know'st that we two went to school together:
  Even for that our love of old, I prithee
  Hold thou my sword-hilts, whilst I run on it.
Vol. That's not an office for a friend, my lord.   [*Alarum still.*
Cli. Fly, fly, my lord, there is no tarrying here.   30
Bru. Farewell to you; and you; and you, Volumnius.
  Strato, thou hast been all this while asleep;
  Farewell to thee too, Strato.—Countrymen,
  My heart doth joy that yet in all my life
  I found no man but he was true to me.   35

28. sword-hilts] *Malone;* Sword Hilts *F.* 33. to thee too, Strato.—Countrymen,] *Theobald;* to thee, to *Strato,* Countrymen: *F.*

13. *vessel full of grief*] Cf. *Wint.,*
III. iii. 21, "I never saw a vessel of
like sorrow / So fill'd and so becoming."
 17. *The ghost of Cæsar*] If there could
be any doubts of the identity of the
apparition in IV. iii, these words would
settle them.
 22. *the world . . . how it goes*] how
things are going on now.
 23. *the pit*] the pit into which wild
animals are driven when they are to be
captured, with the sense of "grave"
implied as well.
 26. *to school together*] From Plutarch.
 28. *sword-hilts*] The plural, presumably used because the hilt of a
sword has more than one part, is regular in Shakespeare; cf. v. iii. 43.
According to A. C. Partridge (*The
Accidence of Ben Jonson's Plays,* 1953),
the singular form *hilt* is found in only
one early Shakespearian text, the
seventh Quarto of *R 3* (1629).

I shall have glory by this losing day
More than Octavius and Mark Antony
By this vile conquest shall attain unto.
So fare you well at once; for Brutus' tongue
Hath almost ended his life's history.   40
Night hangs upon mine eyes; my bones would rest,
That have but labour'd to attain this hour.

        [Alarum. Cry within, "Fly, fly, fly!"

Cli. Fly, my lord, fly!
Bru.   Hence! I will follow.

        [Exeunt Clitus, Dardanius, and Volumnius.]
I prithee, Strato, stay thou by thy lord.
Thou art a fellow of a good respect;   45
Thy life hath had some smatch of honour in it.
Hold then my sword, and turn away thy face,
While I do run upon it. Wilt thou, Strato?
Stra. Give me your hand first. Fare you well, my lord.
Bru. Farewell, good Strato.—Cæsar, now be still;   50
I kill'd not thee with half so good a will.   *[Dies.*

    Alarum. Retreat. Enter ANTONY, OCTAVIUS, MESSALA,
              LUCILIUS, *and the Army.*

Oct. What man is that?
Mes. My master's man. Strato, where is thy master?
Stra. Free from the bondage you are in, Messala.
The conquerors can but make a fire of him;   55
For Brutus only overcame himself,
And no man else hath honour by his death.
Lucil. So Brutus should be found. I thank thee, Brutus,
That thou hast prov'd Lucilius' saying true.

40. life's] *Q 1691;* liues *F.*   43. S.D. *Exeunt . . . Volumnius.] Capell; not in F.*

38. *vile conquest*] No doubt it is vile, in the eyes of Brutus, because it entails the destruction of freedom in Rome. He still believes that the death of Cæsar was necessary.

42. *this hour*] "Death is no calamity according to the Stoic belief of Brutus, but, if nobly attained, a rest from the evils of life" (Kittredge). Cf. l. 36.

45. *of a good respect*] of good reputation. Cf. I. ii. 58.

46. *smatch*] smack, taste.

50. *Cæsar, now be still*] Cæsar's ghost, having been avenged, may now rest.

55. *can but make a fire of him*] can only burn his body, not capture him alive.

59. *Lucilius' saying*] See above, v. iv. 21–2.

Oct. All that serv'd Brutus, I will entertain them.   60
  Fellow, wilt thou bestow thy time with me?
Stra. Ay, if Messala will prefer me to you.
Oct. Do so, good Messala.
Mes. How died my master, Strato?
Stra. I held the sword, and he did run on it.   65
Mes. Octavius, then take him to follow thee,
  That did the latest service to my master.
Ant. This was the noblest Roman of them all.
  All the conspirators save only he
  Did that they did in envy of great Cæsar;   70
  He only, in a general honest thought
  And common good to all, made one of them.
  His life was gentle, and the elements
  So mix'd in him, that Nature might stand up
  And say to all the world, "This was a man!"   75
Oct. According to his virtue let us use him,
  With all respect and rites of burial.
  Within my tent his bones to-night shall lie,

---

71. He only,] *Q 1691;* He, onely *F.* 77. With all] *F3;* Withall *F1.*

60. *entertain*] take into my service. Cf. *Gent.*, II. iv. 105, "entertain him / To be my fellow-servant to your ladyship".

62. *prefer*] recommend. Cf. *2 H 6*, IV. vii. 77, "my book preferr'd me to the king."

67. *latest service*] Strato's act is accepted as a genuine service to Brutus.

68–75. *This was the noblest . . . a man*] Essentially from Plutarch. In bidding farewell to Brutus, Shakespeare emphasizes, in the magnanimous words of his enemy, the purity of his motives in killing Cæsar, and, too, his wrong estimate of the motives of his colleagues.

71–2. *general honest . . . good to all*] with an honourable purpose towards the community, and for the common good of all Romans.

73. *gentle*] noble, magnanimous. Cf. *Cor.*, II. i. 189, "Nay, my good soldier, up; / My gentle Marcius, worthy

Caius"; *Tp.*, I. ii. 467, "Make not too rash a trial of him, for / He's gentle, and not fearful"; Spenser, *F.Q.*, I. i. 1, "A gentle knight was pricking on the plaine"; Jonson, *Discoveries*, LXIV, "had an excellent phantasy, brave notions, and gentle expressions"; Fuller, *Worthies* (Nottinghamshire), "Robert Hood [sic] was . . . the gentlest thief that ever was". In *Shakespeare's Motley* (1952), pp. 24–5, Leslie Hotson establishes this sense of the word as a common Shakespearian usage.

the elements] Loosely used for the humours, as fairly frequently elsewhere in Shakespeare: e.g., *Ado.*, II. i. 359, *Tw.N.*, II. ii. 10. Cf. Marlowe, *1 Tamburlaine*, II. vii. 18, "Nature, that fram'd us of four elements".

75. *This was a man*] Cf. *Ham.*, I. ii. 187, "He was a man, take him for all in all, / I shall not look upon his like again." Cf. also *Ham.*, III. iv. 62.

Most like a soldier, order'd honourably.
So call the field to rest, and let's away,   80
To part the glories of this happy day.   [*Exeunt omnes.*

79. *Most like a soldier*] Cf. *Ham.*, v. ii.
407, "Let four captains / Bear Hamlet,
like a soldier, to the stage."

order'd honourably] treated with all
honour.
81. *part*] share.

Appendix A

THE SOURCE FOR *JULIUS CÆSAR*

The following extracts from North's *Plutarch* are the principal
passages on which Shakespeare's *Julius Cæsar* is based. They are
given in the modernized version of Skeat,[1] whose selection from the
Lives is more easily available than any reprint of the Elizabethan
editions, such as that in the Tudor Translations series. Anyone who
wishes to have a full understanding of what Shakespeare has done
with his source should of course read more widely in the source-
lives than the passages provided here.

I begin with a few passages in which Plutarch discusses the leading personages of the play in general terms. Thereafter the extracts
follow the order in which the events they describe are presented by
Shakespeare.

THE CHARACTER OF CÆSAR

Now Cæsar immediately wan many men's good wills at Rome,
through his eloquence in pleading of their causes, and the people
loved him marvellously also, because of the courteous manner he
had to speak to every man, and to use them gently, being more
ceremonious therein than was looked for in one of his years. Furthermore, he ever kept a good board, and fared well at his table, and
was very liberal besides: the which indeed did advance him forward, and brought him in estimation with the people. His enemies,
judging that this favour of the common people would soon quail,
when he could no longer hold out that charge and expense, suffered
him to run on, till by little and little he was grown to be of great
strength and power. But in fine, when they had thus given him the
bridle to grow to this greatness, and that they could not then pull
him back, though indeed in sight it would turn one day to the destruction of the whole state and commonwealth of Rome; too late
they found, that there is not so little a beginning of any thing, but
continuance of time will soon make it strong, when through con-

1. *Shakespeare's Plutarch*, ed. Walter W. Skeat (Macmillan, 1875). Page
references are to this edition.

tempt there is no impediment to hinder the greatness.[1] (*Life of Cæsar*, p. 45.)

Now Cæsar's self did breed this noble courage and life in them. First, for that he gave them bountifully, and did honour them also, shewing thereby, that he did not heap up riches in the wars to maintain his life afterwards in wantonness and pleasure, but that he did keep it in store, honourably to reward their valiant service: and that by so much he thought himself rich, by how much he was liberal in rewarding of them that had deserved it. Furthermore, they did not wonder so much at his valiantness in putting himself at every instant in such manifest danger, and in taking so extreme pains as he did, knowing that it was his greedy desire of honour that set him on fire, and pricked him forward to do it: but that he always continued all labour and hardness, more than his body could bear, that filled them all with admiration. For, concerning the constitution of his body, he was lean, white, and soft-skinned, and often subject to headache, and otherwhile to the falling sickness (the which took him the first time, as it is reported, in Corduba, a city of Spain:) but yet therefore yielded not to the disease of his body, to make it a cloak to cherish him withal, but contrarily, took the pains of war as a medicine to cure his sick body, fighting always with his disease, travelling continually, living soberly, and commonly lying abroad in the field. (*Life of Cæsar*, p. 57.)

But the chiefest cause that made him mortally hated was the covetous desire he had to be called king: which first gave the people just cause, and next his secret enemies honest colour, to bear him ill-will. This notwithstanding, they that procured him this honour and dignity gave it out among the people that it was written in the Sibylline prophecies, 'how the Romans might overcome the Parthians, if they made war with them and were led by a king, but otherwise that they were unconquerable.' And furthermore they were so bold besides, that, Cæsar returning to Rome from the city of Alba, when they came to salute him, they called him king. But the people being offended, and Cæsar also angry, he said he was not called king, but Cæsar. Then every man keeping silence, he went his way heavy and sorrowful. When they had decreed divers honours for him in the Senate, the Consuls and Praetors, accompanied with the whole assembly of the Senate, went unto him in the market-place, where he was set by the pulpit for orations, to tell him what honours they had decreed for him in his absence. But he, sitting still in his majesty, disdaining to rise up unto them when they came

1. With this last sentence compare Brutus's reasoning when he is soliloquizing in his orchard.

in, as if they had been private men, answered them: 'that his honours had more need to be cut off than enlarged.' This did not only offend the Senate but the common people also, to see that he should so lightly esteem of the magistrates of the commonwealth: insomuch as every man that might lawfully go his way departed thence very sorrowfully. Thereupon also Cæsar rising departed home to his house, and tearing open his doublet-collar, making his neck bare, he cried out aloud to his friends, 'that his throat was ready to offer to any man that would come and cut it.' Notwithstanding it is reported, that afterwards, to excuse his folly, he imputed it to his disease, saying, 'that their wits are not perfit which have this disease of the falling evil, when standing on their feet they speak to the common people, but are soon troubled with a trembling of their body, and a sudden dimness and giddiness.' But that was not true, for he would have risen up to the Senate, but Cornelius Balbus one of his friends (or rather a flatterer) would not let him, saying: "What, do you not remember that you are Cæsar, and will you not let them reverence you and do their duties?" (*Life of Cæsar*, pp. 94–5.)

THE CHARACTER OF BRUTUS

Marcus Brutus came of that Junius Brutus, for whom the ancient Romans made his statue of brass to be set up in the Capitol, with the images of the kings, holding a naked sword in his hand: because he had valiantly put down the Tarquins from the kingdom of Rome. But that Junius Brutus, being of a sour stern nature not softened by reason, being like unto sword-blades of too hard a temper, was so subject to his choler and malice he bare unto the tyrants, that for their sakes he caused his own sons to be executed. But this Marcus Brutus in contrary manner, whose life we presently write, having framed his manners of life by the rules of virtue and study of philosophy, and having employed his wit, which was gentle and constant, in attempting of great things, me thinks he was rightly made and framed unto virtue. So that his very enemies which wish him most hurt, because of his conspiracy against Julius Cæsar, if there were any noble attempt done in all this conspiracy, they refer it wholly unto Brutus; and all the cruel and violent acts unto Cassius, who was Brutus' familiar friend, but not so well given and conditioned as he. (*Life of Brutus*, pp. 105–6.)

He was properly learned in the Latin tongue, and was able to make long discourse in it: beside that he could also plead very well in Latin. But for the Greek tongue, they do note in some of his epistles, that he counterfeited that brief compendious manner of speech of the Lacedaemonians. As, when the war was begun, he wrote unto the Pergamenians in this sort: "I understand you have given Dolabella money: if you have done it willingly, you confess you have offended me; if against your wills, shew it then by giving me willingly." Another time again unto the Samians: "Your councils be long, your doings be slow, consider the end." And in another Epistle he wrote unto[1] the Patareians: "The Xanthians, despising my goodwill, have made their country a grave of despair; and the Patareians, that put themselves into my protection, have lost no jot of their liberty: and therefore, whilst you have liberty, either choose the judgment of the Patareians, or the fortune of the Xanthians." These were Brutus' manner of letters, which were honoured for their briefness. (*Life of Brutus*, p. 107.)

Afterwards, when the empire of Rome was divided into factions, and that Cæsar and Pompey both were in arms one against the other, and that all the empire of Rome was in garboil and uproar: it was thought then that Brutus would take part with Cæsar, because Pompey not long before had put his father to death. But Brutus, preferring the respect of his country and commonwealth before private affection, and persuading himself that Pompey had juster cause to enter into arms than Cæsar, he then took part with Pompey; though oftentimes meeting him before, he thought scorn to speak to him, thinking it a great sin and offence in him, to speak to the murtherer of his father. . . Brutus, being in Pompey's camp, did nothing but study all day long, except he were with Pompey; and not only the days before, but the self-same day also before the great battle was fought in the fields of Pharsalia, where Pompey was overcome. . . Furthermore, when others slept, or thought what would happen the morrow after, he fell to his book, and wrote all day long till night, writing a breviary of Polybius. . . So, after Pompey's overthrow at the battle of Pharsalia, and that he fled to the sea, when Cæsar came to besiege his camp, Brutus went out of the camp-gates unseen of any man, and leapt into a marish full of water and reeds. Then when night was come, he crept out, and went unto the city of Larissa: from whence he wrote unto Cæsar, who was very glad that he had scaped, and sent for him to come unto him. When Brutus was come, he did not only pardon him, but also kept him always about him, and did as much honour and esteem him as any man he had in his company. . . Furthermore, Brutus obtained pardon of Cæsar for Cassius. . . For as Brutus' gravity and constant mind would not grant all men their requests

1. A mistranslation by North. It should be *about the Patareians*; Amyot has *des Patareïens*, Plutarch περὶ Παταρέων.

that sued unto him, but, being moved with reason and discretion, did always incline to that which was good and honest: even so, when it was moved to follow any matter, he used a kind of forcible and vehement persuasion, that calmed not till he had obtained his desire. For by flattering of him a man could never obtain any thing at his hands, nor make him do that which was unjust. Further, he thought it not meet for a man of calling and estimation, to yield unto the requests and entreaties of a shameless and importunate suitor, requesting things unmeet. (*Life of Brutus*, pp. 107–10.)

But Brutus, in contrary manner, for his virtue and valiantness, was well beloved of the people and his own, esteemed of noblemen, and hated of no man, not so much as of his enemies; because he was a marvellous lowly and gentle person, noble-minded, and would never be in any rage, nor carried away with pleasure and covetousness, but had ever an upright mind with him, and would never yield to any wrong or injustice; the which was the chiefest cause of his fame, of his rising, and of the goodwill that every man bare him: for they were all persuaded that his intent was good. . . For it was said that Antonius spake it openly divers times, that he thought, that of all them that had slain Cæsar, there was none but Brutus only that was moved to do it, as thinking the act commendable of itself: but that all the other conspirators did conspire his death for some private malice or envy, that they otherwise did bear unto him. Hereby it appeareth, that Brutus did not trust so much to the power of his army as he did to his own virtue, as it is to be seen by his writings. (*Life of Brutus*, pp. 129–30.)

THE CHARACTER OF CASSIUS

And surely (in my opinion) I am persuaded that Brutus might indeed have come to have been the chiefest man of Rome, if he could have contented himself for a time to have been next unto Cæsar, and to have suffered his glory and authority, which he had gotten by his great victories, to consume with time. But Cassius, being a choleric man, and hating Cæsar privately more than he did the tyranny openly, he incensed Brutus against him. It is also reported, that Brutus could evil away with the tyranny, and that Cassius hated the tyrant: making many complaints for the injuries he had done him; and amongst others, for that he had taken away his lions from him. . . And this was the cause (as some do report) that made Cassius conspire against Cæsar. But this holdeth no water: for Cassius, even from his cradle, could not abide any manner of tyrants. (*Life of Brutus*, pp. 111–12.)

Now Cassius would have done Brutus much honour, as Brutus

did unto him, but Brutus most commonly prevented him, and went first unto him, both because he was the elder man as also for that he was sickly of body. And men reputed him commonly to be very skilful in wars, but otherwise marvellous choleric and cruel, who sought to rule men by fear rather than with lenity: and on the other side, he was too familiar with his friends, and would jest too broadly with them... And as for Cassius, a hot, choleric, and cruel man, that would oftentimes be carried away from justice for gain, it was certainly thought that he made war and put himself into sundry dangers, more to have absolute power and authority than to defend the liberty of his country. (*Life of Brutus*, pp. 129–30.)

THE CHARACTER OF ANTONY

Now Antonius being a fair young man, and in the prime of his youth, he fell acquainted with Curio, whose friendship and acquaintance (as it is reported) was a plague unto him. For he was a dissolute man, given over to all lust and insolency, who, to have Antonius the better at his commandment, trained him on into great follies and vain expenses upon women, in rioting and banqueting...

Thereupon he left Italy, and went into Greece, and there bestowed the most part of his time, sometimes in wars, and otherwhile in the study of eloquence. He used a manner of phrase in his speech called Asiatic, which carried the best grace and estimation at that time, and was much like to his manners and life: for it was full of ostentation, foolish bravery, and vain ambition... And in all other great battles and skirmishes which they fought, being many in number, Antonius did many noble acts of a valiant and wise captain: but specially in one battle, where he compassed in the enemies behind, giving them the victory that fought in front, whereby he afterwards had such honourable reward as his valiantness deserved. So was his great courtesy also much commended of all, the which he shewed unto Archelaus: for having been his very friend, he made war with him against his will while he lived; but after his death he fought for his body, and gave it honourable burial. For these respects he wan himself great fame of them of Alexandria, and he was also thought a worthy man of all the soldiers in the Romans' camp. But besides all this, he had a noble presence, and shewed a countenance of one of a noble house: he had a goodly thick beard, a broad forehead, crooked-nosed, and there appeared such a manly look in his countenance, as is commonly seen in Hercules' pictures, stamped or graven in metal...

Furthermore, things that seem intolerable in other men, as to boast commonly, to jest with one or other, to drink like a good fellow with everybody, to sit with the soldiers when they dine, and to eat and drink with them soldier-like, it is incredible what wonderful love it wan him amongst them. And furthermore, being given to love, that made him the more desired, and by that means he brought many to love him. For he would further every man's love, and also would not be angry that men should merrily tell him of those he loved. But besides all this, that which most procured his rising and advancement, was his liberality, who gave all to the soldiers, and kept nothing for himself: and when he was grown to great credit, then was his authority and power also very great, the which notwithstanding himself did overthrow by a thousand other faults he had. (*Life of Antonius*, pp. 154–7.)

Then was Antonius straight marvellously commended and beloved of the soldiers, because he commonly exercised himself among them, and would oftentimes eat and drink with them, and also be liberal unto them, according to his ability. But then in contrary manner, he purchased divers other men's evil wills, because that through negligence he would not do them justice that were injured, and dealt very churlishly with them that had any suit unto him: and besides all this, he had an ill name to intice men's wives. To conclude, Cæsar's friends, that governed under him, were cause why they hated Cæsar's government (which indeed in respect of himself was no less than tyranny) by reason of the great insolencies and outrageous parts that were committed: amongst whom Antonius, that was of greatest power, and that also committed greatest faults, deserved most blame. But Cæsar, notwithstanding, when he returned from the wars of Spain, made no reckoning of the complaints that were put up against him: but contrarily, because he found him a hardy man, and a valiant captain, he employed him in his chiefest affairs, and was no whit deceived in his opinion of him. (*Life of Antonius*, p. 159.)

But by this means he got the ill will of the common people; and on the other side, the noblemen (as Cicero saith) did not only mislike him, but also hate him for his naughty life: for they did abhor his banquets and drunken feasts he made at unseasonable times, and his extreme wasteful expenses upon vain light huswives; and then in the day-time he would sleep or walk out his drunkenness, thinking to wear away the fume of the abundance of wine which he had taken over night. In his house they did nothing but feast, dance, and mask: and himself passed away the time in hearing of foolish plays, and in marrying these players, tumblers, jesters, and such sort of people. (*Life of Antonius*, p. 161.)

THE EVENTS OF THE PLAY

Cæsar's Triumph

He wan this battle [Munda] on the very feast-day of the Bac-
chanalians, in the which men say that Pompey the Great went out
of Rome, about four years before, to begin this civil war. For his
sons, the younger scaped from the battle; but, within few days
after, Didius brought the head of the elder. This was the last war
that Cæsar made. But the triumph he made into Rome for the same
did as much offend the Romans, and more, than any thing that ever
he had done before: because he had not overcome captains that
were strangers, nor barbarous kings, but had destroyed the sons of
the noblest man of Rome, whom fortune had overthrown. And because he had plucked up his race by the roots, men did not think it
meet for him to triumph so for the calamities of his country, rejoicing at a thing for the which he had but one excuse to allege in his
defence unto the gods and men, that he was compelled to do that
he did. And the rather they thought it not meet, because he had
never before sent letters nor messengers unto the commonwealth at
Rome, for any victory that he had ever won in all the civil wars: but
did always for shame refuse the glory of it. (*Life of Cæsar*, pp. 91–2.)

Antony Offers Cæsar a Diadem

Besides these occasions and offences, there followed also his shame
and reproach, abusing the tribunes of the people in this sort. At
that time the feast *Lupercalia* was celebrated, the which in old time
men say was the feast of shepherds or herdmen, and is much like unto the feast of the Lycæans in Arcadia. But howsoever it is, that day
there are divers noblemen's sons, young men, (and some of them
magistrates themselves that govern then), which run naked through
the city, striking in sport them they meet in their way with leather
thongs, hair and all on, to make them give place. And many noble-
women and gentlewomen also go of purpose to stand in their way,
and do put forth their hands to be stricken, as scholars hold them
out to their schoolmaster to be stricken with the ferula: persuading
themselves that, being with child, they shall have good delivery;
and so, being barren, that it will make them to conceive with child.
Cæsar sat to behold that sport upon the pulpit for orations, in a
chair of gold, apparelled in triumphant manner. Antonius, who
was Consul at that time, was one of them that ran this holy course.
So when he came into the market-place, the people made a lane for
him to run at liberty, and he came to Cæsar, and presented him a
diadem wreathed about with laurel. Whereupon there rose a cer-

tain cry of rejoicing, not very great, done only by a few appointed
for the purpose. But when Cæsar refused the diadem, then all the
people together made an outcry of joy. Then Antonius offering it
him again, there was a second shout of joy, but yet of a few. But
when Cæsar refused it again the second time, then all the whole
people shouted. Cæsar having made this proof, found that the
people did not like of it, and thereupon rose out of his chair, and
commanded the crown to be carried unto Jupiter in the Capitol.
After that, there were set up images of Cæsar in the city, with diadems upon their heads like kings. Those two tribunes, Flavius
and Marullus, went and pulled down, and furthermore, meeting
with them that first saluted Cæsar as king, they committed them to
prison. The people followed them rejoicing at it, and called them
Brutes, because of Brutus, who had in old time driven the kings out
of Rome, and that brought the kingdom of one person unto the
government of the Senate and people. Cæsar was so offended withal, that he deprived Marullus and Flavius of their tribuneships, and
accusing them, he spake also against the people, and called them
Bruti and Cumani, to wit, beasts and fools. (*Life of Cæsar*, pp. 95–6.)

The Romans by chance celebrated the feast called Lupercalia,
and Cæsar, being apparelled in his triumphing robe, was set in the
Tribune where they use to make their orations to the people, and
from thence did behold the sport of the runners. The manner of this
running was thus. On that day there are many young men of noble
house, and those specially that be chief officers for that year, who
running naked up and down the city, anointed with the oil of olive,
for pleasure do strike them they meet in their way with white leather thongs they have in their hands. Antonius, being one among the
rest that was to run, leaving the ancient ceremonies and old customs
of that solemnity, he ran to the Tribune where Cæsar was set, and
carried a laurel crown in his hand, having a royal band or diadem
wreathed about it, which in old time was the ancient mark and
token of a king. When he was come to Cæsar, he made his fellow-
runners with him lift him up, and so he did put his laurel crown
upon his head, signifying thereby that he had deserved to be king.
But Cæsar, making as though he refused it, turned away his head.
The people were so rejoiced at it, that they all clapped their hands
for joy. Antonius again did put it on his head: Cæsar again refused
it; and thus they were striving off and on a great while together.
As oft as Antonius did put this laurel crown unto him, a few of his
followers rejoiced at it: and as oft also as Cæsar refused it, all the
people together clapped their hands. And this was a wonderful
thing, that they suffered all things subjects should do by command-

ment of their kings: and yet they could not abide the name of a king, detesting it as the utter destruction of their liberty. Cæsar, in a rage, arose out of his seat, and plucking down the collar of his gown from his neck, he shewed it naked, bidding any man strike off his head that would. This laurel crown was afterwards put upon the head of one of Cæsar's statues or images, the which one of the tribunes plucked off. The people liked his doing therein so well, that they waited on him home to his house, with great clapping of hands. Howbeit Cæsar did turn them out of their offices for it. (*Life of Antonius*, pp. 163-4.)

Cæsar's Mistrust of Lean Men

It is reported that Cæsar answered one that did accuse Antonius and Dolabella unto him for some matter of conspiracy: "Tush," said he, "they be not those fat fellows and fine combed men that I fear, but I mistrust rather these pale and lean men," meaning Brutus and Cassius, who afterwards conspired his death and slew him. (*Life of Antonius*, p. 163.)

Cæsar also had Cassius in great jealousy, and suspected him much: whereupon he said on a time to his friends, "what will Cassius do, think ye? I like not his pale looks." Another time when Cæsar's friends complained unto him of Antonius and Dolabella, that they pretended some mischief towards him: he answered them again, "As for those fat men and smooth-combed heads," quoth he, "I never reckon of them; but these pale-visaged and carrion-lean people, I fear them most," meaning Brutus and Cassius. (*Life of Cæsar*, p. 97.)

The Growth of the Conspiracy

Now they that desired change, and wished Brutus only their prince and governor above all other, they durst not come to him themselves to tell him what they would have him to do, but in the night did cast sundry papers into the Prætor's seat, where he gave audience, and the most of them to this effect: "Thou sleepest, Brutus, and art not Brutus indeed." Cassius, finding Brutus' ambition stirred up the more by these seditious bills, did prick him forward and egg him on the more, for a private quarrel he had conceived against Cæsar: the circumstance whereof we have set down more at large in Brutus' life. (*Life of Cæsar*, p. 97.)

But for Brutus, his friends and countrymen, both by divers procurements and sundry rumours of the city, and by many bills also, did openly call and procure him to do that he did. For under the image of his ancestor Junius Brutus, (that drave the kings out of

Rome), they wrote: "O, that it pleased the gods thou wert now alive, Brutus!" and again, "that thou wert here among us now!" His tribunal or chair, where he gave audience during the time he was Prætor, was full of such bills: "Brutus, thou art asleep, and art not Brutus indeed."

. . . Now when Cassius felt his friends, and did stir them up against Cæsar: they all agreed, and promised to take part with him, so Brutus were the chief of their conspiracy. For they told him that so high an enterprise and attempt as that, did not so much require men of manhood and courage to draw their swords, as it stood them upon to have a man of such estimation as Brutus, to make every man boldly think, that by his only presence the fact were holy and just. If he took not this course, then that they should go to it with fainter hearts; and when they had done it, they should be more fearful: because every man would think that Brutus would not have refused to have made one with them, if the cause had been good and honest. Therefore Cassius, considering this matter with himself, did first of all speak to Brutus, since they grew strange together for the suit they had for the praetorship. So when he was reconciled to him again, and that they had embraced one another, Cassius asked him if he were determined to be in the Senate-house the first day of the month of March, because he heard say that Cæsar's friends should move the council that day, that Cæsar should be called king by the Senate. Brutus answered him, he would not be there. "But if we be sent for," said Cassius, "how then?" "For myself then," said Brutus, "I mean not to hold my peace, but to withstand it, and rather die than lose my liberty." Cassius being bold, and taking hold of this word: "Why," quoth he, "what Roman is he alive that will suffer thee to die for thy liberty? What? knowest thou not that thou art Brutus? Thinkest thou that they be cobblers, tapsters, or suchlike base mechanical people, that write these bills and scrolls which are found daily in thy praetor's chair, and not the noblest men and best citizens that do it? No; be thou well assured that of other praetors they look for gifts, common distributions amongst the people, and for common plays, and to see fencers fight at the sharp, to shew the people pastime: but at thy hands they specially require (as a due debt unto them) the taking away of the tyranny, being fully bent to suffer any extremity for thy sake, so that thou wilt shew thyself to be the man thou art taken for, and that they hope thou art." Thereupon he kissed Brutus and embraced him: and so each taking leave of other, they went both to speak with their friends about it. (*Life of Brutus*, pp. 112–13.)

The Prodigies that Preceded Cæsar's Death

Certainly destiny may easier be foreseen than avoided, considering the strange and wonderful signs that were said to be seen before Cæsar's death. For, touching the fires in the element, and spirits running up and down in the night, and also the solitary birds to be seen at noondays sitting in the great market-place, are not all these signs perhaps worth the noting, in such a wonderful chance as happened? But Strabo the philosopher writeth, that divers men were seen going up and down in fire: and furthermore, that there was a slave of the soldiers that did cast a marvellous burning flame out of his hand, insomuch as they that saw it thought he had been burnt; but when the fire was out, it was found he had no hurt. Cæsar self also doing sacrifice unto the gods, found that one of the beasts which was sacrificed had no heart: and that was a strange thing in nature, how a beast could live without a heart. Furthermore there was a certain soothsayer that had given Cæsar warning long time afore, to take heed of the day of the Ides of March, (which is the fifteenth of the month), for on that day he should be in great danger. That day being come, Cæsar going unto the Senate-house, and speaking merrily unto the soothsayer, told him, "the Ides of March be come": "so they be," softly answered the soothsayer, "but yet are they not past." And the very day before, Cæsar, supping with Marcus Lepidus, sealed certain letters, as he was wont to do, at the board: so, talk falling out amongst them, reasoning what death was best, he, preventing their opinions, cried out aloud, "death unlooked for." Then going to bed the same night, as his manner was, and lying with his wife Calpurnia, all the windows and doors of his chamber flying open, the noise awoke him, and made him afraid when he saw such light: but more, when he heard his wife Calpurnia, being fast asleep, weep and sigh, and put forth many fumbling lamentable speeches: for she dreamed that Cæsar was slain, and that she had him in her arms. Others also do deny that she had any such dream, as, amongst other, Titus Livius writeth that it was in this sort: the Senate having set upon the top of Cæsar's house, for an ornament and setting forth of the same, a certain pinnacle, Calpurnia dreamed that she saw it broken down, and that she thought she lamented and wept for it. Insomuch that, Cæsar rising in the morning, she prayed him, if it were possible, not to go out of the doors that day, but to adjourn the session of the Senate until another day. And if that he made no reckoning of her dream, yet that he would search further of the soothsayers by their sacrifices, to know what should happen him that day. Thereby it seemed that Cæsar likewise did fear or suspect somewhat, because his wife Calpurnia until that time was never given to any fear and superstition: and that then he saw her so troubled in mind with this dream she had. But much more afterwards, when the sooth-sayers having sacrificed many beasts one after another, told him that none did like them: then he determined to send Antonius to adjourn the session of the Senate. (*Life of Cæsar*, pp. 97–8.)

The Prestige of Brutus. His Troubled Thoughts

Furthermore, the only name and great calling of Brutus did bring on the most of them to give consent to this conspiracy: who having never taken oaths together, nor taken or given any caution or assurance, nor binding themselves one to another by any re-ligious oaths, they all kept the matter so secret to themselves, and could so cunningly handle it, that notwithstanding the gods did reveal it by manifest signs and tokens from above, and by predic-tions of sacrifices, yet all this would not be believed. Now Brutus, who knew very well that for his sake all the noblest, valiantest, and most courageous men of Rome did venture their lives, weighing with himself the greatness of the danger: when he was out of his house, he did so frame and fashion his countenance and looks that no man could discern he had anything to trouble his mind. But when night came that he was in his own house, then he was clean changed: for either care did wake him against his will when he would have slept, or else oftentimes of himself he fell into such deep thoughts of this enterprise, casting in his mind all the dangers that might happen: that his wife, lying by him, found that there was some marvellous great matter that troubled his mind, not being wont to be in that taking, and that he could not well determine with himself. (*Life of Brutus*, pp. 114–15.)

Antony's Life is Spared

This was a good encouragement for Brutus and Cassius to con-spire his death, who fell into a consort with their trustiest friends, to execute their enterprise, but yet stood doubtful whether they should make Antonius privy to it or not. All the rest liked of it, sav-ing Trebonius only. He told them that, when they rode to meet Cæsar at his return out of Spain, Antonius and he always keeping company, and lying together by the way, he felt his mind afar off: but Antonius, finding his meaning, would hearken no more unto it, and yet notwithstanding never made Cæsar acquainted with this talk, but had faithfully kept it to himself. After that, they con-sulted whether they should kill Antonius with Cæsar. But Brutus would in no wise consent to it, saying, that venturing on such an

enterprise as that, for the maintenance of law and justice, it ought
to be clear from all villainy. Yet they, fearing Antonius' power, and
the authority of his office, appointed certain of the conspiracy, that
when Cæsar were gone into the senate, and while others should
execute their enterprise, they should keep Antonius in a talk out of
the senate-house. (*Life of Antonius*, p. 164.)

All the conspirators, but Brutus, determining upon this matter,
thought it good also to kill Antonius, because he was a wicked man,
and that in nature favoured tyranny: besides also, for that he was
in great estimation with soldiers, having been conversant of long
time amongst them: and especially having a mind bent to great
enterprises, he was also of great authority at that time, being Consul with Cæsar. But Brutus would not agree to it. First, for that he
said it was not honest: secondly, because he told them there was
hope of change in him. For he did not mistrust but that Antonius,
being a noble-minded and courageous man, (when he should know
that Cæsar was dead), would willingly help his country to recover
her liberty, having them an example unto him to follow their courage and virtue. So Brutus by this means saved Antonius' life. (*Life
of Brutus*, pp. 119–20.)

Cicero Excluded from the Conspiracy

After that time they began to feel all their acquaintance whom
they trusted, and laid their heads together, consulting upon it, and
did not only pick out their friends, but all those also whom they
thought stout enough to attempt any desperate matter, and that
were not afraid to lose their lives. For this cause they durst not
acquaint Cicero with their conspiracy, although he was a man
whom they loved dearly, and trusted best: for they were afraid that
he being a coward by nature, and age also having increased his
fear, he would quite turn and alter all their purpose, and quench
the heat of their enterprise, (the which specially required hot and
earnest execution), seeking by persuasion to bring all things to such
safety, as there should be no peril. (*Life of Brutus*, pp. 113–14.)

Ligarius Joins the Conspiracy

Now amongst Pompey's friends, there was one called Caius Ligarius, who had been accused unto Cæsar for taking part with Pompey, and Cæsar discharged him. But Ligarius thanked not Cæsar
so much for his discharge, as he was offended with him for that he
was brought in danger by his tyrannical power; and therefore in
his heart he was always his mortal enemy, and was besides very
familiar with Brutus, who went to see him being sick in his bed, and

said unto him: "Ligarius, in what a time art thou sick?" Ligarius rising up in his bed, and taking him by the right hand, said unto him: "Brutus," said he, "if thou hast any great enterprise in hand worthy of thyself, I am whole." (*Life of Brutus*, p. 113.)

Portia Wishes to Share Brutus's Troubles

This young lady, being excellently well seen in philosophy, loving her husband well, and being of a noble courage, as she was also wise: because she would not ask her husband what he ailed before she had made some proof by her self: she took a little razor, such as barbers occupy to pare men's nails, and, causing her maids and women to go out of her chamber, gave herself a great gash withal in her thigh, that she was straight all of a gore blood: and incontinently after a vehement fever took her, by reason of the pain of her wound. Then perceiving her husband was marvellously out of quiet, and that he could take no rest, even in her greatest pain of all she spake in this sort unto him: "I being, O Brutus," said she, "the daughter of Cato, was married unto thee; not to be thy bed-fellow and companion in bed and at board only, like a harlot, but to be partaker also with thee of thy good and evil fortune. Now for thyself, I can find no cause of fault in thee touching our match: but for my part, how may I shew my duty towards thee and how much I would do for thy sake, if I cannot constantly bear a secret mischance or grief with thee, which requireth secrecy and fidelity? I confess that a woman's wit commonly is too weak to keep a secret safely: but yet, Brutus, good education and the company of virtuous men have some power to reform the defect of nature. And for myself, I have this benefit moreover, that I am the daughter of Cato, and wife of Brutus. This notwithstanding, I did not trust to any of these things before, until that now I have found by experience that no pain or grief whatsoever can overcome me." With those words she shewed him her wound on her thigh, and told him what she had done to prove herself. Brutus was amazed to hear what she said unto him, and lifting up his hands to heaven, he besought the gods to give him the grace he might bring his enterprise to so good pass, that he might be found a husband worthy of so noble a wife as Porcia: so he then did comfort her the best he could. (*Life of Brutus*, p. 115.)

Decius Brutus Persuades Cæsar to Go to the Senate

But in the mean time came Decius Brutus, surnamed Albinus, in whom Cæsar put such confidence, that in his last will and testament he had appointed him to be his next heir, and yet was of the conspiracy with Cassius and Brutus: he, fearing that if Cæsar did adjourn the session that day, the conspiracy would be betrayed, laughed at the soothsayers, and reproved Cæsar, saying, "that he gave the Senate occasion to mislike with him, and that they might think he mocked them, considering that by his commandment they were assembled, and that they were ready willingly to grant him all things, and to proclaim him king of all his provinces of the Empire of Rome out of Italy, and that he should wear his diadem in all other places both by sea and land. And furthermore, that if any man should tell them from him they should depart for that present time, and return again when Calpurnia should have better dreams, what would his enemies and ill-willers say, and how could they like of his friends' words? And who could persuade them otherwise, but that they would think his dominion a slavery unto them and tyrannical in himself? And yet if it be so," said he, "that you utterly mislike of this day, it is better that you go yourself in person, and, saluting the Senate, to dismiss them till another time." Therewithal he took Cæsar by the hand, and brought him out of his house. (*Life of Cæsar*, pp. 98–9.)

Portia's Anxiety

Now in the meantime, there came one of Brutus' men post-haste unto him, and told him his wife was a-dying. For Porcia, being very careful and pensive for that which was to come, and being too weak to away with so great and inward grief of mind, she could hardly keep within, but was frighted with every little noise and cry she heard, as those that are taken and possessed with the fury of the Bacchantes; asking every man that came from the market-place what Brutus did, and still sent messenger after messenger, to know what news. At length Cæsar's coming being prolonged (as you have heard), Porcia's weakness was not able to hold out any longer, and thereupon she suddenly swounded, that she had no leisure to go to her chamber, but was taken in the midst of her house, where her speech and senses failed her. Howbeit she soon came to herself again, and so was laid in her bed, and attended by her women. When Brutus heard these news, it grieved him, as it is to be presupposed: yet he left not off the care of his country and commonwealth, neither went home to his house for any news he heard. (*Life of Brutus*, pp. 117–18.)

Artemidorus Presents a Memorial to Cæsar

And one Artemidorus also, born in the isle of Gnidos, a doctor of rhetoric in the Greek tongue, who by means of his profession was very familiar with certain of Brutus' confederates, and therefore knew the most part of all their practices against Cæsar, came and brought him a little bill, written with his own hand, of all that he meant to tell him. He, marking how Cæsar received all the supplications that were offered him, and that he gave them straight to his men that were about him, pressed nearer to him, and said: "Cæsar, read this memorial to yourself, and that quickly, for they be matters of great weight, and touch you nearly." Cæsar took it of him, but could never read it, though he many times attempted it, for the number of people that did salute him: but holding it still in his hand, keeping it to himself, went on withal into the Senate-house. (*Life of Cæsar*, p. 99.)

Popilius Lena Alarms the Conspirators

Another Senator, called Popilius Laena, after he had saluted Brutus and Cassius more friendly than he was wont to do, he rounded softly in their ears, and told them: "I pray the gods you may go through with that you have taken in hand; but withal, despatch, I reade you, for your enterprise is bewrayed." When he had said, he presently departed from them, and left them both afraid that their conspiracy would out. . .

Now it was reported that Cæsar was coming in his litter: for he determined not to stay in the Senate all that day (because he was afraid of the unlucky signs of the sacrifices) but to adjourn matters of importance unto the next session and council holden, feigning himself not to be well at ease. When Cæsar came out of his litter, Popilius Laena (that had talked before with Brutus and Cassius, and had prayed the gods they might bring this enterprise to pass) went unto Cæsar, and kept him a long time with a talk. Cæsar gave good ear unto him: wherefore the conspirators (if so they should be called) not hearing what he said to Cæsar, but conjecturing by that he had told them a little before that his talk was none other but the very discovery of their conspiracy, they were afraid every man of them; and, one looking in another's face, it was easy to see that they were all of a mind, that it was no tarrying for them till they were apprehended, but rather that they should kill themselves with their own hands. And when Cassius and certain other clapped their hands on their swords under their gowns to draw them, Brutus, marking the countenance and gesture of Laena, and considering that he did use himself rather like an humble and earnest suitor than like an accuser, he said nothing to his companion (because there were many amongst them that were not of the conspiracy), but with a pleasant countenance encouraged Cassius. And immediately after Laena went from Cæsar, and kissed his hand; which shewed plainly that it was for some matter concerning himself that he had held him so long in talk. (*Life of Brutus*, pp. 117–18.)

The Assassination of Cæsar

Now Antonius, that was a faithful friend to Cæsar, and a valiant man besides of his hands, him Decius Brutus Albinus entertained out of the Senate-house, having begun a long tale of set purpose. So Cæsar coming into the house, all the Senate stood up on their feet to do him honour. Then part of Brutus' company and confederates stood round about Cæsar's chair, and part of them also came towards him, as though they made suit with Metellus Cimber, to call home his brother again from banishment: and thus prosecuting still their suit, they followed Cæsar till he was set in his chair. Who denying their petitions, and being offended with them one after another, because the more they were denied the more they pressed upon him and were the earnester with him, Metellus at length, taking his gown with both his hands, pulled it over his neck, which was the sign given the confederates to set upon him. Then Casca, behind him, strake him in the neck with his sword; howbeit the wound was not great nor mortal, because it seemed the fear of such a devilish attempt did amaze him and take his strength from him, that he killed him not at the first blow. But Cæsar, turning straight unto him, caught hold of his sword and held it hard; and they both cried out, Cæsar in Latin: "O vile traitor Casca, what doest thou?" and Casca, in Greek, to his brother: "Brother, help me." At the beginning of this stir, they that were present, not knowing of the conspiracy, were so amazed with the horrible sight they saw, they had no power to fly, neither to help him, nor so much as once to make an outcry. They on the other side that had conspired his death, compassed him in on every side with their swords drawn in their hands, that Cæsar turned him no where but he was stricken at by some, and still had naked swords in his face, and was hackled and mangled among them, as a wild beast taken of hunters. For it was agreed among them that every man should give him a wound, because all their parts should be in this murther: and then Brutus himself gave him one wound about his privities. Men report also, that Cæsar did still defend himself against the rest, running every way with his body: but when he saw Brutus with his sword drawn in his hand, then he pulled his gown over his head, and made no more resistance, and was driven either casually or purposedly, by the counsel of the conspirators, against the base whereupon Pompey's image stood, which ran all of a gore-blood till he was slain.

Thus it seemed that the image took just revenge of Pompey's enemy, being thrown down on the ground at his feet, and yielding up the ghost there, for the number of wounds he had upon him. For it is reported, that he had three and twenty wounds upon his body: and divers of the conspirators did hurt themselves, striking one body with so many blows. (*Life of Cæsar*, pp. 100–1.)

Now all the Senators being entered first into this place or chapter-house where the council should be kept, all the other conspirators straight stood about Cæsar's chair, as if they had had something to say unto him. And some say that Cassius, casting his eyes upon Pompey's image, made his prayer unto it, as if it had been alive. Trebonius on the other side drew Antonius aside, as he came into the house where the Senate sat, and held him with a long talk without. When Cæsar was come into the house, all the Senate rose to honour him at his coming in. So when he was set, the conspirators flocked about him, and amongst them they presented one Tullius Cimber, who made humble suit for the calling home again of his brother that was banished. They all made as though they were intercessors for him, and took Cæsar by the hands, and kissed his head and breast. Cæsar at the first simply refused their kindness and entreaties; but afterwards, perceiving they still pressed on him, he violently thrust them from him. Then Cimber with both his hands plucked Cæsar's gown over his shoulders, and Casca, that stood behind him, drew his dagger first and strake Cæsar upon the shoulder, but gave him no great wound. Cæsar, feeling himself hurt, took him straight by the hand he held his dagger in, and cried out in Latin: "O traitor Casca, what dost thou?" Casca on the other side cried in Greek, and called his brother to help him. So divers running on a heap together to fly upon Cæsar, he, looking about him to have fled, saw Brutus with a sword drawn in his hand ready to strike at him: then he let Casca's hand go, and casting his gown over his face, suffered every man to strike at him that would. Then the conspirators thronging one upon another, because every man was desirous to have a cut at him, so many swords and daggers lighting upon one body, one of them hurt another, and among them Brutus caught a blow on his hand, because he would make one in murthering of him, and all the rest also were every man of them bloodied. (*Life of Brutus*, pp. 118–19.)

The Confusion that Followed the Assassination

When Cæsar was slain, the Senate (though Brutus stood in the middest amongst them, as though he would have said something touching this fact) presently ran out of the house, and flying, filled all the city with marvellous fear and tumult. Insomuch as some did shut to the doors, others forsook their shops and warehouses, and others ran to the place to see what the matter was: and others also that had seen it ran home to their houses again. But Antonius and Lepidus, which were two of Cæsar's chiefest friends, secretly conveying themselves away, fled into other men's houses and forsook their own. Brutus and his confederates on the other side, being yet hot with this murther they had committed, having their swords drawn in their hands, came all in a troop together out of the Senate and went into the market-place, not as men that made countenance to fly, but otherwise boldly holding up their heads like men of courage, and called to the people to defend their liberty, and stayed to speak with every great personage whom they met in their way. (*Life of Cæsar*, p. 101.)

Cæsar being slain in this manner, Brutus, standing in the middest of the house, would have spoken, and stayed the other Senators that were not of the conspiracy, to have told them the reason why they had done this fact. But they, as men both afraid and amazed, fled one upon another's neck in haste to get out at the door, and no man followed them. For it was set down and agreed between them, that they should kill no man but Cæsar only, and should intreat all the rest to look to defend their liberty. (*Life of Brutus*, p. 119.)

Even as they had devised these matters, so were they executed: and Cæsar was slain in the middest of the Senate. Antonius being put in a fear withal, cast a slave's gown upon him, and hid himself. But afterwards when it was told him that the murtherers slew no man else, and that they went only into the Capitol, he sent his son unto them for a pledge, and bade them boldly come down upon his word. The selfsame day he did bid Cassius to supper, and Lepidus also bade Brutus. (*Life of Antonius*, pp. 164–5.)

Brutus Speaks to the People

The next morning, Brutus and his confederates came into the market-place to speak unto the people, who gave them such audience, that it seemed they neither greatly reproved nor allowed the fact: for by their great silence they shewed that they were sorry for Cæsar's death, and also that they did reverence Brutus. Now the Senate granted general pardon for all that was past; and, to pacify every man, ordained besides, that Cæsar's funerals should be honoured as a god, and established all things that he had done, and gave certain provinces also and convenient honours unto Brutus and his confederates, whereby every man thought all things were brought to good peace and quietness again. (*Life of Cæsar*, p. 102.)

But Brutus and his consorts, having their swords bloody in their hands, went straight to the Capitol, persuading the Romans as they went to take their liberty again. Now at the first time, when the murther was newly done, there were sudden outcries of people that ran up and down the city, the which indeed did the more increase the fear and tumult. But when they saw they slew no man, neither did spoil or make havoc of anything, then certain of the Senators and many of the people, emboldening themselves, went to the Capitol unto them.

There, a great number of men being assembled together one after another, Brutus made an oration unto them, to win the favour of the people, and to justify that they had done. All those that were by said they had done well, and cried unto them that they should boldly come down from the Capitol: whereupon Brutus and his companions came boldly down into the market-place. The rest followed in troop, but Brutus went foremost, very honourably compassed in round about with the noblest men of the city, which brought him from the Capitol, through the market-place, to the pulpit for orations. When the people saw him in the pulpit, although they were a multitude of rakehels of all sorts, and had a good will to make some stir; yet, being ashamed to do it, for the reverence they bare unto Brutus, they kept silence to hear what he would say. When Brutus began to speak, they gave him quiet audience: howbeit, immediately after, they shewed that they were not all contented with the murther. For when another, called Cinna, would have spoken, and began to accuse Cæsar, they fell into a great uproar among them, and marvellously reviled him; insomuch that the conspirators returned again into the Capitol. (*Life of Brutus*, p. 120.)

Antony's Funeral Oration

Then Antonius, thinking good his testament should be read openly, and also that his body should be honourably buried, and not in hugger-mugger, lest the people might thereby take occasion to be worse offended if they did otherwise: Cassius stoutly spake against it. But Brutus went with the motion, and agreed unto it; wherein it seemeth he committed a second fault. For the first fault he did, was when he would not consent to his fellow-conspirators, that Antonius should be slain, and therefore he was justly accused, that thereby he had saved and strengthened a strong and grievous enemy of their conspiracy. The second fault was, when he agreed

that Cæsar's funerals should be as Antonius would have them, the
which indeed marred all. For first of all, when Cæsar's testament
was openly read among them, whereby it appeared that he bequeathed unto every citizen of Rome 75 drachmas a man; and that
he left his gardens and arbours unto the people, which he had on
this side of the river Tiber, in the place where now the temple of
Fortune is built: the people then loved him, and were marvellous
sorry for him. Afterwards, when Cæsar's body was brought into the
market-place, Antonius making his funeral oration in praise of the
dead, according to the ancient custom of Rome, and perceiving
that his words moved the common people to compassion, he framed his eloquence to make their hearts yearn the more; and taking
Cæsar's gown all bloody in his hand, he laid it open to the sight of
them all, shewing what a number of cuts and holes it had upon it.
Therewithal the people fell presently into such a rage and mutiny,
that there was no more order kept amongst the common people.
For some of them cried out, "Kill the murtherers": others plucked
up forms, tables, and stalls about the market-place, as they had
done before at the funerals of Clodius, and having laid them all on
a heap together, they set them on fire, and thereupon did put the
body of Cæsar, and burnt it in the midst of the most holy places. And
furthermore, when the fire was throughly kindled, some here,
some there, took burning firebrands, and ran with them to the
murtherers' houses that killed him, to set them on fire. Howbeit the
conspirators, foreseeing the danger before, had wisely provided for
themselves and fled. (*Life of Brutus*, pp. 121–2.)

And therefore, when Cæsar's body was brought to the place
where it should be buried, he made a funeral oration in commenda-
tion of Cæsar, according to the ancient custom of praising noble
men at their funerals. When he saw that the people were very glad
and desirous also to hear Cæsar spoken of, and his praises uttered,
he mingled his oration with lamentable words; and by amplifying
of matters did greatly move their hearts and affections unto pity
and compassion. In fine, to conclude his oration, he unfolded before
the whole assembly the bloody garments of the dead, thrust
through in many places with their swords, and called the male-
factors cruel and cursed murtherers. With these words he put the
people into such a fury, that they presently took Cæsar's body, and
burnt it in the market-place, with such tables and forms as they
could get together. Then when the fire was kindled, they took fire-
brands, and ran to the murtherers' houses to set them on fire, and
to make them come out to fight. Brutus therefore and his accom-

plices, for safety of their persons, were driven to fly the city. (*Life of Antonius*, p. 165.)

But when they had opened Cæsar's testament, and found a liberal legacy of money bequeathed unto every citizen of Rome, and that they saw his body (which was brought into the market-place) all bemangled with gashes of swords, then there was no order to keep the multitude and common people quiet, but they plucked up forms, tables, and stools, and laid them all about the body; and setting them afire, burnt the corse. Then when the fire was well kindled, they took the fire-brands, and went unto their houses that had slain Cæsar, to set them afire. Other also ran up and down the city to see if they could meet with any of them, to cut them in pieces: howbeit they could meet with never a man of them, because they had locked themselves up safely in their houses. (*Life of Cæsar*, p. 102.)

Octavius Comes to Rome

Now the state of Rome standing in these terms, there fell out another change and alteration, when the young man Octavius Cæsar came to Rome. He was the son of Julius Cæsar's niece, whom he had adopted for his son, and made his heir, by his last will and testament. But when Julius Cæsar, his adopted father, was slain, he was in the city of Apollonia (where he studied) tarrying for him, because he was determined to make war with the Parthians: but when he heard the news of his death, he returned again to Rome. (*Life of Brutus*, p. 123.)

Now things remaining in this state at Rome, Octavius Cæsar the younger came to Rome, who was the son of Julius Cæsar's niece, as you have heard before, and was left his lawful heir by will, remaining, at the time of the death of his great uncle that was slain, in the city of Apollonia. This young man at his first arrival went to salute Antonius, as one of his late dead father Cæsar's friends, who by his last will and testament had made him his heir; and withal, he was presently in hand with him for money and other things which were left of trust in his hands; because Cæsar had by will bequeathed unto the people of Rome threescore and fifteen silver drachmas to be given to every man, the which he as heir stood charged withal. Antonius at the first made no reckoning of him, because he was very young, and said, he lacked wit and good friends to advise him, if he looked to take such a charge in hand, as to undertake to be Cæsar's heir. But when Antonius saw that he could not shake him off with those words, and that he was still in hand with him for his father's goods, but specially for the ready money, then he spake and did what he could against him. (*Life of Antonius*, p. 166.)

Cinna the Poet is Killed

There was one of Cæsar's friends called Cinna, that had a marvellous strange and terrible dream the night before. He dreamed that Cæsar bad him to supper, and that he refused and would not go: then that Cæsar took him by the hand, and led him against his will. Now Cinna, hearing at that time that they burnt Cæsar's body in the market-place, notwithstanding that he feared his dream, and had an ague on him besides, he went into the market-place to honour his funerals. When he came thither, one of the mean sort asked him what his name was? He was straight called by his name. The first man told it to another, and that other unto another, so that it ran straight through them all, that he was one of them that murthered Cæsar (for indeed one of the traitors to Cæsar was also called Cinna as himself): wherefore taking him for Cinna the murtherer, they fell upon him with such fury that they presently dispatched him in the market-place. This stir and fury made Brutus and Cassius more afraid than of all that was past, and therefore within few days after they departed out of Rome. (*Life of Cæsar*, pp. 102–3.)

But there was a poet called Cinna, who had been no partaker of the conspiracy, but was always one of Cæsar's chiefest friends: he dreamed, the night before, that Cæsar bad him to supper with him, and that, he refusing to go, Cæsar was very importunate with him, and compelled him; so that at length he led him by the hand into a great dark place, where, being marvellously afraid, he was driven to follow him in spite of his heart. This dream put him all night into a fever; and yet notwithstanding, the next morning, when he heard that they carried Cæsar's body to burial, being afraid not to accompany his funerals, he went out of his house, and thrust himself into the press of the common people that were in a great uproar. And because some one called him by his name Cinna, the people, thinking he had been that Cinna who in an oration he made had spoken very evil of Cæsar, they, falling upon him in their rage, slew him outright in the market-place. This made Brutus and his companions more afraid than any other thing, next unto the change of Antonius. Wherefore they got them out of Rome, and kept at the first in the city of Antium, hoping to return again to Rome, when the fury of the people was a little assuaged. The which they hoped would be quickly, considering that they had to deal with a fickle and unconstant multitude, easy to be carried, and that the Senate stood for them: who notwithstanding made no enquiry for them that had torn poor Cinna the poet in pieces, but caused them to be sought for and apprehended that went with firebrands to set fire on the conspirators' houses. (*Life of Brutus*, p. 122.)

The Triumvirate

Therefore he [Octavius Cæsar] sent certain of his friends to Antonius, to make them friends again: and thereupon all three met together (to wit, Cæsar, Antonius, and Lepidus) in an island environed round about with a little river, and there remained three days together. Now as touching all other matters they were easily agreed, and did divide all the empire of Rome between them, as if it had been their own inheritance. But yet they could hardly agree whom they would put to death: for every one of them would kill their enemies, and save their kinsmen and friends. Yet at length, giving place to their greedy desire to be revenged of their enemies, they spurned all reverence of blood and holiness of friendship at their feet. For Cæsar left Cicero to Antonius' will; Antonius also forsook Lucius Cæsar, who was his uncle by his mother: and both of them together suffered Lepidus to kill his own brother Paulus. Yet some writers affirm, that Cæsar and Antonius requested Paulus might be slain, and that Lepidus was contented with it. (*Life of Antonius*, p. 169.)

After that, these three, Octavius Cæsar, Antonius, and Lepidus, made an agreement between themselves, and by those articles divided the provinces belonging to the empire of Rome among themselves, and did set up bills of proscription and outlawry, condemning two hundred of the noblest men of Rome to suffer death, and among that number Cicero was one. (*Life of Brutus*, p. 128.)

Brutus Asks Cassius for Money

Now whilst Brutus and Cassius were together in the city of Smyrna, Brutus prayed Cassius to let him have some part of his money whereof he had great store; because all that he could rap and rend of his side, he had bestowed it in making so great a number of ships, that by means of them they should keep all the sea at their commandment. Cassius' friends hindered this request and earnestly dissuaded him from it, persuading him, that it was no reason that Brutus should have the money which Cassius had gotten together by sparing and levied with great evil will of the people their subjects, for him to bestow liberally upon his soldiers, and by this means to win their good wills, by Cassius' charge. This notwithstanding, Cassius gave him the third part of this total sum. (*Life of Brutus*, pp. 130–1.)

Brutus and Cassius Quarrel

Now as it commonly happened in great affairs between two persons, both of them having many friends and so many captains under them, there ran tales and complaints betwixt them. Therefore, before they fell in hand with any other matter, they went into a little chamber together, and bade every man avoid, and did shut the doors to them. Then they began to pour out their complaints one to the other, and grew hot and loud, earnestly accusing one another, and at length fell both a-weeping. Their friends that were without the chamber, hearing them loud within, and angry between themselves, they were both amazed and afraid also, lest it should grow to further matter: but yet they were commanded that no man should come to them. Notwithstanding, one Marcus Phaonius, that had been a friend and a follower of Cato while he lived, and took upon him to counterfeit a philosopher, not with wisdom and discretion, but with a certain bedlem and frantic motion: he would needs come into the chamber, though the men offered to keep him out. But it was no boot to let Phaonius, when a mad mood or toy took him in the head: for he was a hot hasty man, and sudden in all his doings, and cared for never a senator of them all. Now, though he used this bold manner of speech after the profession of the Cynic philosophers (as who would say, *Dogs*), yet his boldness did no hurt many times, because they did but laugh at him to see him so mad. This Phaonius at that time, in despite of the doorkeepers, came into the chamber, and with a certain scoffing and mocking gesture, which he counterfeited of purpose, he rehearsed the verses which old Nestor said in Homer:

> My lords, I pray you hearken both to me,
> For I have seen mo years than suchie three.

Cassius fell a-laughing at him: but Brutus thrust him out of the chamber, and called him dog, and counterfeit Cynic. Howbeit his coming in brake their strife at that time, and so they left each other. . .

The next day after, Brutus, upon complaint of the Sardians, did condemn and note Lucius Pella for a defamed person, that had been a Prætor of the Romans, and whom Brutus had given charge unto: for that he was accused and convicted of robbery and pilfery in his office. This judgment much misliked Cassius, because he himself had secretly (not many days before) warned two of his friends, attainted and convicted of the like offences, and openly had cleared them: but yet he did not therefore leave to employ them in any manner of service as he did before. And therefore he greatly reproved Brutus, for that he would shew himself so straight and severe, in such a time as was meeter to bear a little than to take things at the worst. Brutus in contrary manner answered, that he should remember the Ides of March, at which time they slew Julius Cæsar, who neither pilled nor polled the country, but only was a favourer and suborner of all them that did rob and spoil, by his countenance and authority. (*Life of Brutus*, pp. 134–5.)

The Death of Portia

And for Porcia, Brutus' wife, Nicolaus the Philosopher and Valerius Maximus do write, that she, determining to kill herself (her parents and friends carefully looking to her to keep her from it), took hot burning coals and cast them into her mouth, and kept her mouth so close that she choked herself. There was a letter of Brutus found written to his friends, complaining of their negligence, that, his wife being sick, they would not help her, but suffered her to kill herself; choosing to die, rather than to languish in pain. Thus it appeareth that Nicolaus knew not well that time, sith the letter (at the least if it were Brutus' letter) doth plainly declare the disease and love of this lady, and also the manner of her death. (*Life of Brutus*, pp. 151–2.)

A Ghost Appears Twice to Brutus

But above all, the ghost that appeared unto Brutus shewed plainly, that the gods were offended with the murther of Cæsar. The vision was thus: Brutus being ready to pass over his army from the city of Abydos to the other coast lying directly against it, slept every night (as his manner was) in his tent; and being yet awake, thinking of his affairs (for by report he was as careful a captain and lived with as little sleep as ever man did) he thought he heard a noise at his tent-door, and looking towards the light of the lamp that waxed very dim, he saw a horrible vision of a man, of a wonderful greatness and dreadful look, which at the first made him marvellously afraid. But when he saw that it did him no hurt, but stood by his bed-side and said nothing; at length he asked him what he was. The image answered him: "I am thy ill angel, Brutus, and thou shalt see me by the city of Philippes." Then Brutus replied again, and said, "Well, I shall see thee then." Therewithal the spirit presently vanished from him. After that time Brutus, being in battle near unto the city of Philippes against Antonius and Octavius Cæsar, at the first battle he wan the victory, and, overthrowing all them that withstood him, he drave them into young Cæsar's camp, which he took. The second battle being at hand, this spirit appeared again unto him, but spake never a word. Thereupon Brutus, knowing that he should die, did put himself to all hazard in battle, but yet fighting could not be slain. So seeing his men put to flight and overthrown, he ran unto a little rock not far off, and there setting his sword's point to his breast, fell upon it and slew himself; but yet, as it is reported, with the help of his friend that despatched him. (*Life of Cæsar*, pp. 103–4.)

Brutus was a careful man, and slept very little, both for that his diet was moderate, as also because he was continually occupied. He never slept in the day-time, and in the night no longer than the time he was driven to be alone, and when everybody else took their rest. But now whilst he was in war, and his head ever busily occupied to think of his affairs and what would happen, after he had slumbered a little after supper, he spent all the rest of the night in despatching of his weightiest causes; and after he had taken order for them, if he had any leisure left him, he would read some book till the third watch of the night, at what time the captains, petty captains, and colonels, did use to come to him. So, being ready to go into Europe, one night very late (when all the camp took quiet rest) as he was in his tent with a little light, thinking of weighty matters, he thought he heard one come in to him, and, casting his eye towards the door of his tent, that he saw a wonderful strange and monstrous shape of a body coming towards him, and said never a word. So Brutus boldly asked what he was, a god or a man, and what cause brought him thither? The spirit answered him, "I am thy evil spirit, Brutus: and thou shalt see me by the city of Philippes." Brutus being no otherwise afraid, replied again unto it: "Well, then I shall see thee again." The spirit presently vanished away: and Brutus called his men unto him, who told him that they heard no noise, nor saw anything at all. Thereupon Brutus returned again to think on his matters as he did before. (*Life of Brutus*, p. 136.)

The Armies Meet at Philippi

For Octavius Cæsar could not follow him because of his sickness, and therefore stayed behind: whereupon they had taken his army, had not Antonius' aid been, which made such wonderful speed, that Brutus could scant believe it. So Cæsar came not thither of ten days after: and Antonius camped against Cassius, and Brutus on the other side, against Cæsar. The Romans called the valley between both camps, the Philippian fields: and there were never seen two so great armies of the Romans, one before the other, ready to fight. In truth, Brutus' army was inferior to Octavius Cæsar's in number of men; but for bravery and rich furniture, Brutus' army far excelled Cæsar's. For the most part of their armours were silver and gilt, which Brutus had bountifully given them: although, in all other things, he taught his captains to live in order without excess. But for the bravery of armour and weapon, which soldiers should carry in their hands, or otherwise wear upon their backs, he thought that it was an encouragement unto them that by nature are greedy of honour, and that it maketh them also fight like devils that love to get, and to be afraid to lose: because they fight to keep their armour and weapon, as also their goods and lands. (*Life of Brutus,* pp. 137–8.)

Unfavourable Omens Precede the Battle

When they raised their camp, there came two eagles that, flying with a marvellous force, lighted upon two of the foremost ensigns, and always followed the soldiers, which gave them meat and fed them, until they came near to the city of Philippes: and there, one day only before the battle, they both flew away. (*Life of Brutus,* p. 137.)

Notwithstanding, being busily occupied about the ceremonies of this purification, it is reported that there chanced certain unlucky signs unto Cassius. For one of his sergeants that carried the rods before him, brought him the garland of flowers turned backward, the which he should have worn on his head in the time of sacrificing. Moreover it is reported also, that another time before, in certain sports and triumph where they carried an image of Cassius' victory, of clean gold, it fell by chance, the man stumbling that carried it. And yet further, there was seen a marvellous number of fowls of prey, that feed upon dead carcases: and bee-hives also were found, where bees were gathered together in a certain place within the trenches of the camp: the which place the soothsayers thought good to shut out of the precinct of the camp, for to take away the superstitious fear and mistrust men would have of it. The which began somewhat to alter Cassius' mind from Epicurus' opinions, and had put the soldiers also in a marvellous fear. (*Life of Brutus,* p. 138.)

Cassius Wishes to Postpone the Battle

Thereupon Cassius was of opinion not to try this war at one battle, but rather to delay time, and to draw it out in length, considering that they were the stronger in money, and the weaker in men and armour. But Brutus, in contrary manner, did alway before, and at that time also, desire nothing more than to put all to the hazard of battle, as soon as might be possible: to the end he might either quickly restore his country to her former liberty, or rid him forthwith of this miserable world, being still troubled in following and maintaining of such great armies together. But perceiving that, in the daily skirmishes and bickerings they made, his men were always the stronger and ever had the better, that yet quickened his spirits again, and did put him in better heart. And furthermore, because that some of their own men had already yielded themselves to their enemies, and that it was suspected moreover divers others would do the like, that made many of Cassius' friends which were of his mind before (when it came to be debated in council, whether the battle should be fought or not) that they were then of Brutus' mind. . . Thereupon it was presently determined they should fight battle the next day. So Brutus, all suppertime, looked with a cheerful countenance, like a man that had good hope, and talked very wisely of philosophy, and after supper went to bed. (*Life of Brutus*, pp. 138–9.)

The Conversations Before the Battle

But touching Cassius, Messala reporteth that he supped by himself in his tent with a few of his friends, and that all supper-time he looked very sadly, and was full of thoughts, although it was against his nature: and that after supper he took him by the hand, and holding him fast (in token of kindness, as his manner was) told him in Greek: "Messala, I protest unto thee, and make thee my witness, that I am compelled against my mind and will (as Pompey the Great was) to jeopard the liberty of our country to the hazard of a battle. And yet we must be lively, and of good courage, considering our good fortune, whom we should wrong too much to mistrust her, although we follow evil counsel." Messala writeth, that Cassius having spoken these last words unto him, he bade him farewell, and willed him to come to supper to him the next night following, because it was his birthday. The next morning, by break of day, the signal of battle was set out in Brutus' and Cassius' camp, which was an arming scarlet coat: and both the chieftains spake together in the midst of their armies. There Cassius began to speak first, and said: "The gods grant us, O Brutus, that this day we may win the field, and ever after to live all the rest of our life quietly one with another. But sith the gods have so ordained it, that the greatest and chiefest things amongst men are most uncertain, and that if the battle fall out otherwise today than we wish or look for, we shall hardly meet again, what art thou then determined to do, to fly, or die?" Brutus answered him, being yet but a young man, and not over greatly experienced in the world: "I trust (I know not how) a certain rule of philosophy, by the which I did greatly blame and reprove Cato for killing himself, as being no lawful nor godly act, touching the gods: nor concerning men, valiant; not to give place and yield to divine providence, and not constantly and patiently to take whatsoever it pleaseth him to send us, but to draw back and fly: but being now in the midst of the danger, I am of a contrary mind. For if it be not the will of God that this battle fall out fortunate for us, I will look no more for hope, neither seek to make any new supply for war again, but will rid me of this miserable world, and content me with my fortune. For I gave up my life for my country in the Ides of March, for the which I shall live in another more glorious world." Cassius fell a-laughing to hear what he said, and embracing him, "Come on then," said he, "let us go and charge our enemies with this mind. For either we shall conquer, or we shall not need to fear the conquerors." After this talk, they fell to consultation among their friends for the ordering of the battle. Then Brutus prayed Cassius he might have the leading of the right wing, the which men thought was far meeter for Cassius, both because he was the elder man, and also for that he had the better experience. But yet Cassius gave it him, and willed that Messala (who had charge of one of the warlikest legions they had) should be also in that wing with Brutus. (*Life of Brutus*, pp. 139–40.)

Brutus is Victorious, Cassius Defeated

In the meantime Brutus, that led the right wing, sent little bills to the colonels and captains of private bands, in the which he wrote the word of the battle; and he himself, riding a-horseback by all the troops, did speak to them, and encouraged them to stick to it like men. So by this means very few of them understood what was the word of the battle, and besides, the most part of them never tarried to have it told them, but ran with great fury to assail the enemies, whereby, through this disorder, the legions were marvellously scattered and dispersed one from the other. For first of all Messala's legion, and then the next unto them, went beyond the left wing of the enemies, and did nothing, but glancing by them overthrew some as they went; and so going on further, fell right upon Cæsar's camp. . .

There was great slaughter in this camp. For amongst others, there were slain two thousand Lacedæmonians, who were arrived but even a little before, coming to aid Cæsar. The other also that had not glanced by, but had given a charge full upon Cæsar's battle, they easily made them fly, because they were greatly troubled for the loss of their camp; and of them there were slain by hand three legions. Then, being very earnest to follow the chase of them that fled, they ran in amongst them hand over head into their camp, and Brutus among them. But that which the conquerors thought not of, occasion shewed it unto them that were overcome; and that was, the left wing of their enemies left naked and unguarded of them of the right wing, who were strayed too far off, in following of them that were overthrown. So they gave a hot charge upon them. But, notwithstanding all the force they made, they could not break into the midst of their battle, where they found them that received them and valiantly made head against them. Howbeit they brake and overthrew the left wing where Cassius was, by reason of the great disorder among them, and also because they had no intelligence how the right wing had sped. So they chased them, beating them into their camp, the which they spoiled, none of both the chieftains being present there. . .

Furthermore, the voward and the middest of Brutus' battle had already put all their enemies to flight that withstood them, with great slaughter: so that Brutus had conquered all on his side, and Cassius had lost all on the other side. For nothing undid them but that Brutus went not to help Cassius, thinking he had overcome them as himself had done; and Cassius on the other side tarried not for Brutus, thinking he had been overthrown as himself was. (*Life of Brutus*, pp. 140–2.)

Cassius Driven Back and Slain

Furthermore perceiving his footmen to give ground, he did what he could to keep them from flying, and took an ensign from one of the ensign-bearers that fled, and stuck it fast at his feet: although with much ado he could scant keep his own guard together.

So Cassius himself was at length compelled to fly, with a few about him, unto a little hill, from whence they might easily see what was done in all the plain: howbeit Cassius himself saw nothing, for his sight was very bad, saving that he saw (and yet with much ado) how the enemies spoiled his camp before his eyes. He saw also a great troop of horsemen, whom Brutus sent to aid him, and thought that they were his enemies that followed him: but yet he sent Titinnius, one of them that was with him, to go and know what they were. Brutus' horsemen saw him coming afar off, whom when they knew that he was one of Cassius's chiefest friends, they shouted out for joy; and they that were familiarly acquainted with him lighted from their horses, and went and embraced him. The rest compassed him in round about on horseback with songs of victory and great rushing of their harness, so that they made all the field ring again for joy. But this marred all. For Cassius, thinking indeed that Titinnius was taken of the enemies, he then spake these words: "Desiring too much to live, I have lived to see one of my best friends taken, for my sake, before my face." After that, he got into a tent where nobody was, and took Pindarus with him, one of his bondsmen whom he reserved ever for such a pinch, since the cursed battle of the Parthians, where Crassus was slain, though he notwithstanding scaped from that overthrow: but then, casting his cloak over his head, and holding out his bare neck unto Pindarus, he gave him his head to be stricken off. So the head was found severed from the body: but after that time Pindarus was never seen more. Whereupon some took occasion to say that he had slain his master without his commandment. By and by they knew the horsemen that came towards them, and might see Titinnius crowned with a garland of triumph, who came before with great speed unto Cassius. But when he perceived, by the cries and tears of his friends which tormented themselves, the misfortune that had chanced to his captain Cassius by mistaking, he drew out his sword, cursing himself a thousand times that he had tarried so long, and so slew himself presently in the field. Brutus in the meantime came forward still, and understood also that Cassius had been overthrown: but he knew nothing of his death till he came very near to his camp. So when he was come thither, after he had lamented the death of Cassius, calling him the last of all the Romans, being unpossible that Rome should ever breed again so noble and valiant a man as he, he caused his body to be buried, and sent it to the city of Thassos, fearing lest his funerals within his camp should cause great disorder. (*Life of Brutus*, pp. 143–4.)

Marcus Cato is Slain

There was the son of Marcus Cato slain, valiantly fighting among the lusty youths. For notwithstanding that he was very weary and over-harried, yet would he not therefore fly; but manfully fighting and laying about him, telling aloud his name, and also his father's name, at length he was beaten down amongst many other dead bodies of his enemies, which he had slain round about him. (*Life of Brutus*, p. 148.)

Lucilius Tries to Save Brutus

Amongst whom there was one of Brutus' friends called Lucilius, who seeing a troupe of barbarous men making no reckoning of all men else they met in their way, but going all together right against Brutus, he determined to stay them with the hazard of his life; and being left behind, told them that he was Brutus: and because they should believe him, he prayed them to bring him to Antonius, for he said he was afraid of Cæsar, and that he did trust Antonius better. These barbarous men, being very glad of this good hap, and thinking themselves happy men, they carried him in the night, and sent some before unto Antonius, to tell him of their coming. He was marvellous glad of it, and went out to meet them that brought him. Others also understanding of it, that they had brought Brutus prisoner, they came out of all parts of the camp to see him, some pitying his hard fortune, and others saying that it was not done like himself, so cowardly to be taken alive of the barbarous people for fear of death. When they came near together, Antonius stayed a while bethinking himself how he should use Brutus. In the meantime Lucilius was brought to him, who stoutly with a bold countenance said: "Antonius, I dare assure thee, that no enemy hath taken nor shall take Marcus Brutus alive, and I beseech God keep him from that fortune: for wheresoever he be found, alive or dead, he will be found like himself. And now for myself, I am come unto thee, having deceived these men of arms here, bearing them down that I was Brutus, and do not refuse to suffer any torment thou wilt put me to." Lucilius' words made them all amazed that heard him. Antonius on the other side, looking upon all them that had brought him, said unto them: "My companions, I think ye are sorry you have failed of your purpose, and that you think this man hath done you great wrong: but I assure you, you have taken a better booty than that you followed. For instead of an enemy you have brought me a friend: and for my part, if you had brought me Brutus alive, truly I cannot tell what I should have done to him. For I had rather have such men my friends, as this man here, than mine enemies." Then he embraced Lucilius, and at that time delivered him to one of his friends in custody; and Lucilius ever after served him faithfully, even to his death. (*Life of Brutus*, pp. 148–9.)

Brutus Meets his Death

Now Brutus having passed a little river, walled in on every side with high rocks and shadowed with great trees, being then dark night, he went no further, but stayed at the foot of a rock with certain of his captains and friends that followed him. . .

Furthermore, Brutus thought that there was no great number of men slain in battle: and to know the truth of it, there was one called Statilius, that promised to go through his enemies, for otherwise it was impossible to go see their camp: and from thence, if all were well, that he would lift up a torch-light in the air, and then return again with speed to him. The torch-light was lift up as he had promised, for Statilius went thither. Now Brutus seeing Statilius tarry long after that, and that he came not again, he said: "If Statilius be alive, he will come again." But his evil fortune was such that, as he came back, he lighted in his enemies' hands and was slain. Now the night being far spent, Brutus as he sat bowed towards Clitus, one of his men, and told him somewhat in his ear: the other answered him not, but fell a-weeping. Thereupon he proved Dardanus, and said somewhat also to him: at length he came to Volumnius himself, and speaking to him in Greek, prayed him for the studies' sake which brought them acquainted together, that he would help him to put his hand to his sword, to thrust it in him to kill him. Volumnius denied his request, and so did many others: and amongst the rest, one of them said, there was no tarrying for them there, but that they must needs fly. Then Brutus, rising up, "We must fly indeed," said he, "but it must be with our hands, not with our feet." Then taking every man by the hand, he said these words unto them with a cheerful countenance: "It rejoiceth my heart, that not one of my friends hath failed me at my need, and I do not complain of my fortune, but only for my country's sake: for as for me, I think myself happier than they that have overcome, considering that I leave a perpetual fame of virtue and honesty, the which our enemies the conquerors shall never attain unto by force or money; neither can let their posterity to say that they, being naughty and unjust men, have slain good men, to usurp tyrannical power not pertaining to them." Having so said, he prayed every man to shift for himself, and then he went a little aside with two or three only, among the which Strato was one, with whom he came first acquainted by the study of rhetoric. He came as near to him as he could, and taking his sword by the hilt with both his hands, and falling down upon the point of it, ran himself through. Others say that not he, but Strato (at his request) held the sword in his hand, and turned his head aside, and that Brutus fell down upon it, and so ran himself through, and died presently. (*Life of Brutus*, pp. 149–51.)

Messala Commends Strato to Octavius

Messala, that had been Brutus' great friend, became afterwards Octavius Cæsar's friend: so, shortly after, Cæsar being at good leisure, he brought Strato, Brutus' friend, unto him, and weeping said: "Cæsar, behold, here is he that did the last service to my Brutus." Cæsar welcomed him at that time, and afterwards he did him as faithful service in all his affairs as any Grecian else he had about him, until the Battle of Actium. (*Life of Brutus*, p. 151.)

Antony Pays Honour to Brutus

Furthermore he [Antony] cast his coat-armour (which was wonderful rich and sumptuous) upon Brutus' body, and gave commandment to one of his slaves enfranchised, to defray the charge of his burial. (*Life of Antonius*, p. 171.)

For it was said that Antonius spake it openly divers times, that he thought, that of all them that had slain Cæsar, there was none but Brutus only that was moved to do it, as thinking the act commendable of itself: but that all the other conspirators did conspire his death for some private malice or envy, that they otherwise did bear unto him. (*Life of Brutus*, p. 130.)

APPENDIX B

From Thomas Platter's account of his visit to England:[1]

Den 21 Septembris [1599] nach dem Imbissessen, etwan umb zwey uhren, bin ich mitt meiner geselschaft über dz wasser gefahren, haben in dem streüwinen Dachhaus die Tragedy vom ersten Keyser Julio Cæsare mitt ohngefahr 15 personen sehen gar artlich agieren; zu endt der Comedien dantzeten sie ihrem gebrauch nach gar überausz zierlich, ye zwen in mannes undt 2 in weiber kleideren angethan, wunderbahrlich mitt einanderen.

1. Reprinted from *Anglia*, xxii (1899), p. 458.